International Studies in Educational Achievement

VOLUME 12

The IEA Preprimary Study:
Early Childhood Care and Education in
11 Countries

International Studies in Educational Achievement

Other titles in the Series include

The IEA Preprimary Study: Early Childhood Care and Education in 11 Countries

Edited by

PATRICIA P. OLMSTED and DAVID P. WEIKART
High/Scope Educational Research Foundation

With National Research Coordinators

Joaquim Bairrão
Arlette Delhaxhe
Helena Hoas
Mikko Ojala
Olayemi Onibokun
Sylvia Opper
Jesús Palacios
Nittaya Passornsiri
Lucio Pusci
Hans-Günther Rossbach
Shi Hui Zhong

Published for the International Association
for the Evaluation of Educational Achievement

PERGAMON

U.K.	Elsevier Science Ltd, The Boulevard, Langford Lane, Kidlington, Oxford OX5 1GB, U.K.
U.S.A.	Elsevier Science, Inc., 660 White Plains Road, Tarrytown, New York 10591-5153, U.S.A.
JAPAN	Elsevier Science Japan, Tsunashima Building Annex, 3-20-12 Yushima, Bunkyo-ku, Tokyo 113, Japan

First edition 1995

Library of Congress Cataloging-in-Publication Data

The IEA Preprimary Study: early childhood care and education in 11 countries/edited by Patricia P. Olmsted and David P. Weikart (High/Scope Educational Research Foundation); with national research coordinators Joaquim Bairrão . . . [*et al.*]. — 1st ed.
   p. cm. — (International studies in educational achievement; v. 12)
   Rev. ed. of: Families speak. c1994.
   "Published for the International Association for the Evaluation of Educational Achievement."
   Includes bibliographical references and index.
   1. Early childhood education—Cross-cultural studies. 2. Child care services—Cross-cultural studies. I. Olmsted, Patricia P. II. Weikart, David P. III. IEA Preprimary Study. IV. High/Scope Educational Research Foundation. V. Families speak. VI. Series.
   LB1139.23I33   1995
   372.21—dc20   94–41672

British Library Cataloguing in Publication Data
A catalogue record for this book is available from the British Library

Elsevier ISBN 0–08–041934–8
High/Scope ISBN 0–929816–89–7

English language hard back edition first published in 1995 by Elsevier Science Limited, The Boulevard, Langford Lane, Kidlington, Oxford OX5 1GB, U.K.
English language soft back edition, *Families Speak: Early Childhood Care and Education in 11 Countries*, first published in 1994 by High/Scope Press, a division of High/Scope Educational Research Foundation, 600 N. River Street, Ypsilanti, MI 48198–2898, U.S.A.

Printed in Great Britain by Biddles Ltd, Guildford, Surrey

Contents

v

List of Tables

Chapter 7

Appendix A

List of Figures

Foreword

T.J. PLOMP
(CHAIRMAN, IEA)

This volume is published as part of IEA's Preprimary Project.

IEA, the International Association for the Evaluation of Educational Achievement, was founded in 1959 for the purpose of conducting comparative studies focusing on educational policies and practices in various countries and education systems around the world. IEA studies have reported on a wide range of topics, each contributing to a deeper understanding of educational processes. IEA membership has grown over the years from a small number of countries to a group of about 55 countries today. The IEA Secretariat is located in The Hague, The Netherlands.

The Preprimary Project was conceived in the late 1970s in response to the need for information about children's care and education experiences prior to formal schooling. It comprises three phases of which Phase 1 focuses on the kinds of early childhood care and education services that families use and on the factors that influence parents' choices of early childhood care/education arrangements. The International Coordinating Center is at the High/Scope Educational Research Foundation in Ypsilanti, MI, U.S.A. With the publication of this volume, Phase I of the Preprimary Project is now complete. The International Coordinating Center is now working on the analysis of the data for Phase 2, which focuses on the processes that occur within various types of early childhood settings.

This volume is the result of the efforts of many individuals. Special thanks must go to the staff of the International Coordinating Center under the leadership of David Weikart and Pat Olmsted, who did an excellent job under difficult budgetary conditions. I would also like to express my gratitude to the group of early childhood researchers who reviewed an early draft of the manuscript and to the following external reviewers of the final manuscript: Dr. Glen Dixon, University of British Columbia and Dr. Anne Smith, University of Otago, New Zealand. My thanks also go to Dr. Richard M. Wolf, Teachers College, Columbia University, who coordinated the external reviews as chair of IEA's Publications and Editorial Committee.

Those readers wishing additional information on this or other IEA studies may directly correspond with IEA at the following address:

IEA Secretariat
Sweelinckplein 14
2517 GK The Hague
The Netherlands
Tel.: + 31 70 346 9679
Fax.: + 31 70 360 9951
E-mail: iea@svo.nl

Preface

The first publication of the IEA Preprimary Project, *How Nations Serve Young Children* (Olmsted & Weikart, 1989), used information from *public records* to draw up profiles of early childhood care and education in various nations. This second publication describes each country's early childhood care and education situation based on information gleaned from conducting *household surveys* in those same countries. As the major work of Phase 1 of the IEA Preprimary Project, it thus provides a "reality check" on the profiles of the earlier work. In addition to describing the three-phase Preprimary Project and revealing its major Phase 1 findings, this volume is able to present for each country a comparison of the information from the household survey with that from public records.

People often wonder how specific countries come to be involved in a study such as the IEA Preprimary Project. Any nation interested in cross-national educational studies may join IEA and then participate in decision-making about the study projects to be undertaken by the organization. Once a project proposal has been officially approved by the IEA General Assembly, any member country can then choose whether to participate in the given study. However, since IEA may be conducting several studies simultaneously, member countries generally participate only in those most relevant to their national needs and goals. Thus, the countries participating in Phase 1 of the IEA Preprimary Project do not constitute the entire set of IEA member countries.

A particular strength of this study is that its participating countries provide variety on a number of dimensions, including form of government, population, and stage of development. In general, the participating countries are those that do not have extremely high infant mortality rates and thus have been able to move from concerns about child survival to concerns about providing adequate education and care services for their young children.

Another strength of the study is that it was conducted with the significant cooperation and contributions of early childhood researchers around the world. Each participating country set up its own coordinating center for the study, usually within a university or government agency (e.g., an education ministry). This coordinating center, under the direction of a National Research Coordinator, procured necessary financial support, ensured that the survey questions were appropriate for families in that country, and supervised the sampling, data collection, and data processing. At all stages of the Phase 1 study, including the writing of this final report, the National Research Coordinators and their staff worked closely with the project's International Coordinating Center in the U.S.A., the High/Scope Educational Research Foundation in Ypsilanti, Michigan.

In developing a report such as this, decisions must be made about how to organize the presentation so it conveys both the national and the international aspects of the study. For example, the report could have been composed of a series of chapters each presenting the findings for an individual country (a chapter on Belgium, a chapter on China, and so on). However, because the editors and authors considered it important to be able to view the IEA Preprimary Project findings for any one nation within an international context, they chose to present the national sample characteristics and the major findings of the study (that is, the information in Chapters 3–6) cross-nationally. This provides readers with a sense of the range of the findings for a specific variable across the group of nations participating in the study. However, for the reader primarily interested in the findings for a particular country, the introductory chapters (Chapters 1 and 2) and Chapter 7 are recommended reading.

Another decision concerned the mode of data presentation. Although figures and graphs sometimes have more "eye appeal" than tables, preparation of clear figures or graphs often requires omitting certain details (such as range and standard deviation). Consequently, in many cases, the editors chose to use tables rather than graphic representations, so their presentation of data could be as complete and useful as possible.

The findings reported in this book have already been used as a basis for Phase 2 of the IEA Preprimary Project, which is an *observational study* of the major types of early childhood care and education settings in participating nations; analysis of Phase 2 data is now under way. Of the 11 nations participating in Phase 1 (the household survey), 9 have continued with Phase 2 (the observational study). Also, 6 additional nations have joined Phase 2: Greece, Indonesia, Ireland, and 3 Eastern European countries—Poland, Romania, and Slovenia.

So far, in connection with the observational study, High/Scope Foundation has produced a series of videotapes of early childhood care and education settings in the Phase 2 countries; a series of monographs dealing with Phase 2 findings is also planned. Thus, this book, together with *How Nations Serve Young Children,* represents only the beginning of what will come from the IEA Preprimary Project.

Patricia P. Olmsted
David P. Weikart
June 1994

A Word about IEA

IEA is the acronym of the International Association for the Evaluation of Educational Achievement, a nongovernmental, nonprofit organization of research institutions in more than 55 countries that is well known for its 30 years of comparative international surveys in science, mathematics, written composition, and other academic areas. IEA research projects have been instrumental in demonstrating the feasibility of large-scale cross-national empirical studies and advancing the methodology of comparative education.

IEA views its comparative educational surveys as a necessary first step in both national and international policy-related research. IEA findings have affected educational systems around the world as specific educational problems have been identified and policymakers have made decisions based on these research findings. Some of the international educational issues IEA has chosen to examine include identifying the effects of different practices in grouping or tracking students, investigating the effects of comprehensive secondary schooling, and examining the effects of specific instructional practices.

Additional information regarding IEA can be obtained from the IEA Secretariat, 14 Sweelinckplein, NL 2519 The Hague, The Netherlands.

Acknowledgements

Our gratitude goes to all those who have assisted in making this book a reality. We acknowledge Carnegie Corporation, the Spencer Foundation, the U.S. Department of Health and Human Services, and the U.S. Department of Education for their support of High/Scope's IEA Preprimary Project activities. We also thank High/Scope Press editor Marge Senninger for her invaluable assistance in all phases of manuscript preparation, and research associate Mei-Yu Yu for her careful attention to the data. Finally, we acknowledge the word-processing assistance of Kay Long and Diana Knepp.

1

The IEA Preprimary Project: Obtaining Knowledge to Improve the Quality of Children's Early Experiences

MARCEL CRAHAY

This book is a report on the first phase of the Preprimary Project being conducted in three phases in 11–15 countries under the sponsorship of the International Association for the Evaluation of Educational Achievement (IEA). Spanning the years 1987–1997, the project represents the first extension of IEA inquiry into the years before children enter the formal educational system. The impetus for such research consists largely of two trends that emerged and converged during the 1960s and 1970s in most IEA member countries, namely:

(1) Increasing acceptance of the proposition that early life experiences make a strong and probably enduring contribution to all subsequent development.

(2) Increasing incidence of families sharing the care and education of their preschool-aged children with others outside the home—a phenomenon that is variously attributed to social, economic, and demographic changes worldwide.

When considering these two trends together, one must keep in mind the probability that the greater the contribution of early experiences to the total development of an individual and of society, the greater the benefits that can accrue to them from good quality early experiences and, by the same token, the greater the harm that can be done to them (the individual and society) by poor quality early experiences. Therefore, any investigation, like the IEA Preprimary Project, that can illuminate the nature and effects of various kinds of early childhood experiences on the long-term development of young children is a welcome addition to existing knowledge.

The IEA Preprimary Project was also initiated in the hope that as a cross-cultural and cross-national study, it would be especially valuable in strengthening and deepening understanding of the impact of early experiences on young children's development. The following benefits that LeVine (1970) attributed to cross-cultural study in child psychology could apply equally well to cross-national study of preprimary education:

> [It provides] a research strategy for using measurable variations among human populations (in behavior patterns, environmental conditions, frequencies) to search systematically for the causes of individual behavior and development. From this perspective, cross-cultural study should serve child psychology as social epidemiology serves pathology in medicine, by expanding the range of observable variation (given ethical restraint on experimental intervention by investigators), by discovering the limits of this range for the human species, by identifying extreme or unusual populations in which experimental or quasi-experimental studies (e.g., longitudinal studies) would shed especially crucial light on etiological issues (p. 559).

Bronfenbrenner (1979) has also pointed to the usefulness of cross-national comparisons. In his discussion of the influence of day care experiences on adult aggressiveness, he noted that cross-cultural investigations have revealed, in some countries, a relationship between early day care experience and adult aggression, but in others, no observable relationship. He went on to say that "the tendency of the peer group in a given culture to predispose children, especially boys, toward greater aggressiveness, impulsivity, and egocentrism appears to be associated with an ideology of individualism and social structure that emphasizes segregation by age" and "the somewhat higher aggressiveness observed in children with day care experience . . . may not be a consequence of early upbringing in group settings per se, but rather a reflection of the general role of peer groups as contexts of socialization in some cultures" (p. 180).

In addition to these earlier investigations, several more-recent multi-national studies and reports focusing on early childhood services have attested to the growing interest in and importance of cross-cultural pre-primary research (e.g., Tobin *et al.*, 1989; UNESCO, 1991; Myers, 1992).

Characteristics of the Field—The Difficulties of Designing an International Comparison

Ideological Dissension

As mentioned earlier, it is largely recognized that early life experiences greatly influence human development. The findings of the Consortium for Longitudinal Studies (Lazar & Darlington, 1979), as well as those of the High/Scope Perry preschool study (Berrueta-Clement *et al.*, 1984; Schweinhart *et al.*, 1993), clearly demonstrate that the effects of early childhood education can extend into adulthood. However, beyond this general agreement concerning the importance of preschool experiences, great dissension exists regarding the kinds of daily experiences that should be provided to foster young children's development.

No doubt all spheres and levels of education are subject to ideological differences. However, preprimary education, perhaps because it is a subject very "close to home," is especially blessed with divergence. The controversies surrounding it are fueled by differences in societal values and attitudes concerning the place of women, the functions of the family, the relevance of schooling, the pressure for industrialization, and so forth. Thus, one might even say that deep ideological differences constitute a *central feature* of the subculture of preprimary education.

One main issue that ideological disputes revolve around concerns the relative merits of young children being placed in out-of-home settings as against their being cared for by a mother or a mother-surrogate at home. The available research on relevant variables (such as attachment, loss, and separation anxiety) and the accumulation of reassuring evidence concerning these variables have little influence on the ideological battle between some moralists or politicians who claim that young children's out-of-home care or education threatens family life, and feminist groups who press for group care/education for the young. Faced with the research evidence, opponents of out-of-home care object that there are some important things that tests cannot measure.

In the field of elementary education, it is obvious to everybody that assessment of children's competency in reading, writing, and mathematics is relevant. Assessment of some other competencies (for example, fluency in a second language) involves more controversial issues, but there is a large social consensus that the task of elementary teachers is at least to teach reading, writing, and computing. Moreover, this consensus is international and allows intercountry comparisons (as in IEA studies). In the field of preprimary education, however, there is very little consensus on a minimal definition of the task that out-of-home teachers/caregivers have to accomplish. According to Katz (1975), "An apparent consequence of the ideological character of early childhood education is the development of encampments: Piagetians, behaviorists, neo-Freudians, open educators, etc. Each camp seems to avoid the examination of counterevidence . . ." (p. 269).

Implicit Rather than Explicit Educational Aims

Amidst the theoretical currents described by Katz (1975), every camp has more-or-less explicitly stated educational objectives and curriculum. However, in the wider field of general preschool care and education, it is often the case that a preprimary setting has no explicit curriculum. In fact, several countries have some out-of-home child care settings that do not subscribe to formal educational objectives. And, of course, this is the case in *all* countries in most family settings. Therefore, how does one rigorously address the issue of the relative merits of in-home versus out-of-home care? Also, how does one rigorously compare the merits of various categories of out-of-home settings if some categories have no explicit educational aims?

Obviously, the IEA Preprimary Project could not be conceived according to the approach traditionally used by IEA. In the present state of the art, it is impossible to look at cross-national variations by treating educational objectives as self-evident and then testing the achievement of these objectives in random samples of children. Since preprimary objectives themselves constitute the core of contemporary controversy, to avoid considering the existing diversity would be to overlook a principal problem in the early childhood field.

In considering this diversity, it may be useful to look at whether children's various socialization settings differ in the extent to which they set objectives. That is, to begin with, it may be useful to take the position that preschool educational institutions can be distinguished from family life by the extent to which their actions are intentional. But this distinction could be viewed in another way: Some preprimary institutions have no rigorously articulated objectives, whereas some families are capable of articulating in detail the intentions behind their practices.

Furthermore, considering preprimary setting diversity, it seems appropriate to replace the term objectives with the term expectations. The latter term is more appropriately applied in the case of the family or some other informal socialization setting. In another sense, expectations could describe the hopes one has with respect to some event or institution; it could also refer to the anticipations one develops concerning the behavior of someone or something one knows of; finally, it could refer to the demands society places on an institution.

Institutional Diversity

As indicated by some hints from the international compilation *How Nations Serve Young Children: Profiles of Child Care and Education in 14 Countries* (Olmsted & Weikart, 1989), the liveliness of the ideological disputes, the degree of educational intentionality, and the importance of the consensus around the merits of out-of-home preprimary education vary from country to country, and these differences are reflected in the types and uses of services that are available:

(1) Some countries have few formal services, and those they have are utilized by very small numbers/proportions of children (e.g., Nigeria).

(2) Some countries offer a wide range of types of care used in a wide variety of ways (e.g., the U.S.A.).

(3) Some countries offer primarily one type of preschool service that is almost universally used by families (e.g., Belgium, Italy, Hong Kong).

(4) In most countries, different services are offered for different age groups (e.g., Finland, the Federal Republic of Germany).

At this level again, the landscape of preschool education differs from that of elementary education, and this difference presented difficulties regarding the design of the preprimary study. Earlier IEA studies, which have dealt with elementary and secondary education, have focused their research on educational institutions. However, to focus the Preprimary Project on educational institutions alone would have run the risk of ignoring the socialization settings that are provided by more informal arrangements, and it was suspected that in some countries, more children were cared for in out-of-home informal settings than in formal settings. So the question arose: Which category (or categories) of child care settings were to be selected for the preliminary study? For some countries (Belgium, Italy, Hong Kong) the choice was easy. As just mentioned, such countries have only one major kind of out-of-home service, which is attended by a high percentage of children. In most of the countries, however, various kinds of services are available. Moreover, the labels used to designate preprimary institutions and the adults who work in them vary from country to country as well as within countries.

In many countries, the personnel working in preprimary settings have no training or qualifications at all. In some countries, their qualifications range all the way from none at all to advanced graduate training. In addition, some countries and regions report extremely high rates of turnover or burnout—so much so that preservice training appears not to be worthwhile for programs. Some countries have adopted, or are in the process of adopting, tested or new strategies for inservice training and a variety of more-or-less permanent support systems for personnel, in accord with the findings of a large-scale study of day care in the U.S.A. The *National Day Care Study Final Report* (Ruopp *et al.*, 1979) indicated that the quality of day care programs is related to relevant training. A more recent study, the High/Scope Training of Trainers Evaluation (Epstein, 1993), has supported and expanded on these findings, providing "strong evidence for the general assertion that inservice training can contribute to program quality and children's development" (p. xv). Understandably, this training aspect of the field is of great interest to many policymakers and planners.

Variations in Sponsoring Agencies

In most countries, the various types of preprimary institutions are only partially or tangentially related to other higher level educational institutions. In some countries, preprimary services are the responsibility of the department of social services; in others, the department of health; in still others, the department of public assistance, family welfare agencies, larger church organizations, and so forth. Even within countries or regions, depending on the age of the clientele or the duration of the services provided, different agencies monitor or subsidize preprimary institutions. One dramatic example of such agency variation can be seen in the successful campaign that was launched in the U.S.A. during the 1970s to keep the nation's Head Start program within the federal Department of Health and Human Services rather than to transfer it to the newly created Department of Education. It is pertinent to this discussion to note that one of the central arguments behind keeping it out of the Department of Education was that Head Start is, by origin and intent, a comprehensive program with nutritional, social, health, and other components, and therefore too broad in scope and function to be turned over to educators.

Partially because of the multiplicity of agencies that fund, license, and monitor settings for young children, there is usually no single agency responsible for collecting basic data concerning what preprimary services are available and who participates in them. Hence, for most countries, there is a serious lack of comprehensive data, especially compared with the more readily available data on such mainstream institutions as elementary and secondary schools.

A Variety of Social Demands

The social demands placed on preprimary education are, as mentioned earlier, a factor to be considered. In the Western world, more and more children are enrolled in preschool institutions; early out-of-home schooling of children is also increasing in the Third World (e.g., UNESCO, 1991; Myers, 1992). This phenomenon seems, at first glance, to be associated with such factors as improved infant survival rates, industrial development, increasing family mobility, and the growing incidence of single-parent and two-parent employment in families with young children. However, some hints from national studies lead one to think that these are not the only factors influencing families' use of out-of-home services for their preschool-aged children. And, indeed, two sets of Phase 1 findings of the IEA Preprimary Project (presented in later chapters) give sense and confirmation to these insights. Phase 1 observations correspond strongly with one preliminary insight of the project concerning the diversity of the social demands placed on child care institutions. It was suspected that in countries where families believe in the educational value of preprimary out-of-home experiences, the demand for good early childhood settings would be strong. In other countries, families would place their children in such settings only when obliged to. In these latter countries, the social demand for high-quality care settings would most likely be weak.

In summary, the domain of interest of the IEA Preprimary Project differs in several important ways from what is usually examined in studies undertaken by IEA. Essentially, preprimary services are less homogeneous and monolithic within and between countries than are elementary or secondary education services. In many respects, *variety is the rule* in the field of young children's education. Because of this variety, the problems of defining and comparing elements or components are significant. Because of the variety of agencies responsible for preprimary institutions, there are great gaps in the early childhood field's basic descriptive and utilization data.

A Two-Level Study

In its earliest planning stages (see "History of the Project"), the IEA Preprimary Project was intended to be a single-phase study, focusing on the quality of life of children in those out-of-home environments specially provided for them (e.g., preschools), with an emphasis on assessing how those environments contribute to children's current and subsequent development. This would entail researchers observing children in selected formal preprimary settings along dimensions considered as crucial and meaningful and then relating these observations to developmental measures.

History of the Project

The idea of expanding the scope of IEA inquiry to the preprimary years was first broached during the late 1970s by a small group of researchers who sensed the importance of educators' knowing what happened to children prior to their encounter with formal schooling. It was clear from the start that this kind of study would present special challenges—much of the needed information could not be obtained from the education agencies who typically collect IEA data. Yet, finding sufficient interest among the IEA member nations, the IEA General Assembly saw fit to establish a preprimary planning group, which began meeting in 1981 in Belgium. Fourteen representatives from 7 member countries made up this initial group: Marcel Crahay, Arlette Delhaxhe, Gilbert De Landsheere, Jean-Pierre Pourtois, Anne-Marie Thirion (Belgium); Rachel Presser (Canada); Annette Marion (France); Wolfgang Tietze (Federal Republic of Germany); Ron Davie, Bill Wall (Great Britain); Suzan Montovani, Antonio Schizzerotto (Italy); Lilian Katz, David Weikart (U.S.A.).

Between 1982 and 1984, the project took further shape. First a draft proposal for the Preprimary Project was approved by the IEA General Assembly, and invitations to participate in the project were extended to all member nations. Next came appointment of a project steering committee (Marcel Crahay of Belgium, Wolfgang Tietze of the Federal Republic of Germany, Lilian Katz and Richard Wolf of the U.S.A.) and selection of the project's International Coordinating Center (High/Scope Educational Research Foundation, Ypsilanti, Michigan, U.S.A.). Thus was the way paved for completion of the final project proposal in early 1984.

Representatives from all interested member nations (17 to start with) met in Singapore in 1984 to discuss the details of participation in the Preprimary Project—establishing national research centers, developing instruments and procedures, and locating within-country funding as well as funding for the international coordination activities. Individual countries then spent the next 2 years actually seeing to these various needs. In 1987, 14 countries launched Phase 1 by each putting together a "national profile" of early childhood data drawn from existing sources. These profiles, based on existing sources and published in Olmsted and Weikart (1989), were a starting point, to be followed by the major effort of Phase 1, a survey of families. This book completes Phase 1 by presenting the findings from that survey.

As work proceeded, it appeared relevant to broaden the scope of the project and to treat the kind of study planned initially as a specific part of a more ambitious enterprise. The project's resultant general framework can be characterized by 5 statements:

(1) The general focus of the study is on the total set of early childhood care/education settings typically experienced by the young child ("total" means that even the child's own home is included as a setting in the study). This choice of focus is based on the reality that many of today's young children experience various settings throughout a typical day or throughout a typical week. Knowing the number and types of settings a child typically experiences each week can provide information about the child's socialization and about the persons who play major roles in this socialization.

(2) The enlarged focus of the study requires selecting one age group

as the point of departure for the research. Four-year-olds have been chosen as the target age. More precisely, the age-range of the children to be studied by the project is 3 years 6 months to 4 years 6 months. In most participating countries, this age-range takes in the child's last full year before entry into a formal school environment; it is also the age-range for which there is the widest variety of early childhood care and education settings.

(3) The study, in each country, of what kinds of provisions are available, and how they are used by a representative sample of 4-year-olds, has been a necessary first step. (This step has produced the Phase 1 findings reported in this volume.) Many countries lack precise statistics concerning child care provisions; they do not know enough about the numbers of various kinds of settings, how and by whom the settings are used, their periods of operation, and so forth.

(4) The expansion of the aims of the study is particularly of interest in that it leads to consideration of the relationships that exist between the diverse preprimary settings used by families. The expression *relationship between settings* refers to:

(i)   The relative importance of various kinds of settings in the life of preschool-aged children.

(ii) The compatibility of the various settings, that is, how preschool-aged children are able to use multiple settings.

By describing the day-to-day life of a typical 4-year-old in each participating country, study findings will point up the relationships that exist between diverse settings. Rather than considering children as elements included in a particular kind of setting, *the research will identify patterns of children's daily lives.* It may be possible to establish a relationship between such data and the diversity and quantity of provisions that are available for the 4-year-olds in various countries.

(5) The impact of various kinds of socialization settings on children's development will also be considered. This calls for an in-depth study of the quality of children's experiences in each kind of setting (Phase 2 of the project) and a longitudinal developmental assessment (Phase 3 of the project). The effects of a socialization setting should ideally be evaluated both in terms of the expressed values within the setting and in terms of the expectations ascribed to it by adults in associated settings. For example, the effect of an out-of-home child care setting should be evaluated in terms of the expressed expectations of the caregivers but also in terms of the expressed expectations of families who place their children in that child care setting. Similarly, what happens within

a setting should be congruent with the values and expectations of the caregivers and of the families who trust that care setting. Furthermore, one must take into account that caregivers have to cope with contextual parameters that constrain or support their practices. Therefore, the in-depth study of the quality of children's experiences in various settings must include the following:

(i)   A direct assessment of the quality of children's experiences in the settings by observing what the children have the opportunity to do and how they interact with adults and peers.

(ii) A long-term evaluation of a wide range of developmental aspects, so some relationships between children's development and the quality of life in their preprimary settings can be established.

(iii) An investigation of the values and expectations of caregivers and parents, in order to assess whether settings are run by caregivers in a way that is congruent with parents' wishes.

(iv) An analysis of the contextual factors that foster or impede the implementation of a high-quality educational environment.

In summary, the IEA Preprimary Project has been designed to be conducted in the following three interrelated phases:

(1) Phase 1: This phase consists primarily of a household survey in each participating nation to determine the types of early childhood care and education services used by families and to determine some of the characteristics of the families and of the services they use. It will also provide a picture of the daily-life patterns of 4-year-olds in each country.

(2) Phase 2: A sample of settings identified in Phase 1 will be studied in depth to ascertain the quality of children's experiences in their various care/education settings. Extensive observational and interview data will be used to examine the interactive and structural characteristics of the major early childhood settings and to explore the impact of programmatic and familial factors on children's developmental status at age 4.

(3) Phase 3: This phase consists of a follow-up, at age 7, of the development of the children studied in Phase 2, and examination of their progress since the end of their preprimary experience.

This report focuses on Phase 1 and on what has been learned from it so far. The following section describes the theoretical framework of this phase of the study.

Phase 1 of the Preprimary Project: A Household Survey of Families

Theoretical Framework

The family plays an important role in the child's weekly and daily life. First of all, it constitutes a background that may or may not be rich in stimulation. It also represents an authority regulating the child's life, because, after all, it is parents who make decisions about their child's weekly and daily routines. However, there are constraints on parents' decisions. For example, the parents' daily schedules may affect the approach taken to a child's care or education. Their expectations regarding the child's development will also play a role. The child's weekly and daily routine will depend not only on the parents' needs and expectations but also on the opportunities offered by the surrounding community.

To solve its problem, the family will probably take advantage of a variety of available services. For example, in Belgium the timetable of the *école maternelle* does not usually correspond to parental schedules, but the institution offers supplementary caretaking systems: morning, midday, and evening nurseries. Although the nurseries constitute resources that families can use, parents who prefer more domestic solutions use care by grandparents, neighbors, or acquaintances for the child's transition from the *école maternelle* to home.

Thus the family can be characterized as an ecosystem that offers the child his or her immediate life-surroundings but also organizes the rest of the child's life according to the family's interactions with other ecosystems: the father's and mother's employment system; the network of neighbors, friends, and relatives; and the formal care/education services. These interactions, which have not been much investigated until now, can be very complex. Many factors must be taken into account: the availability and cost of care/education services; the need for travel to and from care/education settings; the quality of the relationships with neighbors, friends, and relatives; the parents' educational philosophy; the parents' distribution of family roles (in a two-parent family); and the expectations of society.

The Basic Study Method

In relation to this theoretical framework, Phase 1 consisted of a household survey employing a 50–minute Parent/Guardian Interview to collect information about parents' use of early childhood care and education services. This strategy of collecting information about early childhood services directly from families is unique to the IEA Preprimary Project. Most other studies have gone directly to care providers and teachers for information. By interviewing families, the Preprimary Project encompassed even the most informal child care settings, those that would have been missed by a study interviewing only out-of-home sources. Furthermore, the family-interview strategy was able to document children's attendance at multiple care and education settings, thereby giving an unprecedented picture of the total experience of each child studied.

The Parent/Guardian Interview questions, which were jointly developed by the project directors from the participating countries, were designed to yield the following information:

(1) To what extent do today's families use out-of-home services for the care or education of their preschool-aged children? To what extent is care at home by parents the norm?

(2) What factors lead parents to seek out-of-home services for their children? Why do some parents remain their children's sole caretakers? How much choice is involved, and do parents turn to out-of-home care/education for adult- or child-centered reasons?

(3) What within-country and country-to-country variations exist in forms of out-of-home care/education?

(4) In what various ways are care/education programs sponsored or supported? What types of support services (e.g., health, transportation) are offered by early childhood programs?

(5) For children who attend out-of-home settings, how much of their day is spent there? Are multiple settings involved, and how much travel between settings is necessary?

(6) When parents use out-of-home care/education services, how much contact do they have with those responsible for their child? How satisfied are parents with the services provided, and what problems do they encounter?

(7) What persons play important caretaking roles when children are in their own homes and when children are in out-of-home settings?

This wealth of information, never before assembled in precisely this way, in and of itself is already providing baseline data for early childhood policymakers and planners in each of the 11 nations who completed Phase 1 of the Preprimary Project. And, as mentioned earlier, the Phase 1 data allow researchers in each participating country to select a relevant sample of service settings for the Phase 2 study—which examines the quality of children's experiences in their various settings and the age-4 developmental status of those children. Phase 2 data, in turn, will be the basis for the Phase 3 investigation into the relationship between early childhood experiences and later development.

At the time of writing, Phase 1 data collection and analyses have been completed. Phase 2 data collection and analyses are nearing completion, and a series of monographs and videotapes reporting the findings is in preparation. At the same time, instrument design for Phase 3 is also under way.

The 11 nations/territories whose Phase 1 data are reported here are Belgium (French-speaking [Fr.]), China (People's Republic of China [PRC]), Finland, Germany (Federal Republic of Germany [FRG]; note that the study was conducted before unification of the FRG with the German Democratic Republic), Hong Kong, Italy, Nigeria, Portugal, Spain, Thailand, and the U.S.A. At the outset of Phase 1 in 1989, each of these nations assembled a "national profile" of early childhood provisions, based on data sources (mostly government sources) available at the time. This constituted a starting point for the family-based study that was to come—the household survey.

The next two chapters describe the Phase 1 methodology and the national samples, giving an idea of the care taken to assure representativeness and of the characteristics of families involved in the survey. Chapter 4 gives findings about the full variety of arrangements families make for their 4–year-olds' care/education—including everything from care at home by parents to care in highly organized facilities. A special look at organized facility settings is the subject of Chapter 5; Chapter 6 centers on children's daily routines. Two concluding chapters summarize the key findings country-by-country and draws out the implications of the overall findings. They capsulize the information gleaned when families around the world speak about the care and education of their 4–year-old children.

2

Methodology of the Phase 1 Study

PATRICIA P. OLMSTED WITH JOAQUIM BAIRRÃO,
ARLETTE DELHAXHE, HELENA HOAS, MIKKO OJALA,
OLAYEMI ONIBOKUN, SYLVIA OPPER, JESÚS PALACIOS,
NITTAYA PASSORNSIRI, LUCIO PUSCI, HANS-GÜNTHER ROSSBACH,
AND SHI HUI ZHONG

As described in Chapter 1, the IEA Preprimary Project (IEA/PPP) is a cross-national three-phase study investigating the nature, quality, and effects of the experiences of children prior to formal schooling. The major objectives of Phase 1 of the project were: (1) to develop a representative picture of the variety of care and education settings attended by 4-year-old children in each of the participating countries; (2) to examine certain basic features of each country's early childhood settings; (3) to explore, in each country, the relationships between use of early childhood settings and family characteristics; and (4) to describe the daily care patterns for 4-year-old children in each country.

To achieve these four objectives, Phase 1 researchers used household survey techniques to collect data directly from parents (or guardians) about their use or nonuse of extraparental care or education services for their 4-year-old children. This chapter presents general information about the Phase 1 sampling plans and data collection procedures, and it describes and summarizes the specific methodology used by each of the 11 countries taking part in Phase 1.

General Sampling Information

The International Sampling Referee

Leslie Kish serves as international sampling referee for the IEA Preprimary Project. Dr. Kish is a professor emeritus at the University of Michigan, where he was a founder of the Institute for Social Research. In the past he has served as president of the American Statistical Association (1977) and of the International Association of Survey Statisticians (1983–1985).

15

In his role as sampling referee for the IEA/PPP, Dr. Kish worked closely with the ICC in supervising the preparation of the project's sampling documents, monitoring the development of national sampling plans, and granting formal approval of each national plan.

The Target Population

The target population for Phase 1 sample selection was defined as children $3\frac{1}{2}$ to $4\frac{1}{2}$ years old (4 years ± 6 months) at the time of Phase 1 data collection (i.e., at the time of the interview with each child's parent/guardian). In each participating country, the target population excluded children living out-of-country or in institutions, as well as children with serious physical or mental handicaps. In most participating countries, the 4 years ± 6 months age-range takes in the child's last full year before entry into a formal school environment; it is also the age-range for which there is the widest variety of early childhood care and education services. However, for funding reasons, IEA/PPP researchers in Hong Kong found it necessary to begin their project operations before determination of this international target age-range. Thus, the range used for sample selection in Hong Kong was 4–5 years of age.

Sample Selection

In general, in each participating nation, researchers hoped to identify a probability sample of children in the target age-range. However, the sampling referee and the ICC faced several challenges in attempting to obtain probability samples while maintaining high sampling standards. First, educational researchers having little or no national survey sampling experience or training would be carrying out the sampling operations. Second, since most national research teams had limited resources, national samples would have to be small—generally between 400 and 1,000 children; the challenge would come in spreading these small samples over large populations of households. Finally, since generally only 4–10% of households contain a 4-year-old child, researchers in some countries would have to screen large numbers of households to find the relatively small proportion with 4-year-old children.

A Sampling Plan for Each Country

Generally, in cross-national household survey studies, constructing *similar* sample frames for all participating countries is not attempted, because the procedure would be prohibitively expensive and at the same time counterproductive, in light of the different sources of population information available in various countries. In the IEA/PPP the International

Coordinating Center (ICC) and the sampling referee assisted each National Research Coordinator (NRC) in custom-designing a national sampling plan that would produce a probability sample of children. In doing so they used the most recent, most accurate sources of population information that each country had available.

As Dr. Kish noted in the *IEA/PPP Phase 1 Interim Sampling Report* (Weikart *et al.*, 1988), "We want to emphasize that flexibility in sample design in comparative and cooperative studies is permissible; it is also desirable, in order to better utilize the distinct resources and selection frames to be found in the participating countries. It is common to use distinct designs for separate domains, even within single countries" (p. 4). In each country, the sampling referee required a probability sample that was as close to perfect as local conditions would allow.

The Sampling Questionnaire

To assist NRCs in understanding general sampling issues, locating sources of population information, and developing a proposed sampling plan, the ICC, with the help of Dr. Kish, designed an IEA/PPP Phase 1 Sampling Questionnaire (Olmsted *et al.*, 1987). The questionnaire, which used a question-and-answer format with skip patterns to accommodate the variety of situations found in the participating countries, was based on two of the sampling referee's published works (Kish, 1965, 1987). The major sections of the questionnaire covered the following topics: sample size and subpopulations of special interest; existing sets of survey data; population registers; and national census data.

To complete the sample-size section of the Sampling Questionnaire, each NRC obtained national population information, considered subpopulations of special interest (e.g., regional or ethnic subgroups), considered the resources available for Phase 1 of the IEA/PPP, and estimated a proposed sample size. To complete the remaining three sections of the questionnaire (on existing sets of survey data, population registers, national census data), the NRC contacted the national statistical office, research organizations, and other agencies, to determine the existence and availability of various types of information that might be useful for developing the sampling plan or for selecting the sample. Using the information collected in completing the Sampling Questionnaire, the NRC then developed a proposed national sampling plan. After reviewing this proposed plan, the ICC and the sampling referee, together with the NRC, determined a proposed sample design and a proposed sample size that would be both feasible and produce sufficient data to meet specified confidence limits for the estimation of population values.

To accompany the Sampling Questionnaire, the ICC developed a supplementary-information document that included: (1) definitions of sampling terminology; (2) proposed sampling designs; and (3) special considerations (e.g., types of recently conducted surveys that might provide sample frames useful for the IEA/PPP Phase 1 study). Members of the IEA Technical Advisory Committee reviewed the IEA/PPP Phase 1 Sampling Questionnaire and the supplementary-information document, and the IEA General Assembly approved the documents in September 1987.

Weighting the Data

Although the aim of each national sampling design was equal probability of selection, departures from equal probability occurred in a few nations for various reasons. However, in each country where this happened, the NRC provided the probabilities of selection for every case, enabling the ICC to assign weights to individual cases and examine weighted versus unweighted findings. After the sampling referee reviewed the unweighted and weighted results for several key variables, he recommended whether weighting should be used in calculating the Phase 1 results. The three major reasons for weighting the data of a few countries were the following: (1) selection of fixed-size samples (of children) from unequal-sized units (villages, regions); (2) unequal response rates; and (3) a need to obtain national estimates from provincial estimates.

General Data Collection Information

The Parent/Guardian Interview

Phase 1 employed a 50-minute Parent/Guardian Interview (P/G Interview) to collect information about families' use or nonuse of early childhood care and education services (the P/G Interview is given in Appendix C). A major portion of the interview concerned the care or education arrangements parents made for their 4-year-olds during a typical week. Interviewers asked parents why they selected certain care or education settings, what problems they encountered in those settings, and how satisfied they were with each setting. Additional information collected concerned how much parents paid for care or education arrangements, what distances children had to travel to their various settings, and what means of transportation they used. The P/G Interview also asked questions about the family background, including parental education levels and occupations, living accommodation, and household composition.

Another part of the interview, the daily routine chart, asked parents for a detailed description of a typical 24-hour day in their child's life, including the child's whereabouts and caregiver(s) throughout the day previous to the interview. (Some countries—Belgium, Finland, Germany, and Spain—formatted this part of the interview into a Daily Routine Booklet, which children carried with them for a day or a week to have various caregivers "log into" throughout the day.) This daily routine chart or booklet sought to establish the typical "care patterns" children experienced in each country.

Researchers from each participating country contributed to the development of the P/G Interview by indicating areas of interest or by suggesting specific questions. One objective of involving the NRCs in the development was to design an instrument that would (1) provide sufficient information about the use of early childhood care and education services within each participating country, and (2) allow for cross-national comparisons of various types of information. The challenge, then, was to create an instrument that would address issues of national as well as international concern without overburdening every country's interview with questions relevant to only one or a few of the countries. Researchers met this challenge by designating three types of interview items: *international core* items, *international option* items, and *national option* items.

International Core Items

The international core items were those questions that every country participating in the project included in its P/G Interview. Core items were, by definition, questions of cross-national interest. For a question to be designated an international core item, every participating country had to indicate that the item was nationally relevant. For example, all the participating countries expressed interest in learning more about the range of formal and informal care or education arrangements that families make for their 4-year-old children. Therefore, the core items included questions about the types of early childhood care or education services families used; the characteristics of those services (e.g., cost, distance from home, problems encountered); parents' reasons for making their particular arrangement(s) for the care or education of their child; the range of services offered by the child's major extraparental caregiver; and the extent of parental involvement in the child's care setting. In addition, the core items included questions about household composition (e.g., the numbers and ages of the household's adults and children) and about family-background characteristics (e.g., parental education, occupation, income). Also designated as core items were questions about the child's care pattern, or daily routine.

A country could exclude a core item from its version of the P/G Interview only if the item was one that would produce a uniform response across the entire national sample (e.g., if every family in the sample would answer yes to having a source of light in their home, or if every family in the national sample would answer yes to having a private kitchen). Also, if necessary, a country could modify a core item's phrasing to clarify it or make it culturally appropriate. Similarly, where necessary, a country could use alternative methods to obtain some of the information requested in core items, as will be explained later in the discussion of Hong Kong's methodology.

International Option Items

In addition to the core items, the ICC also developed some questions that many but not all countries considered relevant. These were designated as *international option items*. For example, several international option items asked parents about types of health examinations their child may have had. These questions were excluded by a few countries simply to limit the length of the interview procedure. Each country could determine whether to include a specific international option item, depending on the appropriateness or applicability of the item.

National Option Items

Several countries, on their own, developed and formatted additional items for their version of the P/G Interview. These were designated as *national option items*. Since each such item was unique to a specific country, this chapter will not include a discussion of the national option items.

Pilot-Testing of the International P/G Interview

After the countries had agreed on the questions to include in the international interview instrument and designated each question as an international core item or an international option item, the ICC prepared the final international instrument, based on the countries' decisions. The ICC then conducted two forms of pilot-testing on the international instrument.

First, to determine the stability of responses across time, on two separate occasions 2 weeks apart, ICC staff interviewed 25 families with children between the ages of 3 and 5 years. (This procedure is similar to the test-retest method of measuring reliability.) The 25 families varied with respect to family structure, annual household income, family size, use of early childhood services, and so forth. They were from both rural and urban areas in southeastern Michigan. For each of 10 P/G Interview items for which a respondent's answers would be expected to remain the same over the 2-week interval (e.g., questions about annual household income, or about parental years of full-time education), ICC staff calculated the percentage of families whose answers agreed on the two separate occasions. The results were as follows: Of the 10 items, 1 item produced 100% agreement, 5 items produced 90–99% agreement, and 4 items produced 80–89% agreement. Since 80% agreement was considered adequate, ICC staff deemed the items to have sufficient stability.

Second, the ICC pilot-tested the daily routine questioning procedure, to insure that parents' recollections of their 4-year-old child's whereabouts and care providers on the day previous to the interview would be sufficiently accurate to make this an appropriate data-collection procedure. The method used for the pilot test involved an ICC staff member observing 10 4-year-old children for a minimum of 6 hours each during a single day and recording all changes of caregivers, settings, and social context (i.e., the number of other adults and children present) that each child experienced. The following day, an ICC staff member administered the P/G Interview to each child's family and compared the information parents provided in the instrument's daily routine chart with the observations of the previous day. The results indicated that parents' recollections were extremely accurate concerning the caregivers and settings for their children.

Preparation of the National P/G Interview Instruments

After developing the national option items that they wanted to add to the international core and option items, project staff in each country prepared their national P/G Interview instruments. National researchers then conducted within-country pilot tests to assess the clarity, cultural appropriateness, and usefulness of the national instrument. To insure that the instrument would be effective across all populations in the sample areas, most countries selected pilot-test families from geographically dispersed areas. Some countries conducted a two- or three-stage pilot test, making revisions in the instrument after each stage. The sample sizes for these pilot tests ranged from 25 to 200.

Procedures for Data Collection

The Data Collection Period

The time span for data collection was from October 1987 to September 1989; in general, countries collected most of their data between May and November 1988. The data collection period differed from country to country because of factors such as availability of funds, time constraints governing the use of funds, and holiday and seasonal schedules.

Selection of Interviewers

Each country was responsible for selecting its own interviewers. As a result, the criteria for interviewer selection varied according to the specific characteristics that national project staff considered important. Generally the interviewers were university students or graduates, preprimary teachers or caregivers, or persons with prior experience in conducting surveys. In many countries, a person's level of education was the major factor influencing his or her selection as an interviewer, while in a few countries, previous experience with research was the major factor. Several countries also considered familiarity with the care or education settings, with children and families, or with a specific geographical area as an important selection criterion.

Training of Interviewers

Since each country developed its own interviewer training methods and materials, the duration and type of training varied from country to country. In almost every country, national project staff conducted the interviewer training sessions. Topics addressed during training included the goals and design of the study; the various sections of the P/G Interview; administration of the P/G Interview (e.g., how to contact families, how to interview, how to handle potential problems); and the role of the interviewer/data collector. Almost all countries developed a training or instruction manual for the interviews, and most used a combination of the following methods along with the manual: examination of the interview instrument, practice interviews, training videotapes, role play, trial runs of the interview with local families, and group discussion. In some countries the training was a two-stage process wherein project staff trained several interviewers, who subsequently returned to local areas and recruited and trained additional interviewers.

Preparation of Data for Analysis

For countries to use in coding their P/G Interview data, the ICC prepared and distributed a coding manual for the international core and option items. In addition, ICC staff developed and distributed guidelines for cleaning the data, building data files, and sending the data to the ICC. Using these materials, national project staff coded their interview data, built a complete raw data file, cleaned the data, and transmitted it to the ICC.

When the ICC received a set of data from a country, to verify the correctness of the data, the data manager examined the descriptive statistics for a large number of major variables. If the data manager detected errors in a data set (e.g., missing data or miscoded data), the ICC requested additional information from the NRC and, as necessary, corrected the data set. After checking (and, if necessary, correcting) a data set, the data manager prepared weighted and unweighted printouts for a basic set of 20 variables, for examination by the sampling referee. Three project participants—China (PRC), Hong Kong, and Nigeria—used weighted data for analysis.[1]

Methodology in Specific Nations

Sampling and Data Collection in Belgium (Fr.)

In French-speaking Belgium the target population included all non-handicapped children who were between the ages of $3\frac{1}{2}$ and $4\frac{1}{2}$ and living at home. Using two-stage cluster sampling and PPS (probability proportional to size) sampling procedures, researchers first selected 106 PSUs (primary sampling units), which fell into 73 communes (from a total of 279 communes). Then, for each PSU, researchers randomly selected 4 children for the primary sample and 4 children for replacements.

The Belgian sampling frame for the selection of communes consisted of documents from the National Institute of Statistics. The sampling frame for selection of children consisted of commune-level, index card files of inhabitants, which are updated regularly.

Belgium's overall response rate was only 67%, with approximately half of nonresponses due to refusals. The achieved sample size was 424. Due to the large number of nonresponses and the differences in nonresponse rates among communes, the sample was not entirely self-weighting. Comparisons between weighted and unweighted statistics for several variables revealed no appreciable differences, and therefore, unweighted results were recommended by the sampling referee (Delhaxhe & Hindryckx, 1989).

The main data collection instrument used in Belgium was the P/G Interview. The international option items Belgium added included questions relating to the degree of parental satisfaction with the care and education services their child received and to the child's health status. Researchers pilot-tested the P/G Interview by conducting 90 interviews. The pilot test made possible an analysis of (1) the content of the interview (to determine where adaptations were needed), (2) the English-to-French

---

[1]By agreement with the sampling referee, sampling errors were not computed. This departure from preferred statistical procedures (which are often violated) was based on the following reasons: First, though the possible errors of measurement and response may have been more dominant and important in these surveys than the sampling errors, it would not have been feasible to design experiments to measure *all* these types of errors. Second, computing sampling errors for all 11 countries would have been costly and difficult because of each country's distinct and complex sample design. Third, a presentation of the results of sampling error computations would have been inappropriate for the intended audiences of this book. Moreover, it may be that the well-known formulas for standard errors, such as $p + t/(pq/n)$, are underestimates of the actual variabilities present in the data.

translation of items, and (3) the clarity of the interviewer's instructions to the respondents.

Belgium's interviewers were students in the field of psychology or education, persons hired part-time for this job, and "job-workers" (generally, unemployed friends, former students, or relatives of the researchers). All interviewers had a high level of education, and the majority were 20–25 years of age. Their training consisted of two 3-hour group sessions conducted by a researcher. During these sessions, interviewers learned the goals and expected uses of the research and examined the P/G Interview in detail, with attention to the sections that the pilot study had revealed to be of particular importance. After each interviewer conducted a trial run with parents of a 4-year-old, the results were discussed in one of the group sessions.

The Belgian interviewers collected Phase 1 data between December 1987 and January 1989. They administered the P/G Interview face to face, primarily in the respondents' homes, and recorded all responses in writing. National project staff maintained contact with all interviewers by phone, mail, or in person. Project staff reviewed a sample of the completed questionnaires to assess the quality of the data collected (Hindryckx & Delhaxhe, 1989).

Sampling and Data Collection in China (PRC)

China's target population included all nonhandicapped children who were in the target age-range and living at home. First, national project researchers formed 10 strata from the 30 provinces by combining economic, cultural, and geographic information, and then they selected 1 province (PSU) from each stratum. Using multistage stratified cluster sampling, within each province chosen, the statisticians used PPS sampling procedures to select 10 urban areas (secondary sampling units, or SSUs) and 10 rural areas (SSUs).

In each urban SSU chosen, the sampling frame for selecting children was the set of citizen registers that are maintained at police stations and updated regularly. The researchers used computer procedures to randomly select 400 target children from the many citizen registers that covered the urban areas within a given province. For each rural SSU chosen, statisticians selected 68 towns and townships using PPS sampling procedures. For each town selected, they randomly selected 20 registration books from the complete set of citizen registers and then randomly chose 13 children from these books for the primary sample and 7 additional children for replacements. For each township selected, project staff randomly chose 4 villages and then, using random-walk procedures, selected 13 target children from across these villages. The final proposed sample for China consisted of

12,840 children from 10 provinces, including 4,000 from urban and 8,840 from rural areas.

China's overall response rate was 99%, and the final achieved sample size was 12,835. Because the sample was not entirely self-weighting, weights were computed for each case by combining the probabilities of the 10 provinces with the probabilities in two stages of (1) selecting urban areas, towns, and townships and (2) selecting children within them. For national results, the 10 provincial results were weighted by populations of 4-year-olds in the respective strata (Shi, 1989b).

Chinese researchers used the international core P/G Interview to collect Phase 1 data. Because of the magnitude of their data collection project, the researchers chose to take full advantage of the opportunity it afforded to study issues of national interest as well as issues of interest to the IEA/PPP. Thus, China's interview instrument contained many national option items (e.g., questions about parents' attitudes toward the sex of their child and parents' expectations for their child). Chinese researchers conducted a pilot test of their version of the P/G Interview with 200 families from several geographical areas of the country.

In 1987 project staff set up a national research center in Beijing and 9 other provincial research centers to train interviewers and collect data. The NRC and two members of the technical group of the national research center conducted a trial training-session in Beijing, after which training was conducted for data collectors in the remaining 9 provinces.

Interviewers were high-level early childhood education officers (at or above the level of the county board of education) or kindergarten head teachers or administrators. Other interviewer qualifications included completion of at least junior middle school, interest in early childhood education and educational research, and a certificate from the national research center stating that one's work met required standards. Before training, researchers videotaped a properly conducted interview and distributed the tapes and accompanying instructions to each of the 10 provinces. Approximately 1,000 interviewers (60–120 per province) attended 7–9 days of training. Besides the videotapes, training included a highly detailed manual (explaining the P/G Interview, administration procedures, and solutions to potential problems); demonstrations of proper interviewing techniques; practice interviews and tests; an examination; and, in some provinces, field practice after the examination.

China's interviewers collected data between October 1987 and July 1988. They worked in pairs, with one person asking questions while the other recorded the answers. Using this method, the two interviewers were able to check each other's work (Shi, 1989a).

Sampling and Data Collection in Finland

Finland's target population included all nonhandicapped children who were in the target age-range and living at home, except for those residing on the island of Åland (who constituted less than 1% of the age group). Using a complete set of population information for all counties and two-stage stratified cluster sampling, researchers first used PPS procedures to select a sample of 80 PSUs that fell into 68 counties. For each PSU selected, research staff determined a sampling ratio that would produce a national self-weighting, Epsem (equal probability of selection method) sample.

The Finnish sampling frame for the selection of children was a central population register that is maintained and updated every month or so by the National Population Central Register Office in Helsinki. For each PSU, researchers used systematic sampling procedures to select individual children's names from this register. The final proposed sample for Finland consisted of 680 children from 28 urban areas and 40 rural areas, both spread throughout the country.

Finland's initial overall response rate was 68%. However, with extra effort a final response rate of 85% was attained, and only a third of the nonresponses were refusals. Since the achieved sample ($N = 576$) was an Epsem sample, and because the nonresponse was low and uniform across PSUs, the sampling referee did not consider it necessary to weight the data (Ojala & Siekkinen, 1989b).

Data collection in Finland employed the P/G Interview, including most of the international option items. In April 1987 four interviewers conducted a pilot study with 31 families from an urban and a rural community in eastern Finland. As a result of the pilot study, researchers determined that it was important to conduct the interview only with the child's mother or female guardian.

Interviewers were 145 student volunteers from 11 kindergarten teacher-training institutes, the University of Joensuu, and a training institute of social pedagogy. Most were in their second or third year of teacher training. All of the interviewers had completed a matriculation examination and were at least 19 years old. Prior to training, national project staff had developed a detailed manual that described the study and provided general and specific guidelines for the P/G Interview. They had also developed a videotape illustrating the proper approach for arranging and completing an interview. Three members of the national project staff trained the interviewers in two sessions (totaling 8 hours), using the manual and videotape along with role-playing techniques and discussion.

Finnish interviewers collected data from September 1988–September 1989. National research staff closely monitored the interviewers, who submitted their completed P/G Interviews on a monthly basis. Using the completed interviews, staff contacted 5% of the sample families by phone to verify their responses to 10 P/G Interview items and found no problems (Ojala & Siekkinen, 1989a).

Sampling and Data Collection in Germany (FRG)

The German study was conducted in the "old" states of the Federal Republic of Germany. The target population for the IEA study consisted of nonhandicapped children who were between the ages of $3\frac{1}{2}$ and $4\frac{1}{2}$ and living in a household (1) maintained by a German-surnamed householder, and (2) containing the child's genetic or "social" mother. Using multistage cluster sampling and PPS procedures, a survey research institute hired by the researchers selected 525 districts from a total of 50,000 electoral districts. After using random-route procedures to develop a master sample containing 110 households from each of the 525 electoral districts chosen, 3,826 households were randomly selected (from all eligible households) for the Preprimary Project Phase 1 sample. Germany's national study actually encompassed children from birth to 6 years of age, and their researchers estimated that for purposes of the cross-national study, this sample size would yield a minimum of 400 households with children in the target age-range of $3\frac{1}{2}$ to $4\frac{1}{2}$ years.

Germany's sampling frame consisted of a household listing developed through random-route procedures. The final proposed sample consisted of 400 children from 525 electoral districts throughout the country. The country's overall response rate was only 67%, and its refusal rate was 15%. The achieved sample ($N = 509$) was not entirely self-weighting, hence weights were computed for every case. Because comparison between weighted and unweighted statistics for several variables revealed no appreciable differences, unweighted results were recommended (Rossbach, 1989b).

The research team in Germany used the format of the international P/G Instrument as the basis for their national version. Owing to the nature of their fundraising process, German researchers had to begin to develop and pilot-test their P/G Interview before completion of the international version. Also, the German researchers found it necessary to expand the age-range and scope of the project within their country. Thus their final P/G Interview included a few international and several national option items, such as questions relating to paternal involvement in child care, the care history of the child, and parental preferences regarding care arrangements. GFM-GETAS, the survey research institute hired by the national research center, conducted a pilot test with 88 families between February and April 1988. In addition, the national research center conducted a small number of pilot tests.

GFM-GETAS selected interviewers from members of their own staff.

All interviewers had previous experience with social surveys and training in general interview procedures. To train the interviewers for this particular study, the national project center and GFM-GETAS developed materials that included both general and detailed descriptions of the various sections of the P/G Interview, explanations of rules and procedures of data collection, and an explanation of how to use the daily routine materials (the booklet mentioned earlier).

GFM-GETAS conducted the data collection between May and October 1988. Most of the interviews were carried out in person, and responses were recorded immediately. GFM-GETAS, in checking the administration of all interviews completed by approximately 20% of the interviewers, found no problems with the data collection. Also, after each interviewer sent completed interview materials back to the survey research center, GFM-GETAS reviewed them for thoroughness and accuracy (Rossbach, 1989a).

Sampling and Data Collection in Hong Kong

Hong Kong's target population included all nonhandicapped Cantonese-speaking children between the ages of 4 and 5 who were enrolled in early childhood facilities (96% of the age group). Hong Kong researchers first developed 12 strata that reflected geographic location, type of facility, and size of facility, and then, using PPS procedures, they selected early childhood service facilities within each stratum. Within each facility chosen, a single classroom of children was designated for inclusion, and 15 of the classroom's children were randomly selected.

The sampling frame for the selection of facilities was demographic statistics from the Hong Kong government census and affiliated departments, while the sampling frame for the selection of children was classroom registration lists. The final proposed sample consisted of 1,000 children from 65 early childhood facilities in the various areas of Hong Kong. Hong Kong had a response rate of 95% and no refusals; their achieved sample size was 947. Since the sample was not entirely self-weighting, weights were computed for every case. Comparisons between weighted and unweighted statistics for several variables revealed many appreciable differences, and therefore weighted results were recommended by the sampling referee (Opper, 1989b).

The Hong Kong research team used the P/G Interview with several international option items and 3 national option items related to parents' educational aspirations for their child, the child's activities at home, and the family's religious affiliation. The NRC at the University of Hong Kong conducted three separate pilot tests with a total of 50 children and their parents. Researchers first administered the P/G Interview to staff members of the university and collected feedback about the interview questions. The second pilot test demonstrated that some questions were too sensitive or personal and would not be answered honestly in a face-to-face interview. Consequently, researchers divided the P/G Interview into two parts: an interview to be administered face to face and a written questionnaire to be completed by the respondent and returned directly to the NRC. When the final pilot test used the interview-and-questionnaire format with positive results, the research team adopted this format for the study.

The caregivers of the target children—preschool teachers and child care workers—served as interviewers. Principals and heads of participating preschools selected the interviewers in their respective schools and acted as their supervisors. Training consisted of 15 four-hour sessions, each conducted by the research team and attended by 20–25 of the 220 interviewers and their supervisors. The research team made allowance for the fact that, as experienced teachers, the interviewers were already familiar with most of the procedures used in conducting interviews with parents. During training, researchers provided an overview of the study and familiarized interviewers with their role as data collectors.

Data collection took place between October 1987 and June 1988. The NRC received the completed interviews in three waves, each of which was checked carefully by researchers for accuracy; if there were any problems, researchers contacted the interviewer to discuss them. The NRC then sent out the next set of interview and questionnaire forms with a letter emphasizing specific points and suggesting ideas for preventing future difficulties. The research team contacted each interviewer at least once during data collection and strongly encouraged interviewers to contact their supervisors or the NRC at any time for assistance (Opper, 1989a).

Sampling and Data Collection in Italy

Italy's target population included all nonhandicapped children who were in the target age-range and living at home. Using multistage stratified cluster sampling, the research team first defined 4 geographic strata (northern, central, and southern Italy, and the islands of Sardinia and Sicily) and then subdivided each geographic stratum into 4 substrata representing different population densities. From the resulting 16 substrata, researchers used systematic sampling procedures and PPS strategies to select 50 communes. From each commune chosen, they then selected 24 children using systematic sampling procedures.

The Italian sampling frame for selecting children within each chosen commune consisted of commune-level lists of 4-year-olds. The final proposed sample for Italy consisted of a total of 1,200 children from the 50 communes selected throughout Italy. The achieved sample size was 1,000, with an overall response rate of 85% and a refusal rate of 7%. Since the sample was not entirely self-weighting, weights were computed to assess the necessity of weighting during data analysis. Because comparisons between weighted and unweighted statistics for several variables revealed no appreciable differences, the sampling referee recommended that unweighted results be reported (Pusci, 1989b).

For data collection, Italy used the P/G Interview with all the international option items. They added two national option items related to the care history of the child and parent–child activities. A pilot test of the interview with 50 Italian households during the winter of 1987–1988 revealed that the instrument needed several revisions before being used for actual data collection.

The NRC, who was responsible for training interviewers, asked primary education inspectors and headteachers of schools in each of the 50 sample communes to select 3–6 competent preprimary teachers who they felt could be trained to conduct interviews. Of the 160 potential interviewers selected in this way, 145 were chosen to undergo a 3-day training course (20–35 candidates at a time) at the national project center. Before training, the NRC sent copies of the P/G Interview training manual to each of the course participants. During the 3-day course, participants received copies of the interview instrument, so they could practice and make audiotapes of themselves role-playing interviews. After reviewing the quality of the practice interviews on the audiotapes, the NRC selected 136 course participants to be interviewers.

Italy's NRC organized two periods of data collection between May and November 1988. In many communes, before data collection, parents and teachers of preprimary school children received information about the purpose of the study, to increase the likelihood of families' agreeing to participate. All interviews were conducted face to face, and all responses were recorded in writing only. Research staff contacted a sample of approximately 100 families by telephone to verify their responses to 5 or 6 interview items (Pusci, 1989a).

Sampling and Data Collection in Nigeria

In Nigeria, the target population included nonhandicapped children who were between the ages of 3 and 5 and living at home. Using multistage stratified cluster sampling, Nigerian researchers first used a combination of educational, religious, sociopolitical, linguistic, and geographical information to form the country's 19 states into 5 strata. Then, from each stratum, they selected 1 state by judgment. Working from the master sample developed by the Nigerian Federal Office of Statistics (120 enumeration areas per state), for each of the 5 states chosen, the researchers used PPS procedures to select 56 enumeration areas. Within each enumeration area chosen, they then used systematic sampling procedures to select 12 households for screening. According to estimates, after screening, approximately 5 households in each enumeration area would contain children in Nigeria's target age-range.

The sampling frame for the selection of households was a household listing for each enumeration area. Nigeria's final proposed sample consisted of 1,400 children from the 5 selected states. Data to calculate the response rate were not available, but the response rate for another household survey conducted using similar procedures in these 5 states during the same period of time was approximately 96%. The achieved sample size was 1,295. Within each of the 5 states, the urban and rural samples were separately self-weighting. For national results, the 10 sets of results (5 states, urban and rural) were weighted by total census populations in the respective strata (Onibokun, 1989).

The main data collection instrument in Nigeria was the P/G Interview, including all international option items and one national option item relating to the child's developmental status. Pilot-testing took place in September 1987 with a judgment sample of 40 urban and rural households in one state. Results revealed both strengths and weaknesses of the P/G Interview procedure: Strengths included the effectiveness of using interviewers from the Federal Office of Statistics (FOS) to collect data, while weaknesses included problems encountered in eliciting accurate responses to income-related questions.

The Nigerian research team consisted of the NRC (at the University of Ibadan), 5 state research coordinators, and five assistant coordinators (state supervisors from the FOS). The FOS state supervisors selected from their offices a minimum of 10 interviewers per state. Criteria used for interviewer selection were completion of secondary education, familiarity and experience with household survey techniques and procedures, and being a native of the state in which the interview would be conducted.

The NRC held 4-hour workshops to train the state research co-ordinators. After these coordinators had been introduced to the study, the P/G Interview and training manual, and the interviewing procedures, they each role-played an interview with the NRC and received feedback about the interview. After this training, each coordinator returned to his or her respective state and trained the assistant coordinator (the FOS state supervisor) in proper administration of the P/G Interview. The FOS interviewers also attended 3 training sessions organized by the research coordinators in their states. (The interviewers had also been trained by the FOS for a previous household study.)

Data collection took place in October and November 1988. All interviews were conducted face to face, and responses were recorded in writing. The NRC kept in close touch with each of the coordinators and the assistant coordinators. To ensure that problems were handled correctly, assistant coordinators (FOS state supervisors) accompanied interviewers on their field assignments. The coordinators also checked each interview form carefully to ensure that it had been completed properly (Onibokun, 1991).

Sampling and Data Collection in Portugal

In Portugal, the target population included all nonhandicapped native-born children between ages $3\frac{1}{2}$ and $4\frac{1}{2}$ and living at home, except for those who were residents of the autonomous regions of the Azores and Madeira archipelagoes (approximately 1% of the age group). Using two-stage stratified cluster sampling, researchers first divided Portugal's 275 counties into 26 strata, using a combination of socioeconomic, demographic, health, and education information. Next, they used systematic sampling procedures and PPS strategies to select 76 PSUs, which fell into 57 counties. From each PSU chosen, the researchers used systematic sampling procedures to select 10 children.

The Portuguese sampling frame for the selection of children consisted of county-level birth-registration records. Through a pilot study, Portuguese researchers found that although birth records were several years old, over 85% of children in the target age-range could still be located from information contained in them. The final proposed sample for Portugal consisted of 580 children in 57 counties.

Overall, Portugal's response rate was 76%, and its refusal rate was 3%. The achieved sample size was 581. The sample was not entirely self-weighting; so weights were computed to assess the necessity of weighting for data analysis. Comparisons between weighted and unweighted statistics for several variables revealed no appreciable differences. Therefore, the sampling referee recommended that unweighted results be used for data analysis (Abreu *et al.*, 1989).

Researchers in Portugal used the P/G Interview with international option items relating to the child's health status. Pilot-testing of the P/G Interview took place in October 1987. For a pilot test with 35 families (18 in northern Portugal, 17 in southern Portugal), 4 nonprofessional interviewers used the May 1987 version of the P/G Interview. The pilot-testing resulted in a decision to eliminate some national option items and revise the international option items. Researchers also thought the length of the interview should be decreased (pilot-test interviews ranged from just over 30 minutes to just under 2 hours).

Because of concerns about the quality of interviewers, the national project staff based selection primarily on the criterion of having a degree in psychology or another human science. Field-work coordinating centers for training and data collection were set up in Porto and Lisbon (northern and southern Portugal, respectively), and the research team, using a manual that explained the P/G Interview, trained interviewers at these centers in two 1-day sessions. At the first training session, researchers gave each interviewer two interviews to complete; a week later the interviewers attended a second 1-day session to review and receive feedback on the interviews they had completed and to meet individually with the research team. A total of 34 interviewers successfully completed training in Porto and Lisbon.

During data collection, which took place between April and June 1988, interviewers completed 581 interviews. When researchers contacted 204 respondents by telephone to verify their responses, they found no problems with the data collection (Bairrão *et al.*, 1989).

Sampling and Data Collection in Spain

In Spain, the target population included all nonhandicapped children who were between the ages of 3½ and 4½ and living at home. Using two-stage cluster sampling, Spanish researchers first used PPS procedures to select 160 PSUs, which fell into 45 provinces. From each PSU, they then selected 3 children, using random selection procedures when listings of 4-year-olds were available and random-route procedures when such listings were not.

For most PSUs, the sampling frame for the selection of children was a local register. For the few remaining areas, the researchers did not have access to a sampling frame and thus used random-route procedures. Spain's final proposed sample consisted of 480 children from 160 localities throughout the country.

The overall response rate for Spain was 29%, and the refusal rate was 35%. The country had an achieved sample size of 480. The low response rate is partly due to the fact that when a family could not easily be contacted, the researchers often substituted another home rather than recontacting the original home several times. The sample was not entirely self-weighting, hence weights were computed to assess the necessity of weighting during data analysis. Since comparisons between weighted and unweighted statistics for several variables revealed no appreciable differences, the sampling referee recommended that unweighted data be used for the analysis (Palacios, 1989).

The research team in Spain used the P/G Interview with a majority of the international option items and a few national option items. Two of the national option items involved expanding the daily routine chart to ask about the previous Sunday and to record not only the child's whereabouts and caregivers but also the child's activities throughout the day. The researchers pilot-tested the interview with approximately 30 families from three geographical regions with various social, economic, and cultural characteristics.

Interviewers were aged 21–35 with a university degree or in their last 2 years of study for a degree. Preference was given to interviewers affiliated with private firms having expertise in conducting field surveys as well as experience with qualitative and random-route survey procedures. Training lasted an average of 6–8 hours and was conducted in 1 or 2 sessions by 2 members of the national project center staff. Topics covered included the background, design, and goals of the study; the P/G Interview and its training manual; and proper interview techniques and procedures. In addition to studying the P/G Interview in detail, interviewers completed and reviewed practice interviews and discussed any problems encountered in the practice.

Spain collected data in May and June 1989. The research team required all interviewers to maintain telephone contact with the national project center and to send in their completed interviews to be checked. Project staff contacted a sample of families by phone or in person to verify that their interviews had been conducted and to confirm their responses to a selected set of questions (Palacios *et al.*, 1989).

Sampling and Data Collection in Thailand

The target population for Thailand included all nonhandicapped children who were in the target age-range and living at home. Researchers first identified 5 geographic regions (strata) and then divided each region into municipal and nonmunicipal areas. Using multistage stratified cluster sampling and PPS procedures, research staff next selected 38 PSUs (9 municipal, 29 nonmunicipal) in 33 provinces in these 5 strata. They then selected 149 SSUs (blocks/villages) from the 38 PSUs. The information used to construct the 5 strata consisted of 1980 population and housing census data as well as 1987 population projection figures. The final proposed sample consisted of 2,400 children from 9 municipal and 29 nonmunicipal areas in the 5 geographic regions.

The overall response rate was 99%, and the achieved sample size was 2,466. Because the sample was not entirely self-weighting, weights were computed for every case. When comparisons between weighted and unweighted statistics for several variables revealed no appreciable differences, the sample referee recommended that unweighted data be used for analysis (Passornsiri, 1989b).

For data collection, the Thai research team used the P/G Interview with all of the international option items. Researchers conducted two pilot studies with the interview, one in 1987 and one in 1988. First, using the May 1987 version of the P/G Interview, the research team interviewed 52 families in 4 geographic regions (urban and rural) and metropolitan Bangkok to detect any linguistic or cultural problems. Later, using the revised interview instrument, the team interviewed families in two provinces to check families' comprehension of questions and the usability of the administration manual.

The time required to administer the interview ranged from 30 minutes to 1 hour.

Major interviewers were 6 faculty members from Sukhothai Thammathirat Open University (STOU) and 31 health officers from 33 provinces, most of whom had at least a bachelor's degree in nursing or health science. These health officers were invited to attend training at the national project center (STOU) and to act as coordinators for the data collection. Using a P/G Interview training manual, national project staff trained interviewers in a 3-day seminar. Training procedures included an explanation of the project, in-depth study of the interview and manual, presentation of guidelines for data collection, practice interviews with STOU staff and with families in a nearby village, and discussion of problems encountered during interviews. Acting as coordinators, the 31 health officers recruited and trained other provincial health care workers as interviewers. Also, two STOU faculty members trained a health officer in one province and helped with the interviews. In Bangkok, interviewers included the national project staff, STOU faculty, health workers, teachers, and graduate students. Data collection took place between March and July 1989 (Passornsiri, 1989a).

Sampling and Data Collection in the United States

For the U.S.A., the target population included nonhandicapped children between the ages of $3\frac{1}{2}$ and $4\frac{1}{2}$ living at home but was restricted to a set of 11 sites. These 11 sites were selected so that, as a group, they covered all 4 U.S. census regions, included both urban and rural sites, and included families from all major racial/cultural and socioeconomic groups. For each site, statistical staff used PPS procedures to select 12 area segments. For most area segments, all households with children in the target age-range were included in the sample, but for the few extremely large segments, random households were selected with equal probability. In each area segment that was selected, trained staff used carefully developed household listing and screening procedures to ensure that all families with children in the target age-range were located for inclusion in the study.

The sampling frame for selecting area segments for 10 of the sites was the U.S. Bureau of the Census computer file of the 1980 population and housing data for census blocks and enumeration districts. For the 11th site, the sampling frame was a state register that is updated yearly. The final proposed sample consisted of 600 children from 11 sites located around the country.

The United States achieved an overall response rate of 85%, and its refusal rate was 6%. Achieved sample size was 432. Within each of the 11 sites, the research staff selected samples with equal probability that were self-weighting. The weights for the national findings were based on pseudostrata constructed to represent the 11 sites. When weighted and unweighted results for several variables were compared, there were no appreciable differences. Consequently, the sampling referee recommended that unweighted results be reported (Hoas & Olmsted, 1989).

The major data collection instrument in the U.S.A. was the P/G Interview with all of the international option items and several national option items. National project staff conducted 2 pilot tests, 2 weeks apart, with the instrument. For the pilot tests, they used both in-person and telephone interviews with 25 families of children between the ages of 3 and 5 in urban and rural areas of southeastern Michigan.

A panel of Head Start directors from 11 sites representing the four U.S. census regions (the Head Start Research Cooperative Panel) was responsible for selecting interviewers and coordinating data collection. The panel selected 41 interviewers (2–7 per site) from Head Start staff and parents and from other hired persons; all interviewers were at least 22 years old, and most had some college background. The director and 1 staff member from each site attended a full 2 days of training at the national project center. Training included following a detailed training manual, role-playing interviews with emphasis on critical areas within the interview (with feedback from project staff), and watching videotapes illustrating professional interviews and ways to handle potential difficulties. Each trainee also conducted a trial interview with a member of the national research center staff. Project staff carefully reviewed the trial interviews and provided feedback to ensure understanding of and familiarity with the interview. On returning to their respective sites, the director and staff member trained additional interviewers with materials and guidelines provided by the national project staff. Approval as an interviewer required successful completion of 2 audiotaped interviews, as determined by national research center staff.

Data collection extended from October 1988 to August 1989. Interviews were conducted in person or by phone, and responses were recorded in writing and on audiotape (unless the interviewee did not consent to audiotaping). This double recording assisted interviewers and coders in checking the accuracy and thoroughness of written responses. Throughout data collection, Head Start directors closely supervised the interviewers while national project staff monitored their progress by continually reviewing the quality of interviews submitted to them (Hoas, 1990).

3

The Phase 1 National Samples

PATRICIA P. OLMSTED

Before considering the Phase 1 study's major findings about families' care and education arrangements for their 4-year-olds, it is useful to know something about the life circumstances of the families and children who took part in the study in each of the 11 countries. Therefore, this chapter describes the major parental, family, household, and child health characteristics for each of the national samples. It also addresses the question of how the national samples compared with the general populations in their respective countries.

The national sample descriptions include data about parents' ages, educational attainment, and employment status; about family size and whether children live in two- or one-parent households; about how much time parents spend away from their 4-year-olds; and about other key household features and amenities. The last category—key household features and amenities—gives some idea of family resources or affluence (e.g., by indicating whether families had telephones, automobiles, few or many rooms to live in). However, attempts to determine amounts and sources of family *income* encountered a variety of problems (e.g., a high percentage of nonresponses, indications of underreporting of amounts), and therefore this chapter does not include information about family income.

Characteristics of Parents

Parental Age

Table 3.1 contains data about the ages of mothers and fathers in the national samples. The data indicate that mothers in the 11 national samples were, on average, between 30.0 and 32.8 years old. The average age of national sample fathers was between 31.9 and 35.5 years. Because the national samples were made up of families having young children, in each country the average ages of sample mothers and fathers were less than

37

Table 3.1
Mean Age (in Years) of National Sample Mothers and Fathers

Country/ Territory	Mothers		Fathers	
	n	Mean (*SD*)	*n*	Mean (*SD*)
Belgium (Fr.)	407	31.0 (4.5)	398	33.6 (5.4)
China (PRC)⁺	12,402	30.1 (3.9)	11,729	31.9 (4.1)
Finland	561	32.8 (5.0)	525	35.5 (5.7)
Germany (FRG)	497	30.9 (4.6)	453	34.0 (5.3)
Hong Kong⁺	–	–	–	–
Italy	983	31.3 (5.2)	970	35.5 (5.9)
Nigeria⁺	–	–	–	–
Portugal	572	30.0 (5.4)	543	32.9 (6.1)
Spain	473	31.3 (5.1)	457	34.2 (5.5)
Thailand	2,321	30.3 (6.2)	2,087	33.9 (7.2)
U.S.A.	418	30.5 (5.7)	298	33.8 (5.9)

The symbol ⁺ indicates that weighted data were used for analysis. A dash indicates that no data were available.

the average age in the country's general adult population. Consequently, differences were to be expected when we compared certain key characteristics of sample parents with those of the general adult population in a specific nation. Educational attainment, which follows, is one such age-dependent characteristic.

Parents' Educational Attainment

Table 3.2 presents the years of education completed by national sample mothers and fathers in the 11 countries. Sample parents in Thailand averaged the lowest number of years of education, whereas sample parents in the U.S.A. averaged the highest. In 8 of the 11 nations, fathers had 0.5–1.5 more years of education than mothers. In each of the remaining 3 countries (Finland, Italy, and Portugal) the number of years of education completed by sample mothers was nearly the same as the number of years completed by sample fathers.

Researchers in several countries were able to locate information about the average number of years of education completed by adults in the

Table 3.2
Years of Education Completed by National Sample Mothers and Fathers

Country/ Territory	Mothers		Fathers	
	n	Mean (*SD*)	*n*	Mean (*SD*)
Belgium (Fr.)	421	12.0 (3.7)	403	12.7 (4.0)
China (PRC)+	12,363	6.9 (4.0)	12,370	8.1 (3.4)
Finland	568	12.4 (3.1)	527	12.1 (3.4)
Germany (FRG)	500	10.3 (2.4)	451	11.0 (3.1)
Hong Kong+	880	9.1 (2.7)	895	9.9 (3.2)
Italy	258	10.3 (4.1)	253	10.5 (4.5)
Nigeria+	677	6.2 (5.2)	711	7.5 (5.1)
Portugal	573	5.6 (3.1)	553	5.7 (3.1)
Spain	458	11.4 (4.8)	428	12.0 (5.2)
Thailand	2,249	4.8 (2.7)	2,194	5.4 (3.2)
U.S.A.	414	12.8 (3.5)	321	13.8 (3.6)

The symbol + indicates that weighted data were used for analysis.

general population. In nearly every one of these countries, national sample parents had slightly higher levels of educational attainment than adults in the general population. This is not surprising, since national sample parents (on average) tended to be younger than the average adult in their respective general populations, and the trend in many countries in recent decades has been for young people to obtain more education.

Parental Employment

The International Standard Classification of Occupations (ISCO) was used to code the occupations of mothers and fathers in all participating nations. This classification system was developed by the International Labour Organization and has been used extensively in cross-national studies because it provides a standard list of occupational groups for international use (International Labour Office, 1990).

Tables 3.3 and 3.4 present employment information for national sample mothers and fathers. The information includes, for each nation,

Table 3.3
Maternal Employment for National Samples

Country/ Territory	N	Percentage active in labor force[a]	Percentage in each occupational category[b]							
			1	2	3	4	5	6	7	8
Belgium (Fr.)	424	57	44	1	23	10	16	0	6	0
China (PRC)[+]	12,835	98	7	2	2	6	0	56	27	0
Finland	576	75	8	1	25	5	42	6	13	0
Germany (FRG)	509	43	22	0	29	12	22	5	9	2
Hong Kong[+]	947	51	24	4	27	10	6	2	27	0
Italy	1,000	46	26	2	25	8	14	0	22	3
Nigeria[+]	1,295	67	29	3	9	23	0	32	1	3
Portugal	581	65	7	0	14	10	24	13	31	1
Spain	480	35	21	1	25	15	28	1	9	0
Thailand	2,466	57	4	0	1	16	4	60	15	0
U.S.A.	432	50	22	7	26	5	29	1	10	0

The symbol [+] indicates that weighted data were used for analysis.

[a]Includes mothers working for pay either in the home or outside the home.

[b]1=Professional, technical; 2=administrative, managerial; 3=clerical; 4=sales; 5=service; 6=agricultural, forestry, fishery; 7=production; 8=no classification, armed forces.

Table 3.4
Paternal Employment for National Samples

Country/ Territory	N	Percentage active in labor force[a]	Percentage in each occupational category[b]							
			1	2	3	4	5	6	7	8
Belgium (Fr.)	424	92	32	3	11	5	12	2	32	3
China (PRC)[+]	12,835	98	7	4	5	4	0	48	31	1
Finland	576	98	13	4	3	11	13	13	41	2
Germany (FRG)	509	98	26	1	12	6	2	4	42	7
Hong Kong[+]	947	99	17	6	9	15	6	2	45	0
Italy	1,000	91	13	5	16	6	7	5	45	3
Nigeria[+]	1,295	78	24	8	2	25	6	28	1	6
Portugal	581	98	5	1	9	8	9	11	57	0
Spain	480	94	16	8	15	8	13	6	32	2
Thailand	2,466	95	4	1	1	6	3	54	30	1
U.S.A.	432	94	20	22	6	5	11	3	32	1

The symbol [+] indicates that weighted data were used for analysis.

[a]Includes fathers working for pay either in the home or outside the home.

[b]1=Professional, technical; 2=administrative, managerial; 3=clerical; 4=sales; 5=service; 6=agricultural, forestry, fishery; 7=production; 8=no classification, armed forces.

the percentage of mothers and fathers in the labor force and the percentage of mothers and fathers employed in various occupational categories. As Table 3.3 indicates, 7 of the 11 nations reported 43–67% of sample mothers working for pay either in the home or outside the home. The highest rates of labor force participation for mothers were in China and the lowest rate was in Spain. Researchers in several countries were able to locate general population statistics regarding the proportion of women in the labor force. However, in most cases, the statistics covered all adult women; so, as expected, the sample's proportion of women active in the labor force (the sample consisting only of mothers with at least one 4-year-old child) was generally lower than the corresponding proportion for the entire adult female population. However, in a few countries where the population statistics were several years old (e.g., from 1980), the sample's proportion of labor-force active women was *larger* than the general population's proportion. This is explained by the fact that in most countries of the world, female participation in the labor force has been on the increase for the last few decades.

A study of the proportion of sample mothers employed in various occupational.categories shows that in 7 nations, about one quarter were employed in *clerical* positions (category 3). In 6 nations, about one quarter worked in *professional/technical* jobs (category 1—as doctors/nurses, accountants, teachers, social workers, etc.) although in Belgium 44% of sample mothers were employed in such positions. Only 3 countries (China, Hong Kong, Portugal) reported more than one quarter of sample mothers employed in *production* jobs (category 7—as textile workers, laundry workers, produce graders/packers, etc.).

As Table 3.4 indicates, in 10 of the 11 nations, over 90% of sample fathers were working for pay, with only Nigeria having a percentage lower than this. In 3 countries (China, Nigeria, and Thailand) the occupational category with the largest percentage of sample fathers was *agriculture, forestry, fishery* (category 6). In 7 other countries *production* (category 7) was the predominant occupational category for sample fathers (this category includes such occupations as machine operator, textile worker, truck/bus driver).

Only a few countries had available population statistics concerning the distribution of general population men and women among the various occupational categories. In the few cases where comparisons could be made between sample parents and general population men and women, either there was rough agreement, or expected differences were found, based on the relatively young ages of sample parents. For example, when compared with Hong Kong's general adult population, Hong Kong's sample parents had higher proportions in the *professional/technical* category and lower proportions in the *production* and *service* categories. The Hong Kong project coordinator considered this difference to be consistent with the higher levels of educational attainment found among Hong Kong's sample parents.

Parental Time away from Children

One factor that relates directly to children's need for nonparental supervision is the amount of time that parents spend away from their children. Thus, researchers gathered data about the number of hours that each national sample parent spent away from their 4-year-old child in a typical week (e.g., for purposes of employment, education, other family duties, social/community activities). Tables 3.5 and 3.6 present this information for national sample mothers and fathers, respectively.

Table 3.5 indicates that for the 10 countries reporting data, the average number of hours per week that sample mothers were away from their 4-year-

Table 3.5
Percentage Distribution of National Sample Mothers According to Weekly Hours away from 4-Year-Old Child

Country/ Territory	N	Mothers responding n (% of N)	% of n Absent the following number of hours				Mean hours absent (SD)
			1–20	21–40	41–60	>60	
Belgium (Fr.)	424	252 (59)	27	47	23	3	32.2 (15.7)
China (PRC)+	12,835	9,255 (72)	6	18	56	20	52.2 (25.4)
Finland	576	457 (79)	21	44	33	2	33.9 (16.8)
Germany (FRG)	509	237 (47)	64	24	11	1	18.5 (16.6)
Hong Kong+	–	–	–	–	–	–	–
Italy	1,000	164 (16)	18	63	18	1	30.8 (12.5)
Nigeria+	1,295	713 (55)	31	39	23	7	31.0 (21.2)
Portugal	581	386 (66)	18	21	50	11	42.8 (21.2)
Spain	480	230 (48)	30	49	18	3	31.3 (16.9)
Thailand	2,466	1,116 (45)	26	25	23	26	43.7 (31.4)
U.S.A.	432	285 (66)	43	36	20	1	26.7 (16.8)

The symbol + indicates that weighted data were used for analysis. A dash indicates that no data were available.

Table 3.6
Percentage Distribution of National Sample Fathers According
to Weekly Hours away from 4-Year-Old Child

Country/ Territory	N	Fathers responding n (% of N)	% of n Absent the following number of hours				Mean hours absent (SD)
			1–20	21–40	41–60	>60	
Belgium (Fr.)	424	367 (87)	2	27	59	12	48.8 (14.4)
China (PRC)[+]	12,835	10,429 (81)	2	11	51	36	65.1 (34.8)
Finland	576	491 (85)	5	28	56	11	47.2 (17.5)
Germany (FRG)	509	373 (73)	2	13	71	14	51.9 (14.6)
Hong Kong[+]	–	–	–	–	–	–	–
Italy	1,000	235 (24)	3	34	52	11	47.2 (15.6)
Nigeria[+]	1,295	810 (63)	6	17	44	33	53.9 (20.7)
Portugal	581	530 (91)	2	9	51	38	63.8 (28.1)
Spain	480	435 (91)	2	37	42	19	51.1 (20.5)
Thailand	2,466	1,873 (76)	3	11	26	60	76.4 (42.1)
U.S.A.	432	310 (72)	5	18	61	16	52.1 (21.5)

The symbol [+] indicates that weighted data were used for analysis. A dash indicates that no data were available.

olds varied from 18.5 hours (in Germany) to 52.2 hours (in China). Sample mothers in China, Portugal, and Thailand spent the most time away, with more than half of them being away over 40 hours a week. Sample mothers in Germany and the U.S.A. spent the least time away from their 4-year-olds. This is surprising, considering that both are highly industrialized nations, where one would expect high participation of mothers in the labor force and consequent high needs for extraparental care for young children.

For the 10 countries reported in Table 3.6, the average number of hours per week that national sample fathers spent away from their 4-year-olds ranged from 47.2 hours (in Italy and Finland) to 76.4 hours (in Thailand). As Table 3.6 illustrates, 60% of Thailand's sample fathers were typically away for more than 60 hours a week. The 3 countries whose sample mothers averaged the most time away from their young children

(China, Portugal, and Thailand) also reported sample fathers averaging the most time away.

Household and Family Characteristics

Two-Parent Households

Ten countries reported the percentage of sample families in which the parents were married and both present in the household. As shown in Table 3.7, all but 1 of the 10 countries reported a high percentage (86% or higher) of *married spouse present* households. The U.S. sample stands alone with a relatively low percentage (69%) of such households. Two of the 10 countries were able to compare their samples with their general populations on this characteristic, and in both cases the national sample and the general population were similar.

Table 3.7
Family and Residence Characteristics of National Samples

Country/ Territory	*n*	% With married spouse present	Average number of members in family (*SD*)	% Owning home	Average number of rooms in home (*SD*)
Belgium(Fr.)	424	95	4.4 (1.2)	65	6.4 (2.4)
China(PRC)[+]	12,835	91	4.0 (1.3)	75	2.6 (1.4)
Finland	576	87	4.4 (1.3)	78	4.5 (1.4)
Germany(FRG)	509	91	3.9 (1.0)	–	4.3 (1.4)
Hong Kong[+]	947	–	–	41	2.9 (1.2)
Italy	1,000	94	4.2 (1.1)	59	4.1 (1.5)
Nigeria[+]	1,295	92	–	67	4.0 (2.3)
Portugal	581	90	4.4 (1.4)	44	3.7 (1.4)
Spain	480	93	4.4 (1.3)	70	4.3 (2.4)
Thailand	2,466	86	5.1 (1.8)	76	2.1 (1.1)
U.S.A.	432	69	4.5 (1.4)	53	5.7 (1.9)

The symbol [+] indicates that weighted data were used for analysis. A dash indicates that no data were available.

Family Size

Table 3.7 also presents the average family size for 9 of the 11 national samples. The 9 countries exhibit a fairly small range of family sizes, with the smallest average size found in Germany and the largest average size being found in Thailand. In 7 countries, researchers compared the average family size of the sample with the average family size in the general population. In 4 of these countries the sample's average family size and the population's average family size were similar. In the other 3 countries, the sample had a slightly larger average family size than the population.

Home Ownership

As Table 3.7 indicates, the sample families in Hong Kong and Portugal reported considerably lower rates of home ownership than the sample families from other nations. In China, Finland, Spain, and Thailand, 70% or more of sample families owned their homes. Only U.S. researchers were able to compare sample and general population statistics for rates of home ownership, and they found the percentages (53% and 56%, respectively) to be very similar.

Number of Rooms in Home

As can be seen in Table 3.7, sample families in Thailand and China had the smallest average home sizes. Sample families in Belgium and the U.S.A. had the largest average home sizes.

When statistics about family size and number of rooms in the home are combined, the following picture emerges: Of all the national sample families, Thailand's had the most family members, but they were living in the least number of rooms. Belgium and the U.S.A. fell in the middle range of the nations with regard to family size, but they had the largest averages regarding number of rooms to live in. Portugal's average family size was approximately equal to family size in Belgium and the U.S.A., yet the Portuguese homes had, on average, at least 2 fewer rooms than Belgian and U.S. homes.

Household Amenities

The presence or absence of certain kinds of living amenities in sample family households was also of interest in this study. Researchers believed that the amenities, listed in Table 3.8, could relate to the amount of time parents had available to devote to their children. Some of them (e.g., forms of private transportation and communication) could also indicate how much access children had to people and events beyond the immediate household.

Table 3.8
Percentages of National Samples Having Various Amenities

Country/ Territory	N	Indoor water[a]	Auto- mobile	Bicycle	Tele- phone	Tele- vision	Clothes washing machine	Refrig- erator
Belgium (Fr.)	424	100	93	–	83	97	97	100
China (PRC)[+]	12,835	35	1	74	0	56	29	10
Finland	576	99	95	98	98	–	–	–
Germany (FRG)	509	100	–	–	–	–	–	–
Hong Kong[+]	947	100	17	13	97	98	89	97
Italy	1,000	98	95	70	81	99	98	99
Nigeria[+]	1,295	42	11	13	6	31	3	25
Portugal	581	83	46	39	–	56	53	88
Spain	480	100	–	–	–	–	–	–
Thailand	2,466	18	8	56	2	44	2	21
U.S.A.	432	100	87	67	93	99	80	100

The symbol [+] indicates that weighted data were used for analysis. A dash indicates that no data were available.

[a]This question was not asked in Belgium and Germany, but official information indicates that 100% of families in those countries have indoor running water.

Indoor Running Water

Although the interviewers asked families whether their homes had heat, light, or running water, only the data for indoor running water is given in Table 3.8. The other two features, because they were almost universally present where appropriate, are not included here.

As Table 3.8 shows, 7 of the 11 countries reported at least 98% of sample families having indoor running water. In Nigeria, China, and Thailand more than half the families needed to carry water daily from an outdoor source.

Private Transportation

In many countries, moving a 4-year-old child beyond his or her immediate surroundings depends on the availability of private transportation. Therefore, interviewers asked families if they owned a working automobile, bicycle, or other form of transportation. In 7 of the 9 nations asking this question, at least approximately half of the sample families owned an automobile or a bicycle. In Hong Kong, public transportation is frequently used by nearly all families, so the low percentages of sample families owning cars or bicycles were not unexpected. In Nigeria, where public transportation is not generally available, very small percentages of sample families owned a car or bicycle, which means that for their children, the world was likely to be limited to the immediate surroundings.

Telephone and Television

Table 3.8 shows that the 8 countries reporting data about telephone ownership fell into two groups: a group in which nearly all sample families had telephones (5 countries) and a group in which no sample families or relatively few sample families had telephones (China, Nigeria, Thailand).

The sample families in the 8 countries also split into two groups regarding ownership of television sets: a group in which at least 97% of sample families owned at least 1 television set (Belgium, Hong Kong, Italy, and the U.S.A.) and a group in which a moderate percentage of families (31–56%) owned 1 or more television sets (China, Nigeria, Portugal, and Thailand).

Household Appliances

The two household appliances included in Table 3.8 are ones that relate to the amount of time families spend in the major tasks of washing family clothes and obtaining and storing food. In 4 of the 8 countries reporting on these appliances, at least 80% of sample families had clothes washing machines. In Portugal and China moderate percentages had washing machines. Two countries, Nigeria and Thailand, reported virtually no families owning a machine for washing clothes.

When examining the percentages of sample families owning a refrigerator, we must keep in mind that in some countries, a refrigerator is viewed as essential for food storage, whereas in other countries, common food-preservation methods do not necessitate this appliance. In the 5 industrialized nations reporting on ownership of refrigerators (Belgium, Hong Kong, Italy, Portugal, and the U.S.A.) at least 88% of sample families owned this appliance. In the remaining 3 nations (China, Nigeria, and Thailand) 10–25% of sample families owned this appliance.

Child Health Information

Although only indirectly related to the use of early childhood services, national sample data about children's health status, examinations, and problems were also obtained by researchers in 10 of the 11 countries participating in the study.

Over 90% of sample families in 5 countries (China, Finland, Nigeria, Spain, and the U.S.A.) reported their 4-year-old children to be in *excellent* or *good health*. In the remaining 5 countries (Belgium, Hong Kong, Italy, Portugal and Thailand) the corresponding percentages (for *excellent* or *good health*) ranged from 55% (for Hong Kong) to 85% (for Belgium).

Table 3.9
Percentages of National Sample 4-Year-Olds Having Various
Health Examinations and Exhibiting Vision/Hearing Problems

Country/ Territory	N	% With					
		Medical exam	Dental exam	Vision exam	Vision problem[a]	Hearing exam	Hearing problem[a]
Belgium (Fr.)	424	–	–	–	–	–	–
China(PRC)[+]	12,835	40	–	–	–	–	–
Finland	576	98	95	93	7	91	4
Germany (FRG)	509	–	–	–	–	–	–
Hong Kong[+]	947	–	–	–	–	–	–
Italy	1,000	93	16	21	22	33	47
Nigeria[+]	1,295	53	10	10	–	3	–
Portugal	581	92	10	10	33	13	46
Spain	480	91	–	–	–	–	–
Thailand	2,466	42	9	1	9	1	21
U.S.A.	432	94	56	44	6	53	12

The symbol [+] indicates that weighted data were used for analysis. A dash indicates that no data were available.

[a]Percentage is based on the number who had vision (or hearing) checked.

Health Examinations and Health Problems

As Table 3.9 shows, 8 countries reported data about the percentage of 4-year-olds who had undergone a *medical* examination during the previous year. In 5 of these countries (Finland, Italy, Portugal, Spain, and the U.S.A.) over 90% of the children had been examined during the previous year. In China, Nigeria, and Thailand the medical examination percentages ranged from 40 to 53%.

Six nations reported information about children's *dental, vision,* and *hearing* examinations. In Finland over 90% of national sample children had undergone all three types of examinations during the past year—much higher percentages than those reported by any of the other 5 countries. Also in Finland, only small percentages of those undergoing vision and hearing check-ups were found to have related problems. In the U.S.A. approximately half of the national sample parents reported that their children had received each of the three (dental, vision, and hearing) examinations, and only small percentages of those examined were found to have vision or hearing problems.

The remaining countries (Italy, Nigeria, Portugal, and Thailand) reported no more than a third of national sample children having received vision or hearing tests. Three of these countries (Italy, Portugal, and Thailand) reported information about problems, and although only small percentages of children received the check-ups, at least one-fifth of those examined were found to have problems in vision or hearing.

Summary—Comparing National Samples with General Populations

As noted earlier in this chapter, parents in any given national sample represented a relatively young segment of the nation's adult population. Consequently, when researchers compared characteristics of national samples with characteristics of their respective general populations, certain differences were to be expected. For example, during the past few decades, many nations have increased the requirements for the number of years one must remain in school. Therefore, it was not surprising to find that across the nations, the relatively young parents in the national samples generally averaged more years of education than adults in the general population.

For certain variables, it was difficult to locate corresponding population statistics to compare with the national sample statistics. This was the case for the variable of maternal employment. Whereas the national samples generally consisted of women 25–36 years old with at least one 4-year-old child, general population statistics about women's labor force participation are given for adult women of all ages, or for women between specific ages (e.g., ages 25–39). There are no general population statistics for the subgroup of women who have children of preschool age. Also, in many countries, population statistics are collected and published only every 5–10 years. This sometimes made them outdated and thus inappropriate for a comparison concerning a variable that changes as rapidly as maternal employment.

Despite all these considerations, it is possible to make some statements about whether national samples were representative of their general populations. Earlier in this chapter, data were presented for individual characteristics (e.g., parents' educational attainment, mothers' labor force participation), and for such characteristics, the differences found between samples and general populations were expected, based on the relative youth of parents in samples and the lack of suitable population statistics for comparison. Seven of the 11 participating countries were able to compare their national samples with their general populations on at least 4 different characteristics. Another 2 countries were able to make a comparison on 3 characteristics. In each of these 9 countries, since the differences were generally found in the expected direction, the 9 national samples may be deemed representative of their respective general populations.

In Nigeria the last reliable census was conducted in 1963, and another is planned for 1992–1993. Because of the lack of up-to-date population information, it is not possible to make an accurate assessment of the representativeness of the Nigerian national sample. Spain was also unable to locate population statistics. That fact, combined with Spain's very high nonresponse and refusal rates reported in Chapter 2, make it difficult—if not impossible—to assess the quality of the Spanish national sample.

4

Study Findings: Families' Weekly Use of Early Childhood Services

OLAYEMI ONIBOKUN AND PATRICIA P. OLMSTED

A premise of the IEA Preprimary Project is that care or education provided to young children by someone other than their parents—what we refer to as *extraparental,* or *early childhood,* services—takes many forms. The services can be formal or informal; they can take place in a private home (the child's or someone else's) or in an organized facility; they can involve one-on-one, small- or large-group settings, and these settings can include various kinds of caregivers or teachers, ranging from helpful friends or relatives to highly trained professionals.

This chapter looks at questions such as these regarding the use of early childhood services. In the various countries taking part in the Phase 1 study of the IEA/PPP, how many families typically turn to extraparental care or education for their 4-year-old children? What types of early childhood services do these families choose? When 4-year-olds do receive services, what does their week typically consist of—how many different settings (including caregivers/teachers) do they encounter, and how much time do they spend in each setting? Besides answering these questions and more, this chapter also presents information about the relationships between various household and family characteristics and family use of early childhood services.

Families' Use of Early Childhood Services

The study's 11 participating nations reported great variation regarding the use of extraparental care/education services for 4-year-old children. Table 4.1 presents the proportion of children in each country who attend at least one extraparental early childhood setting each week. (For this study, *attendance at a setting* or *use of an early childhood service* is counted if a 4-year-old is in a given extraparental care/education setting at least 2 hours per week.) The table shows that in Hong Kong and Belgium, nearly every 4-year-old attends an extraparental setting. In the rest of the study's

Table 4.1
Percentage of 4-Year-Olds in at Least One Extraparental
Care/Education Setting Each Week

Country/ Territory	N	Nonservice users (in own home, P/G care, only)		Service users (in at least 1 extraparental setting)		No information	
		No.	% of N	No.	% of N	No.	% of N
Belgium (Fr.)	424	8	2	416	98	0	0
China (PRC)[+]	12,835	7,124	55	5,468	43	243	2
Finland	576	145	25	431	75	0	0
Germany (FRG)	509	92	18	417	82	0	0
Hong Kong[+]	947	–	–	947	100[a]	0	0
Italy	1,000	148	15	852	85	0	0
Nigeria[+]	1,295	841	65	435	33	19	2
Portugal	581	171	29	410	71	0	0
Spain	480	101	21	379	79	0	0
Thailand	2,466	1,555	63	894	36	17	1
U.S.A.	432	168	39	264	61	0	0

The symbol [+] indicates that weighted data were used for analysis. Attendance at a setting, or use of a service, was counted if a 4-year-old was in a given extraparental care/education setting at least 2 hours per week. P/G denotes parent/guardian.

[a]Because 95% of 4-year-old children in Hong Kong attend *organized facility* settings, the Hong Kong sample was selected from those settings.

industrialized European nations (other than Belgium) only approximately 70–85% of families use extraparental services for their 4-year-old children. Sizable, but even lower, are the corresponding percentages for the U.S.A. and China. Of all the study's countries, Nigeria and Thailand have the lowest proportions of parents enrolling their children in early childhood settings.

Before looking into the types of early childhood services families use and the extent of their service use, the reasons why some families in various nations do not use such services will be considered. If a family reported not using extraparental care/education services, the interviewer asked why exclusive parent/guardian care was the family's choice. Research staff coded the responses into the following four major categories: (1) *parent/guardian related* reasons, including (a) *social/emotional* reasons (such as wanting to be the primary adult in the child's early years), (b) *educational* reasons (such as wanting to teach the young child), and (c) *other* parent/guardian-related reasons (such as not having considered any other alternative); (2) *child-related* reasons (such as concern for special physical/developmental needs of the child or concern about the child's emotional closeness to the parent/guardian); (3) *facility-related* reasons (such as unavailability of services or lack of specific desired features); and *other* reasons.

This discussion is limited to the 7 countries in which the majority of sample families responded to the question about their reason for choosing parent/guardian at-home care (i.e., China, Finland, Italy, Portugal, Spain, Thailand, and the U.S.A.).

In all 7 countries more than 50% of sample families gave *parent/ guardian-related* reasons for choosing to be the sole providers of care for their 4-year-olds. This suggests that a lack of availability of early childhood care/education services (such as child care centers or family day care homes) is not the major reason why parents do not use such services.

Within the parent/guardian-related category, *social/emotional* reasons were the most often cited in each of 3 countries (Italy, Spain, and the U.S.A.); *educational* reasons were the most often cited in 2 countries (China and Finland); and *other* reasons were the most often cited in the remaining 2 countries (Portugal and Thailand).

Sizable percentages of families in Italy and Spain gave *child-related* reasons for being the sole providers of care/education for their 4-year-olds. China was the only country in which a sizable percentage (32%) cited *facility-related* reasons.

Details of Families' Use of Early Childhood Services

Types of Settings Used

To obtain data about what types of extraparental settings 4-year-olds in various countries attend each week, the National Research Coordinators (NRCs) jointly decided to categorize extraparental services as follows: (1) care in the child's *own home* (by a nonparent); (2) care in some *other home,* including informal care by a friend or relative as well as formal (licensed, or regulated) care (e.g., in a family day care home); and (3) care in an *organized facility,* including both care-oriented and education-oriented large-group settings. Table 4.2 presents for each country the percentages of service-using 4-year-olds attending these 3 categories of settings. The percentages refer to the extraparental setting in which the child spends the *most time* each week (which the NRCs jointly decided to call the child's *first setting*).

Considering children's *first settings,* in 7 countries the majority of service-using children are in organized facilities. This is true in countries with fairly low rates of extraparental-setting attendance (e.g., in China, with 43% attendance) as well as in countries with high rates of extraparental-setting attendance (e.g., in Italy and Belgium).

In 2 countries (Finland and Portugal), relatively large proportions of

Table 4.2
Percentage Distribution of 4-Year-Old Service-Users
According to Type of First Setting[a]

Country/ Territory	N	n Who attend 1 or more settings (% of N)	% of n Attending the following type of first setting			
			Own home (nonparent)	Other home	Organized facility	Other
Belgium (Fr.)	424	416 (98)	1	4	95	0
China (PRC)[+]	12,835	5,468 (43)	12	10	76	2
Finland	576	431 (75)	7	47	46	0
Germany (FRG)	509	417 (82)	18	22	60	0
Hong Kong[+]	947	947 (100)	–	–	100[b]	–
Italy	1,000	852 (85)	3	3	94	0
Nigeria[+]	1,295	435 (33)	66	9	25	0
Portugal	581	410 (71)	23	35	41	1
Spain	480	379 (79)	6	6	87	1
Thailand	2,466	894 (36)	42	25	33	0
U.S.A.	432	264 (61)	14	28	58	0

The symbol [+] indicates that weighted data were used for analysis.

[a]The child's *first setting* was defined as the extraparental care/education setting in which he/she typically spent the most time each week.

[b]Because 95% of 4-year-old children in Hong Kong attend *organized facility* settings, the Hong Kong sample was selected from those settings.

families choose each of two types of extraparental settings: other home and organized facility. In both Nigeria and Thailand the largest proportion of families use own home (nonparent care) settings. However, whereas Nigerian families principally use this kind of setting, Thailand also reported quite sizable percentages of families using organized facility settings and other home settings.

Subcategories of Types of Settings

Table A.1 in Appendix A, p. 198, presents more detailed information about the types of care/education settings that serve as children's first settings. For the *own home* and *other home* categories, the table gives the percentage breakdown for *relative* and *nonrelative* care; for the *organized facility* category, it gives percentages for the subcategories of *care, education, unclassified,* and *miscellaneous.*

In 4 of the 8 countries reporting at least 5% of children in *own home* care, it is *relatives* who provide all or most of this type of care (in China, Germany, Portugal, and Thailand). In 3 of the 8 countries (Finland, Spain, and the U.S.A.) *relatives* and *nonrelatives* alike provide the own home care, while in 1 of the 8 countries (Nigeria) *nonrelatives* are the usual own home care providers.

In *other home* settings various divisions between *relative* and *non-relative* care can also be seen. Of the 8 countries where at least 5% of children attend other home settings, there are 5 (China, Germany, Portugal, Spain, and Thailand) where *relatives* are most often the caregivers. In the 3 remaining countries (Finland, Nigeria, and the U.S.A.) *nonrelatives* predominate as caregivers in other home settings. In Finland and the U.S.A. the other home setting is usually a family day care home, while in Nigeria the other home setting is more often an informal arrangement among friends.

Examination of the subcategories of *organized facility* across the various countries reveals that *educational* settings are most common in 9 of the 11 countries. In the remaining 2 countries (Portugal and Spain) the subcategory *unclassified* applies to all the organized facilities children attend. In 3 countries (China, Thailand, and the U.S.A.) more than 10% of 4-year-olds attend organized facilities classified as *care* settings. Finally, in Finland approximately 15% of children attend organized facilities classified as *miscellaneous.*

Types of Settings Used in Urban versus Rural Areas

Researchers examined the use of extraparental care/education services for families living in urban areas and also for families living in rural areas. Table A.2 in Appendix A, p. 199 gives the information for these two groups of families across 8 nations. In 6 of the nations (China, Finland, Nigeria, Spain, Thailand, and the U.S.A.) there are notable differences in use patterns. For each of these 6 countries, a chi-square analysis indicated a significant difference between the distribution of urban families and the distribution of rural families among the following categories of settings: (1) *own home, parent care only*; (2) *own home, nonparent care*; (3) *other home*; and (4) *organized facility*. In each of these 6 countries, a higher percentage of rural families than urban families reported caring for their 4-year-olds themselves (*own home, parent care only*). Also, a higher percentage of urban children than rural children attend *organized facilities.*

Number of Settings Used Each Week

In studying children's weekly care patterns, researchers looked at how many different extraparental settings the 4-year-olds of the study's various countries typically experience. Table 4.3 concerns children who are service users (those attending at least one extraparental setting) and distributes them according to how many different settings they typically attend each week. In 8 of the 10 countries with findings reported in Table 4.3, at least two-thirds of service-using children typically attend just one setting per week, and virtually no service-using children attend more than two different settings each week. The exceptions to this finding are Belgium and Germany, where the data indicate that sizable percentages of service-using

Table 4.3
Percentage Distribution of 4-Year-Old Service-Users According to Number of Extraparental Settings Attended Each Week

Country/ Territory	N	n Who attend at least 1 setting (% of N)	% of n Attending the following number of settings			
			1	2	3	4
Belgium (Fr.)	424	416 (98)	31	41	23	5
China (PRC)[+]	12,835	5,468 (43)	84	14	2	0
Finland	576	431 (75)	79	19	2	0
Germany (FRG)	509	417 (82)	48	36	10	6
Hong Kong[+]	947	947[a] (100)	–	–	–	–
Italy	1,000	852 (85)	71	28	1	0
Nigeria[+]	1,295	435 (33)	95	5	0	0
Portugal	581	410 (71)	70	26	4	0
Spain	480	379 (79)	68	29	3	0
Thailand	2,466	894 (36)	88	12	0	0
U.S.A.	432	264 (61)	71	27	1	1

The symbol [+] indicates that weighted data were used for analysis.

[a] Information was requested for one setting only.

4-year-olds attend two settings, and fair percentages even attend three or four settings, each week.

Combinations of Settings Used by Families

Since in many (7) of the nations, at least 20% of service-using 4-year-olds attend at least two extraparental settings each week, it is useful to look at the types of settings that families select as *second settings*. (The NRCs jointly decided to define the child's *second setting* as the extraparental setting in which he or she spends the *second-longest time* each week.) Table 4.4 distributes service-using children in 9 nations according to the type of *second setting* they typically attend. Compared with the findings

Table 4.4
Percentage Distribution of 4-Year-Old Service-Users
According to Type of Second Setting[a] Attended

Country/ Territory	N	n Who attend at least 2 settings (% of N)	% of n Attending the following types of second settings			
			Own home (nonparent)	Other home	Organized facility	Other
Belgium (Fr.)	424	310 (73)	5	25	70	0
China (PRC)[+]	12,835	706 (6)	53	34	4	9
Finland	576	90 (16)	19	22	59	0
Germany (FRG)	509	218 (43)	37	50	13	0
Hong Kong[+]	947	0[b]	–	–	–	–
Italy	1,000	249 (25)	38	56	6	0
Nigeria[+]	1,295	0[c]	–	–	–	–
Portugal	581	124 (21)	39	48	8	5
Spain	480	122 (25)	46	41	6	7
Thailand	2,466	106 (4)	61	28	11	0
U.S.A.	432	77 (18)	27	34	39	0

The symbol [+] indicates that weighted data were used for analysis.

[a]The child's *second setting* was defined as the extraparental setting he/she attended for the second-longest time each week.

[b]Information was requested for one setting only.

[c]Insufficient information was available for inclusion.

about children's first settings, Table 4.4 findings reveal more variety. In only 3 of the 9 nations is *organized facility* the most common second setting; in 3 nations *other home* is most common, and in 3 nations *own home (nonparent)* is most common.

Time Children Spend in Extraparental Settings

When children participate in one or more extraparental settings each week, how much time do they typically spend there? Table 4.5 presents the average number of hours service-using children spend in their first, second, and third settings and in all their extraparental settings combined. The averages for *all settings combined* vary greatly, from 24.5 hours per week in Germany to 55.6 hours per week in Thailand. Besides Thailand, China is the only other nation that reported an average of over 50 hours per week for all settings combined. In 5 countries children average 30–45 hours per week in all settings combined, and in 2 countries (Germany and the U.S.A.) they average fewer hours than this.

In several countries, average time spent in all settings combined equals, or is close to, average time spent in the *first setting*; these are nations in which most of the service-using children attend only one extraparental setting. Nine countries reported enough children participating in at least two settings to permit calculation of the average time spent in each setting, the first and the second. In most of the 9 countries, children are in their second settings for comparatively few hours per week, but in 3 of the 9 countries (China, Spain, and Thailand) children spend more than a third of their "extraparental hours" in their second settings.

When findings about the time children spend in all extraparental settings are combined with findings about the number of settings they attend, the following observations can be made. (1) Service-using children in China and Thailand spend large amounts of their time in their first settings, and if they attend second settings, they spend about half as much time there. (2) Service-using children in Belgium, Germany, and the U.S.A. typically spend relatively small amounts of their time each week in each of two or more extraparental settings (20–26 hours in the first setting and less than 10 hours in the second setting).

Time Children Spend Traveling to First Settings

Because researchers were interested in how convenient families find their children's care/education arrangements, sample families were asked how much time service-using 4-year-olds spent traveling to their first settings (i.e., out-of-home first settings). A cursory look at Table 4.6 reveals that in general, most children attending extraparental settings travel for only a few minutes to reach their first settings. In Belgium, Finland, Germany, Italy, Portugal, Spain, and Thailand at least 50% of children travel less than 6

Table 4.5

Average Hours 4-Year-Old Service-Users Spend Each Week in Individual Settings and in all Settings Combined

	Setting(s)											
	First			Second			Third			Combined		
Country/ Territory	No. of service users	Mean hr. spent	SD	No. of service users	Mean hr. spent	SD	No. of service users	Mean hr. spent	SD	No. of service users	Mean hr. spent[a]	SD
Belgium (Fr.)	416	25.8	6.8	310	8.6	5.1	116	5.2	1.7	416	33.9	11.6
China (PRC)+	5,468	52.6	22.5	686	27.2	28.4	—	—	—	5,468	55.5	24.2
Finland	430	31.9	14.2	88	7.4	6.0	—	—	—	430	33.7	15.2
Germany (FRG)	411	19.6	11.4	207	8.0	6.1	61	4.6	3.3	411	24.5	15.1
Hong Kong+	947	17.2	7.0	—	—	—	—	—	—	—	—	—
Italy	852	32.6	9.2	248	11.2	7.3	—	—	—	852	35.9	11.4
Nigeria+	435	35.1	11.9	—	—	—	—	—	—	—	—	—
Portugal	409	39.7	20.2	124	13.8	9.5	—	—	—	409	44.1	21.5
Spain	379	29.1	11.4	117	17.7	10.9	—	—	—	379	35.0	16.3
Thailand	886	52.9	33.5	106	26.9	24.6	—	—	—	882	55.6	34.9
U.S.A.	263	25.0	16.6	75	8.5	6.9	—	—	—	263	27.8	17.7

The symbol + indicates that weighted data were used for analysis. For China, Finland, Italy, Portugal, Spain, Thailand, and the U.S.A., dashes indicate that there were too few cases with a third setting. In Hong Kong and Nigeria, information was requested for one setting only. Numbers of service-users may be lower than in Tables 4.3 and 4.4 because of missing information.

[a]Because of varying sample sizes, the sum of the mean hours for individual settings does not equal the mean hours for combined settings.

Table 4.6
Percentage Distribution of 4-Year-Old Service-Users According to
Time Spent Traveling to their First Settings

Country/ Territory	N	n Who travel to first settings (% of N)	% of n Traveling the following number of minutes[a]				
			1–5	6–10	11–15	16–30	≥31
Belgium (Fr.)	424	406 (96)	64	26	5	5	0
China (PRC)[+]	12,835	4,890 (38)	0	0	73	24	3
Finland	576	396 (69)	57	23	12	7	1
Germany (FRG)	509	321 (63)	50	33	12	4	1
Hong Kong[+]	947	946 (100)	0	0	81	14	5
Italy	1,000	816 (82)	58	26	10	6	0
Nigeria[+]	1,295	135 (10)	35	31	15	18	1
Portugal	581	308 (53)	54	19	11	11	5
Spain	480	353 (74)	52	26	14	7	1
Thailand	2,466	515 (21)	58	20	10	10	2
U.S.A.	432	213 (49)	47	27	14	9	3

The symbol [+] indicates that weighted data were used for analysis.

[a]In asking about travel times, China and Hong Kong used only three categories: 15 minutes or less, 16–30 minutes, more than 30 minutes.

minutes. In most of these 7 countries an additional 20–30% of children travel 6–10 minutes, so at least 70% of children in these 7 countries live within at most 10 minutes of their first settings.

The percentages for the U.S.A. are close to those for the 7 countries just mentioned; about three-quarters of service-using children in the U.S.A. travel for no more than 10 minutes to reach their first settings. In Nigeria, nearly equal percentages of children travel for 1–5 minutes (35%) and for 6–10 minutes (31%) to reach first settings.

Although, across the 11 countries, most children travel no more than 10–15 minutes to reach the care/education setting where they spend the most time each week, some children must travel for much longer periods of time.

Table 4.6 indicates that in Hong Kong and Portugal, 5% of families live more than 30 minutes from their children's first settings.

Mode of Transportation to First Settings

Knowing travel times is useful only if the *mode* of transportation is also taken into account. Table 4.7 presents the data obtained when families were asked about what form of transportation they and/or their children used to get to first settings.

Traveling by *foot* is the most common form of transportation in 8 countries (China, Germany, Hong Kong, Italy, Nigeria, Portugal, Spain, and Thailand). When Table 4.7 data are combined with Table 4.6 data, it is evident that those countries where walking is most common are generally those where most children travel no more than 5 minutes. The findings are

Table 4.7
Percentage Distribution of 4-Year-Old Service-Users According to Mode of Transportation to their First Settings

Country/ Territory	N	n Traveling to first setting (% of N)	% of n Traveling by			
			Foot	Private auto	Public transport	Other[a]
Belgium (Fr.)	424	394 (93)	41	57	1	1
China (PRC)[+]	12,835	4,903 (38)	59	0	3	38
Finland	576	396 (69)	36	55	2	7
Germany (FRG)	509	321 (63)	46	38	3	13
Hong Kong[+]	947	946 (100)	64	3	8	25
Italy	1,000	826 (83)	85	0	7	8
Nigeria[+]	1,295	137 (11)	79	14	7	0
Portugal	581	306 (53)	63	21	7	9
Spain	480	355 (74)	74	18	8	0
Thailand	2,466	525 (21)	55	17	10	18
U.S.A.	432	220 (51)	15	74	1	10

The symbol [+] indicates that weighted data were used for analysis.

[a]Other includes such forms of transportation as bicycle, motorcycle, boat, and provider-supplied transportation (i.e., van, school bus).

less clear for China and Hong Kong, both of whom included a category of "15 minutes or less" in their P/G Interviews.

In Germany similar percentages of parents reported their children traveling by *foot* and by *private auto*. In 3 countries (Belgium, Finland, and the U.S.A.), the majority of parents reported transporting their children by *private auto*. At least 1% of families in each country reported using *public transport* (i.e., municipal bus, streetcar, subway) to reach the first setting, but the percentages for the various countries are low, and no country's percentage exceeds 10%.

Families in 9 countries reported their children using *other* forms of transportation to first settings. In 5 countries, this category included at least 10% of children.

Meals or Snacks Provided in the First Setting

The auxiliary features of care/education services, such as any nutritional features, were of interest to researchers. Consequently, families were asked what meals or snacks their children received in their first settings. Information is available for all countries except Hong Kong

The findings indicate that in 9 of the 10 countries (i.e., all except Belgium), at least 25% of children are in settings that provide at least two meals/snacks. The type of meal or snack most commonly provided varies from country to country, but it is generally the *morning meal*, the *midday meal*, or the *afternoon snack*. In Belgium, very few children attend a first setting in which meals/snacks are provided, but 17% do receive a *morning snack*. (For nearly all 4-year-olds in Belgium, the first setting is a part-day preschool.) In 4 countries (China, Germany, Nigeria, and Thailand) an *evening meal* is provided for more than 20% of the 4-year-olds attending first settings.

Parental Cost for Various Types of First Settings

Researchers in each country asked sample parents how much they paid for their child's extraparental care or education. Table 4.8 presents cost data for children's first settings. The table indicates the number of sample families *using* each of three types of settings, the number of these same families *who paid for* their child's attendance at the setting, and the average monthly cost for parents who paid.

In Belgium only a small proportion of sample parents pay for their children's attendance at any type of setting. However, in 4 other countries (Germany, Italy, Portugal, and Thailand) relatively large proportions of families using *organized facilities* pay for their children to attend this type of setting, while much smaller proportions pay for *own home* and *other home* settings. In the remaining nations, most families using any of the three types of settings pay for these services.

Table 4.8
Average Monthly Parental Cost in U.S. $ for Various Types of Extraparental Care/Education

Country/Territory	MHI[a]	Own home			Other home			Organized facility		
		No. using	No. paying	Cost/Mo (% of MHI)	No. using	No. paying	Cost/Mo (% of MHI)	No. using	No. paying	Cost/Mo (% of MHI)
Belgium (Fr.)	–	5	0	–	15	2	$132	396	65	$5
China (PRC)[+]	–	–	–	–	–	–	–	–	–	–
Finland	$2,396	31	20	$230 (10)	201	174	$137 (6)	199	154	$136 (6)
Germany (FRG)	$1,910	73	10	$272 (14)	92	12	$166 (9)	252	242	$35 (2)
Hong Kong[+]	$705	–	–	–	–	–	–	947	947	$27 (4)
Italy	$1,800	27	5	$4 (<1)	25	2	–	800	327	$35[b] (2)
Nigeria[+]	–	287	252	$7	40	33	$8	109	87	$2 (2)
Portugal	$347	93	18	$26 (7)	144	54	$26 (7)	168	160	$24 (7)
Spain	–	–	–	–	–	–	–	–	–	–
Thailand	$134	370	34	$18 (13)	225	31	$8 (6)	297	280	$2 (1)
U.S.A.	$2,166	38	21	$100 (5)	74	54	$120 (6)	152	117	$144 (7)

The symbol [+] indicates that weighted data were used for analysis. Dashes indicate that no information was available.

[a]MHI is the average monthly household income for 1988 (or the closest year available) converted into U.S. $. Currency exchange rates for 1988–1989 were used for the conversion.

[b]Because of missing data, cost per month for *organized facility* was provided by Italy's National Research Coordinator.

Examination of monthly parental costs across the various types of settings within a country reveals some patterns. For example, in Portugal parental costs are almost identical for the three different types of settings, while in other countries (e.g., Finland, Germany, Thailand, and the U.S.A.) parents pay quite different amounts, depending on the type of setting. In a few countries, in fact, one type of setting stands out as costing, on average, either much more or much less than the other two types. *Own home* settings in Finland are an example of this.

For some countries, the data present a picture of financial support of one or more types of settings by some agency or organization (such as government or a religious group). For example, in Belgium support of *organized facility* settings is evident, whereas in Finland support of *other home* and *organized facility* settings is clear.

For 6 of the nations in Table 4.8, researchers were able to determine parental cost for services as a percentage of average monthly household income (MHI). Across these 6 countries, they found that the highest percentage (14%) of MHI is paid by the relatively small number of parents in Germany who choose *own home* extraparental care; the lowest percentage (less than 1%) of MHI is paid by the small number of parents in Italy who choose *own home* extraparental care. Overall, in Germany, Italy, and Thailand most families pay, on average, a very small percentage (only 1–2% of MHI) for care/education services. In Hong Kong the majority pay an average of 4%. In Finland, Portugal, and the U.S.A. most families pay an average of 6–7% of MHI for early childhood services.

Table A.3 in Appendix A, p. 200 presents additional information about the various countries' parental costs for 4-year-old children's attendance at three types of settings. The table shows the median hourly cost and the median weekly cost for each type of setting, and it lists the average number of hours per week that children attend each type of setting. As indicated in the table, in most countries parents reported different average attendance hours for the different types of settings. These differences in total attendance hours affect the calculation of average parental cost per week, as shown in Table A.3. (Of course, they also affect calculation of average cost per month, as shown in Table 4.8.)

Parents' Satisfaction with Early Childhood Services

The household-survey approach of this study gave researchers a unique opportunity to gauge parental satisfaction with existing early childhood services. Table 4.9 presents the levels of parental satisfaction with the first setting and with the second setting attended by their children (data was reported by parents in 10 nations and 8 nations, respectively). With first settings in 9 of the 10 countries, more than 50% of parents are *very satisfied*. Only in Hong Kong is the percentage of *very satisfied* parents less

Table 4.9

Percentage Distribution of Service-Using Families According to Level of Satisfaction with First and Second Settings

Country/ Territory	n_1 Rating first setting (n_2) Rating second setting	% of n_1 Rating first setting as				% of n_2 Rating second setting as			
		Very satisfied	Some-what satisfied	Not very satisfied	Not at all satisfied	Very satisfied	Some-what satisfied	Not very satisfied	Not at all satisfied
Belgium (Fr.)	395 (234)	57	38	4	1	61	34	3	2
China (PRC)[+]	5,570 (693)	52	41	6	1	52	43	4	1
Finland	428 (86)	81	18	1	0	85	14	1	0
Germany (FRG)	–	–	–	–	–	–	–	–	–
Hong Kong[+]	906	14	86	0	0	–	–	–	–
Italy	847 (249)	62	32	5	1	72	25	3	0
Nigeria[+]	449	78	16	5	1	–	–	–	–
Portugal	405 (119)	66	32	2	0	66	32	2	0
Spain	376 (121)	78	19	2	1	85	12	3	0
Thailand	890 (105)	80	19	1	0	85	15	0	0
U.S.A.	262 (76)	88	10	2	0	89	11	0	0

The symbol [+] indicates that weighted data were used for analysis. Dashes indicate that no information was available. Cases with missing data were deleted, and percentages were calculated using remaining cases. No country reported more than 10% missing data for this item.

than 50%. Across the 10 countries, the percentages of parents who gave their children's first settings either level of positive rating (*very satisfied* or *somewhat satisfied*) was 93 to 100%.

Inspection of parents' levels of satisfaction with their children's second settings indicates that in every one of the 8 countries with data available for both settings, the percentage of parents reporting *very satisfied* with the second setting is equal to or higher than the percentage reporting *very satisfied* with the first setting. When percentages for the two positive ratings (*very satisfied* and *somewhat satisfied*) are combined, in each of the 8 countries, positive-rating parents make up 95–100% of those rating second settings.

For 9 countries, researchers compared parental satisfaction among the different types of settings. In 4 of the 9 countries (China, Nigeria,

Portugal, and Thailand) they found a significant relationship between type of setting and percentage of parents who are *very satisfied*. In each of these 4 countries, the group of parents using *organized facility* settings contains the lowest percentage of very satisfied users; the percentages of very satisfied users are generally similar for *own home* and *other home* settings. There are similar but nonsignificant relationships between level of satisfaction and type of setting for most of the remaining countries. In general, the lowest percentage of very satisfied parents is found in the group of families using *organized facility* settings.

Researchers also looked at the relationship between level of parental satisfaction with the child's first setting and *mother's years of education, father's years of education,* and *type of setting* across the 10 nations reporting parental satisfaction data. In only 3 nations did they find significant relationships between parental level of satisfaction and either parent's years of education. In Italy and Nigeria families in which fathers have more years of education are more satisfied with their children's care/education settings. In Spain the direction of this relationship is reversed: families in which fathers have fewer years of education are more satisfied with their children's care/education settings.

Problems with Early Childhood Services

Researchers wondered whether parents were giving superficial answers to the generally stated satisfaction question and whether their responses to questions about specific problems with settings might reveal a different picture. However, across the study's 11 countries, only small percentages of sample parents responded that specific problems applied to their children's first settings. Across the 11 countries, a total of 143 specific problems were posed (i.e., Belgian researchers asked parents about 9 possible problems; Chinese researchers, about 15 possible problems). Only 43 (30%) of these 143 posed problems were cited by at least 1% of parents in some nation. Of these 43 problems, 32 (74%) were cited by at most 5% of parents in any given nation.

Researchers coded principal problems into 15 categories: location; hours of operation; exclusion of sick children; personal characteristics of unreliability of caregiver; unqualified caregiver; caregiver disliked by child; philosophy of program; religious orientation; facility/equipment; safety, sanitation, nutrition; negative atmosphere; other children; staff turnover; cost.

The percentages of Nigerian parents reporting problems were small, but parents did report problems in 9 of the 15 possible categories. Chinese parents noted problems in 8 of the 15 categories, with percentages ranging from 3 to 10%. In 2 countries, at least 1% of parents cited problems in every category posed in their country's questionnaire (Germany posed only 4 categories; Hong Kong, only 8 categories).

When the data are examined by problem categories, we note that at least 2% of parents in 6 countries (Belgium, China, Hong Kong, Italy, Nigeria, and Portugal) cited *facility/equipment* problems with high rates for Hong Kong (21%) and China (10%). At least 1% of parents in each of 5 countries (Belgium, China, Germany, Italy, and Nigeria) noted problems with the *hours of operation* of the setting, with 10% of German parents citing this problem. At least 1% of parents in each of 5 countries (Belgium, China, Germany, Hong Kong, and Nigeria) responded that they had problems with *other children* in the setting; this was cited by 13% of parents in Hong Kong. Finally, *cost* was a problem for 2% or more of the parents reporting in each of 5 countries (China, Germany, Hong Kong, Nigeria, and Portugal), with 18% of parents in Hong Kong citing this problem.

It is interesting to note which specific categories of problems were reported by parents in *very few* countries. For example, in only 1 nation (Portugal) were problems of *safety, sanitation, or nutrition* cited by parents, and then only 1%. *Unqualified teacher/caregiver* was noted as a problem by parents in only 3 countries (China, Hong Kong, and Nigeria), although 9% of parents in China mentioned this problem. Also, *staff turnover* was cited as a problem by parents in only 3 countries (Belgium, China, and Hong Kong). Finally, parents in only 3 countries (China, Hong Kong, and Nigeria) responded that the *location* of their children's care/education settings was a problem.

For each country, researchers examined the relationship between level of parental satisfaction and reporting of problems with the first setting. In every country the proportion of *very satisfied* parents who cited first-setting problems was significantly lower than the proportion of less-satisfied families who cited first-setting problems.

Reasons Parents Give for Using Early Childhood Services

Do parents use early childhood services because they are employed and need child care during their working hours, or because they believe that an extraparental care/education experience is important for one or more aspects (e.g., cognitive or social aspects) of their child's development? Table 4.10 presents, for 9 nations, the major reasons sample parents gave for using care/education services (first settings). If parents gave multiple reasons, they were asked to specify the "most important" reason.

In each of 5 countries (Finland, Nigeria, Portugal, Thailand, and the U.S.A.) at least 50% of parents indicated that a *parent-related* reason led to their decision to use the first setting. In each of these 5 countries, *employment or job* was the most frequently cited parent-related reason.

In each of 4 countries (Germany, Hong Kong, Italy, and Spain) at least 50% of parents indicated that a *child-related* reason led to their decision to use the first setting. In 3 of these 4 countries the most frequently cited

Table 4.10

Percentage Distribution of Service-Using Families According to Major Reason for Using First Setting

Country/Territory	N	n Using at least 1 Setting (% of N)	% of n Citing the following type[a] of major reason											No Info
			Parent-related					Child-related						
			Wk	Ed	Ob	Oth	Total	Ed	S/E	Hlth	Oth	Total	Other	
Belgium (Fr.)	424	416 (98)	–	–	–	–	–	–	–	–	–	–	–	–
China (PRC)[+]	12,835	5,468 (43)	–	–	–	–	–	–	–	–	–	–	–	–
Finland	576	431 (75)	76	–	–	–	80	–	14	–	–	19	1	0
Germany (FRG)	509	417 (82)	22	–	5	7	35	6	57	–	–	63	0	2
Hong Kong[+]	947	947 (100)	–	–	–	–	–	29	59	–	–	88	0	12
Italy	1,000	852 (85)	19	–	–	–	22	33	42	–	–	76	1	1
Nigeria[+]	1,295	435 (33)	46	12	–	6	66	15	–	–	–	22	8	4
Portugal	581	410 (71)	52	–	–	–	57	–	22	–	–	28	14	1
Spain	480	379 (79)	28	–	–	–	36	43	12	–	8	63	1	0
Thailand	2,466	894 (36)	70	–	6	–	76	10	8	–	–	19	1	4
U.S.A.	432	264 (61)	36	–	6	–	51	19	21	–	–	42	6	1

The symbol + indicates that weighted data were used for analysis. A dash indicates that no data were available or that the entry is less than 5 percent.

[a]Types of parent-related reasons: Wk=employment or job; Ed=education or training; Ob=obligations to family or community; Oth=other. Types of child-related reasons: Ed=preparation for school; S/E=social/emotional development; Hlth=physical health of child; Oth=other.

child-related reason was the *social/emotional development* of the child, while in the remaining country (Spain) the most frequently cited child-related reason was the *education or training* of the child.

In the U.S.A., the percentages citing *parent-related* and *child-related* reasons were similar to each other. However, if the percentage of American parents citing *education or training* of the child is added to the percentage citing *social/emotional development* of the child, the combined percentage (40%) is greater than the percentage citing parental *employment or job* (36%).

Influences Related to Use of Services

Based on information reported in the early childhood literature, researchers selected family and community variables (e.g., *mother's completed years of education, father's occupational level, marital status, urban/rural residence*) and examined the relationship between each variable and hours of use of early childhood services, in preparation for regression analyses. As a result of this examination, they selected a set of predictor variables for the analysis: (1) *urban/rural residence*, (2) *number of children in the family*, (3) *mother's completed years of education*, (4) *father's completed years of education*, (5) *mother's hours away from the child each week*, and (6) *father's hours away from the child each week*. Tables A.4 and A.5 in Appendix A, pp. 201–202 present the descriptive information for these six independent variables and for the criterion variable *total service hours* used each week, as well as the correlation matrix for these variables for each country.

The results of the ordinary least squares regression analyses for the study's 11 participating nations reveal that the proportion of the criterion variable (*hours of use* of early childhood services) explained by the predictor variables in the regression model ranges from .01 (Hong Kong) to .69 (Thailand), with most values between .27 and .48. In each of the 10 countries with data for *mother's hours away*, this predictor variable has a statistically significant effect. The greater the number of hours that the mother is away from the 4-year-old, the greater the number of hours of extraparental care-education services used. *Father's hours away* as a predictor variable has a statistically significant effect in 4 countries (China, Nigeria, Spain, and the U.S.A.). In each of these countries, the greater the number of hours that the father is away from the child, the greater the number of hours of extraparental care/education services used.

For 3 countries (China, Finland, and Nigeria) the *urban/rural residence* predictor variable has a statistically significant effect. In China and Finland, *urban* families use services for a greater number of hours each week, while in Nigeria, *rural* families use services for a greater number of hours each week.

Table 4.11
Results of Regression Analyses of Hours of Use of
Early Childhood Services on Various Predictor Variables

Country/ Territory	n^a	Beta values for predictor variables						
		Urban/ rural	No. of children	Education mother	Education father	Hours away, mother	Hours away, father	R^2
Belgium (Fr.)	226	.04	−.20**	−.03	−.03	.34**	.03	.19
China (PRC)⁺	8,814	.19**	−.21**	.08**	.05**	.33**	.11**	.35
Finland	385	.07*	−.06	.00	.05	.76**	−.02	.63
Germany (FRG)	178	.00	−.14*	.10	.00	.46**	.10	.27
Hong Kong⁺	866	–	–	.02	.07**	–	–	.01
Italy	158	−.04	−.13	.02	−.07	.39**	.03	.17
Nigeria⁺	242	−.21**	–	−.20**	.46**	.27**	.14**	.32
Portugal	341	–	−.06	.00	.12*	.65**	−.00	.44
Spain	191	−.01	−.00	.05	−.01	.63**	.13*	.43
Thailand	986	−.04	−.06**	.03	.01	.82**	.02	.69
U.S.A.	209	.00	−.18**	.12	−.03	.65**	.12*	.48

The symbol ⁺ indicates that weighted data were used for analysis. The use of weighted data for the multiple regressions analyses in China, Hong Kong, and Nigeria may have affected the findings. A dash indicates that no data were available.

[a]The regression analysis deleted cases with missing values (listwise).

*$p<.05$. **$p<.01$.

In each of 5 countries (Belgium, China, Germany, Thailand, and the U.S.A.) the *number of children* predictor variable has a statistically significant effect. In every country, families with more children use extraparental services for fewer hours each week.

Mother's years of education and/or *father's years of education* as predictor variables have statistically significant effects in 4 countries (China, Hong Kong, Nigeria, and Portugal). In China and Nigeria the educational levels of both parents have significant effects, while in Hong Kong and Portugal, only the father's educational level has a significant effect. In all cases where these predictor variables are significant (except that of Nigerian mothers), the greater the number of years of education completed by the parent, the greater the number of hours of extraparental care/education services used by the family.

In general, the results indicate that *mother's hours away* as a predictor variable has a statistically significant effect in the largest number of countries. In 10 countries, one or more predictor variables in addition to *mother's hours away* also has a statistically significant effect. However, these additional significant predictor variables vary from country to country, and no discernable pattern is evident across countries.

5

Study Findings: Use of Organized Facilities

MIKKO OJALA AND SYLVIA OPPER

Chapter 4 revealed that in every country studied in Phase 1, a certain percentage of 4-year-olds spend some time each week in an *organized facility*, such as a day care center or a kindergarten. This chapter presents the findings on children who experience an organized facility as their first or second setting (as the place where they spend the most or next-to-the-most extraparental time each week).[1]

Some of the topics reported in Chapter 4—time children spend in their first settings, families' reasons for using extraparental services, problems encountered, and satisfaction with settings—will be examined again in this chapter, but with respect to *organized facilities in particular*. Other topics, such as service sponsors and auxiliary services, because they relate especially to programs in organized facilities, will now be explored in more detail. Also of particular interest in this chapter will be (1) the nature of any contacts parents have with the teachers/caregivers in the organized facilities their children attend,[2] (2) the alternative arrangements parents make when organized facility care is occasionally not an option, and (3) children's and parents' satisfaction with organized facilities.

---

[1]If a child's first and second settings were both organized facilities, researchers collected data for the *more educational* of the two settings, even if it was not the child's first (longest-attended) extraparental setting of the week.

[2]*Organized facility* settings comprise both group care programs and group education programs and thus employ different terms to refer to adults working in these settings. Adults in child care centers are usually called *caregivers*, whereas adults in educational programs are called *teachers*. For purposes of simplification, this chapter refers to adults in both of these categories as *educators*. Since researchers chose to gather data about the more educational of a child's two longest-attended organized programs, the term *educator* is appropriate more often than not.

71

Organized Facilities—Extent of Use and Nature of Program

Information about the extent of children's attendance at organized facilities is given in Table 5.1. The table shows, for each of the study's countries, the percentage of sample children who experienced organized group care or group education as their first or second settings. Clearly, in most of the countries, organized group care or education plays an important role in the life of young children. Nigeria and Thailand are at one extreme with the lowest percentages in organized programs, and Belgium and Hong Kong are at the other extreme with the highest percentages in organized programs. The remaining countries are divided into three groups. In one group—China, Finland, Portugal, and the U.S.A.—approximately one-third of children are in organized programs. In another group—Italy and Spain—approximately three-quarters of children are in organized programs. Germany falls between the two groups, with approximately one-half of its children in such programs.

What types of programs do these organized facilities provide? As can be seen from Table 5.2, the basic orientation of organized facility

Table 5.1 Percentage of all Children Attending Organized Facilities as the First or Second Setting

Country/Territory	N	n No. of children in organized facilities (% of N)
Belgium (Fr.)	424	396 (93)
China (PRC)[+]	12,835	4,127 (32)
Finland	576	202 (35)
Germany (FRG)	509	281 (55)
Hong Kong[+]	947	947 (100)
Italy	1,000	813 (81)
Nigeria[+]	1,295	106 (8)
Portugal	581	178 (31)
Spain	480	334 (70)
Thailand	2,466	296 (12)
U.S.A.	432	170 (39)

The symbol [+] indicates that weighted data were used.

Table 5.2
Percentage Distribution of Organized Facility Users (Children)
According to Type of Organized Program They Attend

Country/ Territory	*n*	% of *n* in the following type of organized program			
		Child care	Educational	Unclassified (general)	Miscellaneous
Belgium (Fr.)	396	0	100	0	0
China (PRC)⁺	4,127	14	86	0	0
Finland	202	0	67ᵃ	0	33ᵇ
Germany (FRG)	281	0	100	0	0
Hong Kong⁺	947	4	96	0	0
Italy	813	0	100	0	0
Nigeria⁺	106	9	51	40	0
Portugal	178	0	0	100	0
Spain	334	0	0	100	0
Thailand	296	36	64	0	0
U.S.A.	170	29	71	0	0

The symbol ⁺ indicates that weighted data were used.

ᵃCommunal day care centers.

ᵇDay clubs, part-time.

programs in most countries is educational. In some countries (such as China, Hong Kong, Nigeria, Thailand, and the U.S.A.) a small proportion of programs are oriented toward child care. In Portugal and Spain it is difficult to distinguish between programs that are care- or education-oriented. (In Portugal preprimary programs may operate according to either an educational or a social-services model. Spain has no official curriculum for its preprimary programs, although the Ministry of Education and Science and some autonomous regions have educational plans for these programs.) Nigeria reports three kinds of programs provided by organized facilities: The majority are educational, some operate according to a "general model," and a few have a child care orientation. In Finland the most frequently used organized facilities are day care centers, which have programs that are clearly educational in nature; the remaining organized settings are day clubs, which are sponsored by churches and which operate only about 5 hours per week.

Time Spent in Organized Facilities

One important issue that has educational, developmental, and practical implications is the amount of time children spend in organized facilities. As can be seen from Table 5.3, which shows how long children in different countries attend their organized programs over a typical week, the average

Table 5.3
Average Time Children Spend per Week
in Their Organized Facilities

Country/ Territory	*n*	Hours per week			
		Minimum	Maximum	Mean	*SD*
Belgium (Fr.)	396	10.0	32.0	25.0	3.3
China (PRC)[+]	4,115	2.0	163.0	47.2	12.1
Finland	202	2.0	50.0	26.9	16.6
Germany (FRG)	281	2.0	48.0	19.8	8.9
Hong Kong[+]	947	14.0	55.0	17.2	7.0
Italy	813	2.0	53.0	32.5	8.8
Nigeria[+]	105	15.0	100.0	23.4	7.0
Portugal	168	14.0	80.5	45.4	12.1
Spain	333	12.5	64.5	29.1	8.2
Thailand	296	4.0	60.0	37.8	6.4
U.S.A.	169	2.0	65.0	22.1	15.4

The symbol [+] indicates that weighted data were used.

time varies from country to country. Children in China and Portugal spend the longest time each week in organized facilities, followed by children in Thailand and Italy. In a third group (Belgium, Finland, Nigeria, Spain, and the U.S.A.) the average weekly attendance ranges from 22.1 to 29.1 hours. Children in Germany and Hong Kong spend the least time each week in organized facilities.

Table 5.3 also gives information on the maximum and minimum hours per week that children in various countries spend in organized facilities. Inspection of the maxima reveals that some countries have children who spend great amounts of time in organized facilities. For example, the highest maximum number of hours is found in China and includes children who attend boarding kindergartens for 6 or more days a week. Close behind is Nigeria, while the lowest maximum weekly time is found in Belgium.

Some countries reported little variation in the weekly hours that children spend in organized facilities, while others reported considerable variation. Table 5.4 shows that in Belgium, China, and Hong Kong, most children spend a similar amount of time in organized settings. At the other extreme, in the U.S.A. at least 10% of the children are included in each of the 10-hour categories listed in the table, indicating a wide variation in weekly attendance. In Finland, the data indicate that children spend either a few hours or many hours in organized facilities. In the remaining countries, the majority of children are spread across two or three of the 10-hour categories, indicating moderate variation.

Assuming that 20 hours or less per week in an organized facility

Table 5.4
Percentage Distribution of Children According to Number
of Weekly Hours Spent in Organized Facilities

Country/ Territory	*n*	2–10 hr/wk	10.1–20 hr/wk	20.1–30 hr/wk	30.1–40 hr/wk	Over 40 hr/wk
		\multicolumn{5}{c}{% of children in organized facilities for}				
Belgium (Fr.)	396	1	10	89	0	0
China (PRC)+	4,115	0	1	5	17	77
Finland	202	32	7	9	26	26
Germany (FRG)	281	10	61	18	7	4
Hong Kong+	947	0	94	0	2	4
Italy	813	2	8	28	48	14
Nigeria+	105	0	64	32	3	1
Portugal	168	0	5	8	21	66
Spain	333	0	12	58	22	8
Thailand	296	0	1	12	69	18
U.S.A.	169	32	26	10	18	14

The symbol + indicates that weighted data were used.

represents a half-day program and that over 20 hours per week represents a full-day program, one can describe two groups of countries. In the first—Belgium, China, Finland, Italy, Portugal, Spain, and Thailand—the majority of children are in full-day organized programs. In the second— Hong Kong, Germany, Nigeria, and the U.S.A.—the majority of children are in half-day organized programs.

The number of days children spend in organized facilities may vary from country to country. For example, in some countries, children attend their organized programs Monday through to Saturday, whereas in others, they attend only Monday through to Friday. Consequently, researchers in each country also obtained information on the average time children spend each day in organized programs. Children spend the longest average daily times in organized facilities in China, Portugal, and Thailand (where daily averages range from approximately 7.4 to 9.1 hours). The shortest average daily time is found in Hong Kong (approximately 3.5 hours).

Reasons Parents Give for Using Specific Organized Facilities

What reasons do families give for using a particular organized facility as their child's extraparental care or education setting? The major reasons given by parents can be grouped into the seven general categories shown in Table 5.5: *convenience, positive information* about the setting, *physical characteristics* of the setting, *nonphysical characteristics* of the setting, *cost, no other alternative,* and *other.* (A category generally included several more specific reasons, or subcategories.)

Table 5.5
Percentage Distribution of Parents According to Major Reason for Choice of a Specific Organized Facility

Country/Territory	n	Convenience	Positive information	Physical characteristics	Nonphysical characteristics	Cost	No other alternative	Other
Belgium (Fr.)[a]	—	—	—	—	—	—	—	—
China (PRC)[+]	4,112	60	22	2	2	2	10	2
Finland	201	30	12	6	27	1	24	0
Germany (FRG)	275	35	9	2	38	1	15	0
Hong Kong[+]	—	—	—	—	—	—	—	—
Italy	784	44	22	4	14	1	12	3
Nigeria[+]	61	38	50	0	7	0	0	5
Portugal	177	35	21	4	9	10	20	1
Spain	324	32	32	2	16	2	11	5
Thailand	289	53	13	2	16	3	13	0
U.S.A.	163	11	40	9	23	8	5	4

The symbol + indicates that weighted data were used for analysis. A dash indicates that no information was available.

[a]Belgian researchers collected information about parents' reasons for choice but used a different format for the question. Their findings indicated that *convenience, positive information,* and *nonphysical characteristics* were given as the major reasons for facility choice.

As can be seen from Table 5.5, in general, reasons of *convenience* were the most frequently cited by parents who were asked the major reason for their organized facility choice. This was specifically the case (compared with all other categories) in China, Finland, Italy, Portugal, and Thailand. Also, although some other categories of reasons fared about as well as *convenience* in Germany, Nigeria, and Spain, approximately one-third of parents in these 3 countries mentioned reasons falling in the convenience category. In Finland, Germany, and Portugal, those who cited convenience usually mentioned *location* as the relevant subcategory of convenience.

In Nigeria and the U.S.A., *positive information* about the setting was the most frequently cited reason category. In Spain this category was also very frequently cited—as frequently as convenience. Positive information was also frequently cited in China, Italy, and Portugal, where approximately one-fifth of parents gave this type of reason.

Nonphysical characteristics of the setting was the most frequently cited category in Germany, where parents mentioned these two nonphysical characteristics subcategories: the educator's *philosophy of childrearing,* and *personal characteristics of the caregiver/teacher.* In Finland and the U.S.A. nonphysical characteristics of the setting was parents' second-most frequently cited category.

In some countries, particularly Finland and Portugal, another reason frequently mentioned was *no other alternative. Physical characteristics* of the setting and *cost* were very rarely mentioned as the type of major reason for choosing a particular organized facility.

Sponsors of Organized Facilities

Of the descriptors for the organized facilities attended by children in various nations, perhaps sponsorship shows the greatest variability across countries.[3] Among the 11 participating countries, there were 10 patterns

---

[3]Countries defined sponsor types as follows. *Educational institution*—in almost all cases, this means sponsorship by a school system (e.g., a preprimary program affiliated with the formal educational system). In a very few instances, it means sponsorship by an institution of higher education (e.g., a preprimary program that is affiliated with a college or university). *Government*—sponsorship by a national, regional, or local governmental agency. *Religious Organization*—sponsorship by a specific church or religious group (e.g., the Catholic church in Italy). *Employer*—sponsorship by the company employing one or both parents. *Voluntary Organization*—sponsorship by a charitable organization (e.g., Save the Children) or group (e.g., a women's organization for education of young children). *Private Organization*—sponsorship by a proprietary group (e.g., Kindercare in the U.S.A.) or private individual. Sponsorship may combine two or more of these sponsor types (e.g., the preprimary programs affiliated with government and religious organizations in Portugal).

of sponsorship, with only Finland and Italy having similar patterns (66 and 67% sponsorship by *government* and 23 and 29% sponsorship by *religious organizations* respectively). In several countries the *government* sponsors the highest percentage of the organized facilities, either alone or in combination with one or more other sponsors (Finland, Italy, Portugal, Spain, and Thailand). In Germany and Hong Kong *religious organizations* sponsor the greatest percentage of organized settings, while in Nigeria and the U.S.A. *private organizations* have this position. Only in China do *employers* sponsor the greatest percentage of organized preprimary facilities.

The *government* and *religious organizations* together sponsor 86–95% of the organized facilities in 4 nations (Finland, Germany, Italy, Portugal). In Hong Kong, *religious organizations* and *private organizations* together sponsor 88% of such settings. In the U.S.A., organized facilities are sponsored by several different single sponsors, with the percentage of settings sponsored by each falling within a fairly narrow range. Belgium displays a unique sponsorship situation: 100% of organized facilities are sponsored by the *government*, and most facilities have either an *educational institution* or *other* (i.e., a local authority) as an additional sponsor.

Auxiliary Services in Organized Facilities

It is often assumed that organized facility programs offer many kinds of auxiliary services to parents and children. The Phase 1 study of the IEA Preprimary Project examined this assumption with regard to *health, special education, social services,* and *transportation.*

Health Services

Health services fared better than most other auxiliary services we looked into, yet Belgium is the only country whose organized facilities offer *extensive* health services (Table 5.7). In China, Spain, Hong Kong, Portugal and the U.S.A. more than a third of organized facility children are offered health services. In Finland, Italy, Nigeria, and Thailand, however, organized programs very rarely offer health services.

Although organized programs may *offer* health services, this does not necessarily mean that parents or children make use of the services. As can be seen from Table 5.7, the countries in which children make the most use of available health services are China, Finland, Nigeria, Thailand, and the U.S.A. Although both Nigeria and Thailand have low rates of availability, the health services that are offered are used quite extensively. The lowest usage rates are found in Hong Kong and Spain.

Table 5.6
Percentage Distribution of Children's Organized Facilities
According to Types of Sponsors

Country/ Territory	*n*	% of organized facilities with the following types[a] of sponsors								
		1	2	3	4	5	6	7	8	9
Belgium (Fr.)	396	0	9	0	0	0	0	0	91[b]	0
China (PRC)[+]	4,127	16	16	0	28	9	2	2	0	27
Finland	202	1	66	29	2	1	1	0	0	0
Germany (FRG)	281	0	29	60	0	5	0	5	0	1
Hong Kong[+]	947	1	0	60	0	11	28	0	0	0
Italy	812	0	67	23	0	0	7	1	0	2
Nigeria[+]	195	0	0	18	0	4	26	3	0	49
Portugal	178	0	54	0	0	0	0	0	38[c]	8
Spain	334	0	24	2	1	1	2	1	0	69
Thailand	296	2	40	2	0	0	0	1	16[d]	39
U.S.A.	170	12	15	19	1	3	25	8	0	17

The symbol [+] indicates that weighted data were used for analysis.

[a]1=educational institution; 2=government; 3=religious organization; 4=employer; 5=voluntary organization; 6=private organization; 7=other; 8=multiple sponsors; 9=no information.

[b]2 + 7 = 50%; 2 + 3 = 41%.

[c]2 + 3 = 32%; 2 + 4 = 2%; 2 + 7 = 2%; other combinations combined = 2%.

[d]2 + 5 = 4%; 1 + 2 = 3%; 1 + 2 + 6 = 3%; 2 + 3 = 2%; other combinations combined = 4%.

Table 5.7
Availability and Use of Health Services in
Children's Organized Facilities

Country/ Territory	*N*	Children with access to services		Children using services		
		n	% of *N*	No. of users	Users as % of *n*	Users as % of *N*
Belgium (Fr.)	396	339	86	225	66	57
China (PRC)[+]	4,126	1,795	44	1,425	79	35
Finland	202	43	21	34	79	17
Germany (FRG)	281	–	–	–	–	–
Hong Kong[+]	947	349	37	81	23	9
Italy	813	91	11	43	47	5
Nigeria[+]	105	2	2	2	100	2
Portugal	178	58	33	27	47	15
Spain	334	140	42	41	29	12
Thailand	296	52	18	44	85	15
U.S.A.	170	63	37	47	75	28

The symbol [+] indicates that weighted data were used. *N* = number of children in organized facilities. Dashes mean the question was not asked.

Table 5.8
Availability and Use of Special Education
Services in Children's Organized Facilities

Country/ Territory	N	Children with access to services			Children using services		
		n	% of N		No. of users	Users as % of n	Users as % of N
Belgium (Fr.)	396	100	25		11	11	3
China (PRC)⁺	4,126	35	1		14	40	<1
Finland	202	56	28		9	16	5
Germany (FRG)	281	–	–		–	–	–
Hong Kong⁺	947	197	21		13	7	1
Italy	813	137	17		8	6	1
Nigeria⁺	106	2	2		1	50	1
Portugal	178	24	13		6	25	3
Spain	334	140	42		25	18	8
Thailand	296	12	4		3	25	1
U.S.A.	170	41	24		12	29	7

The symbol ⁺ indicates that weighted data were used. N = number of children in organized facilities. Dashes mean the question was not asked.

Special Education Services

As can be seen from Table 5.8, the figures concerning special education services contrast with those concerning health services, with special education services being considerably less prevalent. Organized settings in Spain are the most likely to offer special education services, followed by Finland, Belgium, the U.S.A., and Hong Kong. Not many organized programs in Italy and Portugal offer special education services, while China, Nigeria, and Thailand offer even fewer.

Are special education services that are available actually used? The data show that in China, Nigeria, Portugal, and Thailand, where only a few organized settings offer special education services, the usage rates are higher than in some other countries with more availability of services. In Finland and Spain usage rates are fairly low, while in Belgium, Hong Kong, and Italy available special education services are even less heavily used.

Social Services

Table 5.9 shows that with the exception of Belgium, a relatively small proportion of organized facilities offer social services. In China, Hong Kong, Italy, Portugal, Spain, and the U.S.A. they are available to 11–27% of children in organized facilities. In China, Finland, Nigeria, and Thailand few organized facilities offer social services.

Table 5.9
Availability and Use of Social Services
in Children's Organized Facilities

Country/ Territory	*N*	Children with access to services		Children using services		
		n	% of *N*	No. of users	Users as % of *n*	Users as % of *N*
Belgium (Fr.)	396	176	44	23	13	6
China (PRC)+	4,126	440	11	321	73	8
Finland	202	15	7	6	40	3
Germany (FRG)	281	–	–	–	–	–
Hong Kong+	947	177	19	26	15	3
Italy	813	115	14	24	21	3
Nigeria+	105	2	2	2	100	2
Portugal	178	48	27	8	17	5
Spain	334	44	13	3	7	1
Thailand	296	21	7	15	71	5
U.S.A.	170	41	24	13	32	8

The symbol + indicates that weighted data were used. *N* = number of children in organized facilities. Dashes mean the question was not asked.

Data about the use of available social services show that in Nigeria all of the small percentage of organized facility children who have access to services do make use of them. In China and Thailand the rate of usage is also quite high.

Transportation

As Table 5.10 indicates, whereas 3 countries (China, Finland, and Nigeria) have very few organized facilities that offer children transportation, in 4 countries (Belgium, Hong Kong, Italy, and Thailand) transportation is offered for 32–40% of children in organized facilities. In Portugal, Spain, and the U.S.A. transportation services are offered for 21–26% of organized facility children.

In China, where organized settings very rarely offer transportation services, 65% of children use their available services. In Hong Kong, Portugal, Thailand, and the U.S.A. available transportation services have 41–55% usage rates. In Belgium, Finland, Italy, and Spain the usage rates range from 22–34%. The lowest usage rate is seen in Nigeria, where no children used the limited transportation services that are available.

A Cross-National Comparison Regarding Auxiliary Services

A cross-national comparison of rates of auxiliary-service usage among *all* children attending organized facilities (users as a percent of the *N* in

Table 5.10
Availability and Use of Transportation
Services in Children's Organized Facilities

| Country/ Territory | N | Children with access to services | | Children using services | | |
		n	% of N	No. of users	Users as % of n	Users as % of N
Belgium (Fr.)	396	125	32	28	22	7
China (PRC)⁺	4,126	122	3	79	65	2
Finland	202	7	4	2	29	1
Germany (FRG)	281	–	–	–	–	–
Hong Kong⁺	947	375	40	185	49	20
Italy	813	288	35	99	34	12
Nigeria⁺	105	2	2	0	0	0
Portugal	178	37	21	15	41	8
Spain	334	77	23	26	34	8
Thailand	296	102	35	56	55	19
U.S.A.	170	44	26	22	50	13

The symbol ⁺ indicates that weighted data were used. N = number of children in organized facilities. Dashes mean the question was not asked.

Tables 5.7–5.10) shows some interesting results. Considering this universe of children, we find that the pattern of percentages of organized facility children who benefit from *special education* and *social services* was similar across countries. For both types of services, "users-as-%-of-N" across all countries was no more than 8%.

For *health services*, we find a very different pattern—one that ranges widely from only 2% benefiting in Nigeria to 57% benefiting in Belgium. "Users-as-%-of-N" for *transportation* services also had a distinctive pattern. Hong Kong and Thailand showed the highest percentages of organized facility children benefiting from transportation (about one-fifth), while in China, Finland, and Nigeria 2% fewer of children benefited from this facility.

In summary, most countries' organized facilities offer relatively few services beyond the regular care and education program. Belgium is the country where auxiliary services are most commonly offered. Countries offering a moderate amount of auxiliary services are Hong Kong, Portugal, Spain, and the U.S.A. Countries offering few additional services are China, Finland, Italy, Nigeria, and Thailand. China does, however, offer health services to a substantial proportion of children, and Thailand and Italy do offer transportation services to over a third of children in organized programs.

Occasional Alternative Arrangements for the Organized Setting

For children regularly attending organized settings, there may be occasions when parents must find alternatives. Some facilities close regularly for vacations or holidays; others close occasionally in emergency situations; some are "closed" in that they are not the setting preferred (or perhaps allowed) when a child is ill. Table 5.11, which indicates the alternative arrangements that parents make on such occasions, indicates that there are slightly different arrangements, depending on whether the closing (or nonattendance) is planned and regular, or unplanned and due to an emergency.

Generally, if the closing is planned, most parents arrange to take care of their children at home. This is the case particularly in China, Finland, Italy, Portugal, Thailand, and the U.S.A. and to a lesser extent in Belgium and Spain. Another common but less frequent arrangement used by fewer than 10% of families in all countries except China is for the child to remain at home under the care of another relative. A third possibility, especially popular in Belgium and Spain, is care in the home of another relative. Other arrangements, such as a (sick) child remaining in the organized setting, the child being cared for by a nonrelative in the home of one or the other, the child attending another organized setting, or the child attending the parent's workplace, are fairly uncommon in every country. Parents in most countries do make alternative arrangements for any regular closing (or nonattendance). In Spain and Thailand, however, 25% and 10%, respectively, report having no plan for such an occurrence.

The parent taking care of the child at home is also the most common arrangement during an emergency closing, although in almost all countries the percentage of families using this option for an emergency closing is considerably lower than the percentage using it for a planned closing. Parents presumably have difficulty changing their regular schedule to fit in with unexpected closings and consequently must rely more on relatives in these instances to take care of their children. For example, care in the child's home by another relative is an option used more frequently during an emergency than during a planned closing in Belgium, China, Finland, Italy, Spain, and the U.S.A. Care in some other home by another relative is also more common during an emergency in Belgium, Italy, Portugal, and the U.S.A. In each country, the percentages of parents making *other arrangements* were similar for planned and unplanned closings. The same can be said for the percentages having *no plans*. Finally, whereas relatively few countries provide care in an organized facility during planned closings, countries such as Finland, Germany, Spain, Thailand, and the U.S.A. still offer at least minimal services during an emergency closing—sometimes in a facility located nearby.

Table 5.11

Percentage Distribution of Service-Using Parents According to the Alternative Arrangement Made During Planned (P) and Unplanned (UP) Closings of Facilities[a]

% of n Citing the following type[b] of arrangement

Each cell below shows **P (UP)**.

Country/Territory	n	1	2	3	4	5	6	7	8	9	10	No Info.
Belgium (Fr.)	396	0 (0)	59 (46)	7 (9)	2 (3)	20 (28)	4 (6)	4 (4)	1 (2)	3 (2)	0 (0)	0 (0)
China (PRC)+	4,420	3 (—)	89 (57)	0 (25)	0 (1)	7 (—)	0 (0)	0 (0)	0 (0)	0 (0)	1 (0)	0 (0)
Finland	202	8 (25)	72 (51)	3 (8)	0 (2)	3 (2)	0 (1)	9 (4)	0 (1)	2 (1)	0 (0)	3 (5)
Germany (FRG)	—	— (8)	— (72)	— (3)	— (0)	— (14)	— (3)	— (0)	— (0)	— (0)	— (0)	— (0)
Hong Kong+	—	—	—	—	—	—	—	—	—	—	—	—
Italy	813	0 (1)	73 (63)	9 (15)	2 (3)	9 (10)	1 (1)	0 (0)	1 (1)	0 (1)	1 (0)	4 (5)
Nigeria+	—	—	—	—	—	—	—	—	—	—	—	—
Portugal	178	2 (0)	78 (44)	8 (9)	1 (3)	7 (20)	1 (2)	0 (4)	2 (5)	0 (0)	0 (1)	1 (12)
Spain	334	3 (15)	64 (75)	9 (9)	6 (0)	18 (3)	1 (0)	1 (0)	0 (0)	0 (0)	0 (1)	0 (0)
Thailand	296	0 (8)	75 (26)	9 (10)	0 (0)	3 (1)	0 (4)	1 (0)	0 (0)	10 (30)	0 (1)	0 (2)
U.S.A.	170	1 (10)	86 (59)	3 (11)	2 (4)	2 (5)	4 (4)	0 (1)	0 (1)	0 (1)	0 (2)	2 (4)

The symbol + indicates that weighted data were used for analysis. Dashes indicate that no data were available.

[a]Planned closing=holiday and staff inservice training; unplanned closing=emergency at setting or child is refused because of illness.

[b]Types of arrangements: 1=(sick child) remaining in facility; 2=own home with parent; 3=own home with other relative; 4=own home with nonrelative; 5=other home with other relative; 6=other home with other relative; 7=other facility; 8=parental workplace; 9=no plan; 10=other arrangement.

Contact between Educators and Parents

It is increasingly recognized that a close partnership between parents and those who provide organized programs for their children results in benefits for all concerned. Parents benefit by becoming informed about program provisions for their children. In turn, these informed parents generally support the programs with which they have direct and meaningful communication, and early childhood educators (both teachers and care-givers) benefit by receiving this active support from parents. Educators also benefit by becoming familiar with the child's experiences in the home and can then build curricular experiences on this knowledge. Most importantly, children benefit from the increased communication between program and parent.

Educators and parents, however, have been slow in promoting partner-ship and cooperation. In many countries parent involvement in organized programs still remains an ideal rather than a reality. This study examined the extent of educator–parent contact in the various countries by asking questions about certain types of contact parents had experienced during the past 3 months, such as informal meetings, formal meetings requested by either the educator or the parent, group meetings, telephone or written communications, and parent assistance in the organized program. Two aspects of educator–parent contacts were studied—availability and frequency.

Availability of Educator–Parent Contacts

Of the various types of educator–parent contacts reported in the study's countries (Table 5.12), perhaps the most widespread is the *informal meeting* between parent and educator. This contact presumably takes place when the child arrives at or leaves the organized setting. Informal meeting is the most common type of contact in all but 3 countries—China, Hong Kong, and Nigeria.

Another common form of contact is the one-on-one *meeting requested by the educator or parent*. Such meetings, requested by the educator, were reported especially in China; they also occur fairly extensively in Belgium, Finland, Italy, and the U.S.A. This type of contact also occurs, but less frequently, in Nigeria, Spain, and Thailand. One-on-one meetings requested by parents are universal in China and relatively frequent in Italy; they were also reported by approximately one-third of the sample (organized facility parents) in both Finland and the U.S.A. In Nigeria, Spain, and Thailand fewer than 10% of sample parents reported having such meetings.

Less common types of contact are *telephone or written communication,* the *group meeting,* or *parent assistance in the setting.* Although *telephone or written communication* is extremely common in Finland and the U.S.A.

Table 5.12
Percentages of Organized Facility Users (Parents) Engaging in Various Kinds of Educator–Parent Contacts

Country/ Territory	n	% of Parents reporting the following types[a] of contact						
		Inf. Mtg.	Mtg./ Ed.	Mtg./ Par.	Tel./ Writ.	Grp. Mtg.	Parent Assist.	Other
Belgium (Fr.)	396	95	44	–	–	–	33	–
China (PRC)[+]	4,127	61	100	100	13	32	–	1
Finland	202	85	54	34	64	71	13	14
Germany (FRG)	281	–	–	–	–	–	–	–
Hong Kong[+]	947	33	–	–	27	37	21	58
Italy	813	81	41	43	23	58	9	2
Nigeria[+]	106	20	23	6	8	4	5	3
Portugal	178	86	–	–	41	50	10	15
Spain	334	88	15	9	17	39	11	4
Thailand	296	60	24	9	9	20	6	0
U.S.A.	170	80	44	36	65	63	49	14

The symbol [+] indicates that weighted data were used. Dashes mean the question was not asked.

[a]Inf. Mtg.=informal meeting; Mtg./Ed.=meeting requested by educator; Mtg./Par.=meeting requested by parent; Tel./Writ.=telephone/written communication; Grp. Mtg.=group meeting; Parent Assist.=parent assistance in setting.

and relatively common in Portugal, it is less so in Hong Kong and Italy and fairly uncommon in Spain, China, Thailand, and Nigeria. Contact through *group meetings* was reported by approximately two thirds of sample families in Finland, Italy, and the U.S.A.; by a third to a half of sample families in China, Hong Kong, Portugal, and Spain; and by only 20% of Thai and 4% of Nigerian sample families. In most countries of the study, parent assistance in the setting is not a common practice. Approximately one-half of American parents, one-third of Belgian parents, and one-fifth of Hong Kong parents assist in the setting, but elsewhere, fewer than 14% of parents do so.

Alternative (*other*) types of contact are rare in most countries, with the exception of Finland, Hong Kong, Portugal, and the U.S.A. In Hong Kong other contact consists of a handbook that the preschool sends regularly to the home. This contains reports on the child's progress, results of tests or examinations (if these are a part of the curriculum), notices of special events, and so on. In Finland other contact consists of parents visiting the educator's home and parents participating in the same hobbies as the educator. In Portugal other contacts occur mostly because a mother works at her child's setting. In the U.S.A. other refers to various kinds of personal contact.

Frequency of Educator–Parent Contacts

Not only is *informal meeting* the type of educator–parent contact that most parents experience, but it is also the type of contact that occurs most frequently for them. It occurs *daily* in Finland for 51% of parents; in Italy, for 48%; in Spain, for 43%; in Portugal, for 39%; in Thailand, for 23%; and in the U.S.A., for 21%. Of Belgian parents, 73% meet informally with the educator *weekly*, as do 23% of Finnish families and 19% of American families. At least one-half of sample parents in Belgium, Finland, Italy, Portugal, and Spain, and 40% in the U.S.A., reported meeting with their children's educators at least *weekly*.

In China, Hong Kong, and Nigeria the informal meeting is less common. It occurs *once a month* for 26% of Chinese and for 15% of Nigerian families and *less than once a month* for 29% of Hong Kong families. In Thailand the situation is bimodal: 23% of parents meet the educator daily, whereas 41% never meet the educator.

Meetings requested by the educator are held infrequently except in Belgium (where they occurred *weekly* for 15% and *twice each month* for a further 16% of the sample) and in Nigeria (where they occurred *twice each month* for 14% of the sample). Parents who attend educator-requested meetings generally attend them *once a month* or *less than once a month* in China, Finland, Italy, Spain, Thailand, and the U.S.A.

Of the 7 countries that report having *meetings requested by parents*, Finland (12%) and Italy (14%) have the largest number of *daily* parent-requested meetings. Of U.S. parents, 15% request meetings at least *once a month*, and a further 16% request them *less than once a month*. In many countries parents report at least *once a month* parent-requested meetings (Finland, 22%; Italy, 33%; Nigeria, 2%; Spain, 4%; Thailand, 6%; U.S.A., 20%).

Group meetings are not very frequent in most of the countries. They occur, but *less than once a month*, for 24% of families in China, 60% in Finland, 37% in Hong Kong, 39% in Italy, 3% in Nigeria, 38% in Portugal, 30% in Spain, 14% in Thailand, and 25% in the U.S.A.

Telephone or written communications are also relatively rare. In most countries parents primarily reported them occurring *less than once a month*. Such communications occur most frequently in Finland and the U.S.A. Of U.S. families, 5% have these contacts *daily*; 17%, *weekly*; and 12%, *twice each month*. In Finland such contacts are also rather frequent: 1% of Finnish families have them *daily*; 13%, *weekly*; 11%, *twice each month*; and 20%, *once a month*. In the findings, no distinction was made between telephone and written communication, although these are very different types of contacts. In Hong Kong, for example, these contacts would be predominantly by telephone, whereas in the U.S.A. written communication, such as a newsletter, might be more popular.

Contact through *parent assistance in the setting* is infrequent in every country. Even in Belgium, where such contacts are the most common, only 14% of parents assist *weekly*; 12%, *twice each month*; and 66%, *never*. In the U.S.A. 30% of parents assist the educator at least *once a month*, but 47% *never* assist. In Finland 87% of parents *never* assist. Similarly large percentages of nonassisting parents exist in other countries: Hong Kong (79%), Italy (87%), Portugal (89%), Spain (88%), and Thailand (93%).

In brief, the two countries with the greatest variety and the highest frequency of contacts between organized programs and the home are Finland and the U.S.A. Countries in which parents have access to the fewest types of contacts and where the various types of contacts have the lowest frequencies are Hong Kong and Nigeria.

Problems with Organized Facilities

Having seen some of the reasons parents give for choosing particular organized programs for their children, we can then ask whether parents are satisfied with the choices they have made. Do organized facilities meet parents' expectations? Once their children begin to attend on a regular basis, what are the problems parents encounter with these types of settings?

Examination of the problems reported by parents should provide some insight into what parents consider to be important dimensions of organized early education and care. The study of parent satisfaction will reveal parents' perceptions of the quality of the available programs. First of all, three main types of problems were identified by sample parents: problems pertaining to the *setting in general,* to the *program* within the setting, and to the *educator*.

Problems Related to the Setting

With respect to parents' problems pertaining to the setting, China, Germany, and Hong Kong reported the highest percentages of general problems. In China the main problems, in order of frequency, are *hours of operation* (for 10% of parents), *cost* (for 9% of parents), and *location* (for 8% of parents). In Germany the main problems are *hours of operation* (for 13%) and *cost* (for 5%), and in Hong Kong the main problems are *cost* (for 18%), and *location* (for 7%). In each of the remaining countries no more than 5% of parents cited any one type of problem related to the setting. The single category receiving the highest number of complaints overall was *cost*. In Finland and Spain *cost* was not cited as a problem; in the other countries the proportions of families reporting *cost* as a problem ranged from 18% (in Hong Kong) to 1% (in Belgium, Italy, Thailand, and the U.S.A.).

Problems Related to the Program

The major program-related problem concerns *facility/equipment* (particularly in China and Hong Kong, and less so in Belgium). This is followed by problems concerning *other children* (particularly in Hong Kong and China, and to a lesser extent in Nigeria, Belgium, and Germany) and problems with the *philosophy of the program* (in Hong Kong). Staff turnover is a problem for only 8% of families in China, 6% in Hong Kong, and 2% in Belgium.

The two countries whose parents reported the most program-related problems are China—particularly for *facility/equipment* (29%), *other children* (10%), and *staff turnover* (8%)—and Hong Kong—for *philosophy* (20%), *facility/equipment* (21%), *other children* (13%), and *staff turnover* (6%). Some Belgian families (6%) also reported a problem with *facility/equipment*. In each of the other countries, no more than 4% of families reported any one type of problem. One program area that was reported as a problem in only 2 countries, Finland and the U.S.A. (1% each), was *religious orientation*.

Problems Related to the Educator

Except in China, Hong Kong, and Belgium, problems related to the educator are not a major concern for parents. Most countries reported fewer than 5%, and in many cases fewer than 1%, of parents having problems with any particular aspect of the educator. There also seems to be no common pattern to the educator problems that parents in various countries cited. In China the problems are that the educator is *unqualified* and the educator's *personal characteristics*. In Hong Kong it is mainly the *unreliability* of the educator, and in Belgium it is *other* unspecified educator problems.

In short, sample parents in most countries reported few problems with their children's organized facilities. Compared with those in other countries, sample parents in China and Hong Kong consistently reported more problems related to the programs, to the settings, and to the educators. In Belgium parents cited a few problems with educators and programs, and in Germany *hours of operation* (a facility-related problem) stood out among the problems cited. *Cost* is the single problem cited in almost all countries, but even that problem was reported with low frequency in every country except Hong Kong and China. Despite the reports about various problems, in every country, most parents reported few actual problems with the program, the setting, or the educator.

Table 5.13

Percentage Distribution of Parents According to Degree of Satisfaction with their Child's Organized Facility

Country/ Territory	*n*	% of Parents reporting the following degree of satifaction				
		Very	Some-what	Not very	Not at all	No answer
Belgium (Fr.)	396	56	38	4	1	1
China (PRC)+	4,126	46	46	7	1	0
Finland	202	80	18	1	1	0
Germany (FRG)	–	–	–	–	–	–
Hong Kong+	947	14	82	0	0	4
Italy	813	61	32	5	1	1
Nigeria+	105	59	31	7	0	3
Portugal	178	53	45	2	0	0
Spain	334	77	19	2	1	1
Thailand	296	68	30	1	0	1
U.S.A.	170	88	9	2	0	1

The symbol + indicates that weighted data were used for analysis. Dashes indicate that no information was available.

Satisfaction with Organized Facilities

The findings on satisfaction with organized facilities support the apparent lack of parental problems with these settings. Table 5.13 indicates that in every country a vast majority of parents are *somewhat* or *very satisfied* with their children's settings. The country with the highest degree of satisfaction is the U.S.A., followed by Finland. Countries with the most dissatisfaction are Italy, China and Nigeria.

The findings about children's enjoyment while attending organized facilities are similar to the findings for parental satisfaction with these settings. In all 10 countries reporting findings for this item (i.e. all but Nigeria), at least 85% of parents reported that their children enjoyed participating in these settings. When *enjoys* and *sometimes enjoys* are combined, in every country, at least 95% of parents indicated that these categories would describe their children's experiences in the organized facilities.

National Summaries

The findings on the various aspects of organized facilities show that whereas some features are common to all countries, other features vary. Perhaps the most consistent finding is the high degree of satisfaction that sample parents of all countries reported with organized settings: 92–100%

of parents are either somewhat or very satisfied with organized settings. Similarly, in almost all countries, a very large proportion of children, ranging from 89% in Spain to 96% in Germany, appear to enjoy the time they spend in organized settings. In Hong Kong, Spain, Italy, and Thailand, however, from 10 to 15% of children do not or only sometimes enjoy these settings. Other characteristics, such as the amount of time children spend in organized facilities, facility sponsors, or the type and frequency of educator–parent contacts, show wide variations across countries. These have been discussed separately by topic in the previous sections of this chapter. This final section presents for each country a brief summary of the distinctive organized facility characteristics that exhibit a range of variation across countries. The purpose is to highlight the unique pattern of services that each country adopts to provide organized early education and care for their young children.

Belgium (Fr.)

Belgium is exceptional among the study's European countries in that organized facilities, all of which are educational, are available for all 4-year-old children and attended by 93% of them. Children spend, on average, 5 hours a day, or 25 hours a week, in these settings, with the majority being there 20–30 hours a week. During facility closings children are cared for at home by their parents (planned closing, 59%; unplanned closing, 46%) or cared for at another home by a relative (planned closing, 20%; unplanned closing, 28%).

All organized facilities are sponsored by the government. Most of them have additional support from local authorities or religious organizations. As reported by Belgian parents, health services are provided and used extensively; 86% of Belgian children attending organized facilities have this type of service available, and 66% of those make use of it. Also, social services are provided for 44%, special education for 25%, and transportation for 32% of Belgium's organized facility users.

The most common educator–parent contact reported by 95% of the organized facility sample is the informal meeting, which occurs weekly for 73% of parents. Two other types of contact reported by Belgian parents are the meeting requested by the educator (44%) and parent assistance in the setting (33%). Parents report very few problems with the organized facilities their children attend.

China (PRC)

China is characterized by moderate provision but heavy use of organized facilities, particularly of facilities with an educational program. Almost one third of China's total study sample attended organized facilities, with the majority of these (86%) enrolled in educational programs and the rest

(14%) enrolled in care-oriented programs. China's children spend a great deal of time in these programs, an average of 8 hours daily, or 47 hours weekly. The majority (77%) spend more than 40 hours each week in such settings. Most of the children attending organized facilities stay at home with their parents during planned closings (89%) or unplanned closings (57%), and another 25% stay in their own home with a relative during unplanned closings.

Organized facilities are sponsored by a variety of organizations, in particular, by employers (28%), government, and educational institutions (each 16%). The most important criterion that parents use when choosing an organized facility is convenience (60%), although positive information about the program is also an important deciding factor for 22% of organized facility parents, and having no other alternative is the deciding factor for 10%. Health care is the most widespread auxiliary service provided by China's organized facilities; it is available for 44% of children and is also used quite extensively (by 79% of those for whom it is available). The social services that organized facilities offer are available for 11% of organized facility children.

The most frequent educator–parent contact consists of informal meetings (reported by 61% of parents), and these occurred weekly for 13% of the organized facility sample. Meetings requested by either the educator or the parent are universally available, although they are held less than once a month. Parents feel that the major problems with organized facilities have to do with equipment and materials (29%), staff qualifications (21%), hours of operation, and the personal characteristics of the educator (each 10%).

Finland

In Finland, organized facilities were used by 35% of the total study sample. Of these children, 67% attended educational programs (day care centers), and the remaining 33% attended part-time day clubs. Although Finnish children average 6 hours a day, or 27 hours a week, in their organized programs, the amount of time individuals spend in such programs varies widely. About one third of the children attend for 1–10 hours, one-third for 30–40 hours, and one-third for over 40 hours. During facility closings, the most common alternative (72% for planned, 51% for unplanned) is care in the child's own home. However, 25% of children are able to be accommodated by another organized facility in the event that their own program announces an unplanned closing.

Organized facilities for the most part are sponsored by the government (66%) and religious organizations (29%). Parents indicate a variety of reasons for choosing their child's particular program, such as convenience (30%), the nonphysical characteristics of the setting (27%), and having no other alternative (24%). Organized facilities offer a moderate level of health services (21%) and special education services (28%), but few social services (7%). Of these, health services are the most widely used (by 79% of those families with access to them).

Various types of educator–parent contacts occur, and these are frequent. The most common are informal meetings (85%), group meetings (71%), telephone/written communication (64%), and meetings requested by the educator (54%) or the parent (34%). Informal meetings took place daily for 51% of the organized facility sample. Finnish parents reported almost no problems with organized settings.

Germany (FRG)

Approximately half of all the German children (55%) attended organized facilities. In line with a long tradition of Froebelian kindergartens, all such settings are educational in orientation. The average time children spend in these settings is shorter than that spent by children in most other countries in the study—4 hours a day, or 20 hours a week. Most children (61%) spend 10–20 hours each week in their kindergartens. Although 29% spend more time than this, their attendance is rarely for more than 30 hours per week. The most common alternatives during unplanned facility closings are care by parents at home (72%) and care at a relative's home (14%).

Most of Germany's organized facilities are sponsored by religious organizations (60%); an additional 29% are sponsored by the government. Sample parents reported that they chose their child's organized facility because of nonphysical characteristics of the setting (38%) and convenience (35%); some parents (15%) had no other alternative. German parents' problems with organized settings are hours of operation (for 13%) and cost (for 5%).

Hong Kong

The distinctive features of organized facilities in Hong Kong are extensive provision and widespread use. Almost every 4-year-old child attends either an educational setting (96%) or a care setting (4%). However, as in Germany, the average time children attend these settings is relatively short—4 hours daily, or 17 hours weekly; most children attend for only 10–20 hours each week.

Organized facilities are sponsored by either religious (60%), private (28%), or voluntary (11%) organizations—government plays no part. On the whole, these settings provide a moderate level of auxiliary services. The most widespread is transportation (for 40% of the sample), followed by health services (37%), special education (21%), and social services (19%). With the exception of transportation, which is used by 49% of families having access to this service, most of the services provided are under-utilized (used by only 7–23% of the families with access).

The most common forms of educator–parent contact are use of a handbook (for 58% of organized facility parents), group meetings (for 37%), informal meetings (for 33%), and telephone/written communication (for 27%). Most contacts occur less than once a month. Parents report having problems with a number of aspects of their children's programs: the facility and equipment (21%), philosophy of the program (20%), cost (18%), other children (13%), and educator unreliability (10%).

Italy

A high proportion (81%) of Italy's 4-year-old children attend organized settings, all of which are educational. On average, children attend their educational programs 6 hours each day, or 33 hours each week. A large number (48%) attend 30–40 hours weekly, and 28% attend 20–30 hours. In the event of a facility closing, most children are cared for at home by their parents (planned closing, 73%; unplanned closing, 63%), although some children stay with a relative at home (9% and 15%, respectively) or at a relative's home (9% and 10%, respectively).

As in Finland, the major sponsors of organized facilities are government (67%) and religious organizations (23%). Parents select their child's facility mainly for convenience (44%) or because of positive information about the setting (22%). The facilities offer a moderate level of auxiliary services: The most widespread is transportation (offered for 35% of organized facility children), followed by special education (for 17%), social services (for 14%), and health services (for 11%). Use of health and transportation services by children who have access is moderate (47% and 34%, respectively), but the percentages of all organized facility users who benefit from auxiliary services are low, only 1–12%.

Italian parents engage in a variety of educator–parent contacts, such as informal meetings (81%), group meetings (58%), and meetings requested by the educator or by the parent (each 41–43%). Informal meetings occurred daily for 48% of the organized facility sample, but other types of contact were relatively infrequent. Meetings requested by the educator generally took place once a month or less, and meetings requested by the parents ranged from daily meetings (for 14%) to less than once a month (for 9%). The vast majority of sample parents reported few or no problems with their children's organized facilities.

Nigeria

Nigeria is characterized by low (only 8%) usage of organized facilities. Of the organized programs attended, 51% are educational, 9% are care-oriented, and 40% provide a "general" setting. Children spend, on average, 5 hours daily, or 23 hours weekly, in these settings, with the majority (64%) attending 10–20 hours a week.

Information available on half the sample parents shows that organized facilities are sponsored by a variety of organizations, the most common being private (26%), religious (18%), and voluntary (4%). Parents base their choice of a setting primarily on having heard positive information about the facility (50%) and also on convenience (38%). Very few organized settings (1–2%) offer health, social, and special education services.

The most common educator–parent contacts are meetings requested by the educator (reported by 23% of parents) about once every 2 weeks, and informal meetings (reported by 20%) once a month or less. Sample parents cited few specific problems with organized settings, the most common having to do with cost (5%) and other children (4%).

Portugal

In Portugal, as in China, Finland, and the U.S.A., there is moderate use of organized facilities (31%), and all of these facilities provide programs that are "general" in nature. Compared with children in most other countries of the study, Portuguese children spend a long time in their organized programs—an average of 9 hours a day, or 45 hours a week. As in China, the majority (66%) attend more than 40 hours each week. During facility closings most children stay at home with their parents (planned closing, 78%; unplanned closing, 44%) or in a relative's home (7% and 20%, respectively).

Of the organized facilities, 54% are government-sponsored, and a further 38% have multiple sponsors, usually government together with religious organizations. Sample parents indicated a variety of reasons for their selection of a setting: convenience (35%), positive information about the setting (21%), and having no other alternative (20%). Children attending organized facilities have a moderate level of auxiliary services provided for them. Health services (available for 33%) are most common; next come social services (for 27%), transportation (for 21%), and special education (for 13%). Among children with access to the services, usage ranges from 17% for social services to 47% for health services.

The most widespread educator–parent contacts are informal meetings (reported by 86% of parents), group meetings (50%), and telephone/written communication (41%). Informal meetings take place daily for 39% of parents, but other types of contacts occur less than once a month. The vast majority of sample parents (90%) reported that their children enjoyed their organized facilities. With the exception of problems with cost, which was mentioned by 5% of the sample, parents appeared to have few problems with organized settings.

Spain

The majority of Spanish children (70%) attend organized facilities. As in Portugal, these settings are described as "general," presumably covering both education and care. Average daily attendance is 6 hours, and average weekly attendance 29 hours, with the majority of children (58%) attending 20–30 hours per week. Although parents use a variety of alternatives during facility closings, the most usual ones are for children to stay at home with their parents (planned closing, 36%; unplanned closing, 26%), or at a relative's home (19% and 18%, respectively). Relatively high proportions of parents have no plan for either planned (25%) or unplanned closings (30%).

Of those sample parents who responded to the question on facility sponsorship (31%), the majority (24%) indicated government sponsorship. Most parents choose their children's settings on the basis of convenience or positive information about the setting (each 32%), or they base their decision on the nonphysical characteristics of the setting (16%). Organized facilities in Spain offer quite extensive auxiliary services for children. The most widely available are health services and special education services (each 42%), and transportation (23%). Available health and transportation services are the most used (by 29% and 34% of the children, respectively).

As is true in many other countries, the most common educator–parent contact is through informal meetings (for 88% of parents); 43% of parents reported having this type of contact daily. Other parents cited group meetings (39%), telephone/written communication (17%), and meetings requested by the educator (15%), although all of these occurred less than once a month. Parents reported few problems with organized settings, and a large majority (89%) believed that their children enjoyed the facilities they were attending.

Thailand

In Thailand there is relatively low use of organized facilities. Only 12% of sample parents reported that their children attended organized facilities. Of these children, 64% were in an educational setting, and 36%, in a care setting. Thai children attend their settings for a relatively long time—an average of 7 hours daily, or 38 hours weekly, with the majority (69%) attending 30–40 hours each week. During facility closings the majority of children stay at home with their parents. However, a small minority of parents reported having no plans for either planned (10%) or unplanned (6%) closings.

The major sponsors of organized facilities are government (40%), or government combined with other institutions (16%). The most important criteria that parents use when choosing a facility are convenience (53%) and nonphysical characteristics of the setting (16%). The most widely offered auxiliary services are transportation (35%) and health care (18%); these are used by 55% and 85% of children with access, respectively.

The most common educator–parent contacts are informal meetings (60%), which occurred daily for approximately one-quarter of the sample. Other types of contacts are meetings requested by the educator and group meetings, both of which usually occur less than once a month. Thai parents reported very few problems with their children's organized settings.

The U.S.A.

Organized facilities in the U.S.A. are used to a moderate extent—by 39% of the total sample, with 71% of these children attending an educational setting, and 29% attending a care setting. Although the average time children attend organized facilities is 5 hours daily, or 22 hours weekly, there is a wide variation among children. Attendance ranges from 2–10 hours (for 32%) to more than 40 hours (for 14%). The common arrangement during facility closings is for children to stay at home with their parents (planned closings, 86%; unplanned closings, 59%). During unplanned closings a few children (11%) are cared for at home by relatives.

A variety of organizations sponsor organized facilities: these are mainly private (25%), religious (19%), government (15%), and educational (12%). The criteria parents usually consider when choosing an organized facility are positive information about the setting (40%) and nonphysical characteristics of the setting (23%). Organized facilities in the U.S.A. offer a moderate level of auxiliary services: health (37%), transportation (26%), special education, and social services (each 24%). Health care and transportation are the two most widely used (used by 75% and 50%, respectively, of the children with access to these services).

Informal meetings between educators and parents occur quite extensively (80%); 21% of these are daily, and 19%, weekly. Also widespread are telephone/written contact (65%), group meetings (63%), parents helping in the setting (49%), and meetings requested either by the educator (44%) or the parent (36%). With the exception of telephone/written communication, which occurs weekly for 17% and every 2 weeks for a further 12%, most contacts occur less than once a month. Parents in the U.S.A. report almost no problems with their children's organized settings.

6

Study Findings: Children's Daily Routines

ARLETTE DELHAXHE, GENEVIEVE HINDRYCKX,
PATRICIA P. OLMSTED, AND ZHENKUI MA

In the Phase 1 household survey, parents in each country were asked to provide a detailed description of a typical day in their child's life. The daily routines that parents outlined for their children's waking hours yielded such country-specific findings as these:

(1) A typical 4-year-old in Portugal may spend up to 2 hours a day with grandparents.
(2) In the U.S.A., mothers usually supervise their preschool-aged children for 10–11 hours a day.
(3) In China, it is common for a 4-year-old to spend nearly 3 hours a day without direct adult supervision.

This chapter examines the daily routine part of the household survey in greater detail, explaining development of the daily routine questionnaire, data collection procedures, and findings from 10 countries.[1]

Methodology

The Daily Routine Chart

The daily routine (DR) chart was jointly developed by the National Research Coordinators (NRCs) from the participating countries. The chart contains spaces for an interviewer to record the parent/guardian's recollections about the child's routine on the day before the interview. The interviewer asked for three types of information for each of 24 hours, beginning at midnight. These three types of information were (1) the child's primary caregiver, (2) the child's location, and (3) the number of

---

[1]This chapter presents findings for only 10 countries because Italy chose not to have its daily routine data included in the cross-national analysis.

99

other adults/adolescents present and the number of other children present (i.e., the social context of the child). The Parent/Guardian Interview in Appendix C includes a copy of the daily routine chart.

As a group, the NRCs developed the following 10 categories of primary caregivers:

Category	Definition of Category
(1) Mother	Mother, stepmother, or female guardian
(2) Two parents	Mother and father, equally responsible
(3) Father	Father, stepfather, or male guardian
(4) Sibling	Brother, sister, stepbrother, stepsister
(5) Grandparent	Grandmother, grandfather, or both
(6) Other relative	Aunt, uncle, cousin, and so forth
(7) Friend/neighbor	Friend or neighbor of the family
(8) Other adult	Family child care provider, nurse, baby sitter, maid, childminder, paraprofessional in organized facility
(9) Teacher/caregiver	Regular staff person in an organized early childhood facility
(10) Nobody	No direct supervisor

They also developed the following nine categories for the location of the child:

Category	Definition of Category
(1) Home	Home of the child/family
(2) Relative's home	Home of grandparent(s), aunt, cousin, and so forth
(3) Friend/neighbor's home	Home of friend or neighbor of child's family
(4) Child care home	Private home in which child care is provided, on a regular basis, to at least one child unrelated to the child care provider
(5) School/center	Organized facility in which staff provide early childhood services to a group of children
(6) Parent's workplace	Location where mother or father works, including such locations as a factory, hospital, educational institution, and marketplace
(7) Play area	Locations, formal or informal, where children play

| (8) Shops/stores | Locations where family buys things, transacts business, or meets with others (i.e., city hall, community center) |
| (9) In transition | In-transit locations, when child moves from one setting to another (e.g., on foot, by car, by public transportation) |

The NRCs agreed to use a 1-hour interval on the DR chart. When the parent/guardian reported more than one location, caregiver, or social context for a given hour, the interviewer was instructed to enter the information that best represented (i.e., described the longest portion of) the 1-hour time interval. For example, if the child was at home alone with the mother for 20 minutes and then went with a grandparent to a nearby public park to play for 40 minutes, the latter situation (grandparent/play area) would be the information recorded for that hour.

Each national research center pilot-tested the DR chart to check the appropriateness of the system of categories, the design of the chart, and the feasibility of the proposed data collection procedures. As a result of this national pilot-testing, minor changes were made in the DR chart.

The International Coordinating Center (ICC) pilot-tested the DR procedures to insure that parents' recollections about their 4-year-olds' care providers and locations on the previous day were sufficiently accurate. The method used for the pilot test is described in Chapter 2. The results indicated that parents' recollections of their children's daily routines were extremely accurate. Also, with the exception of cases in which a parent was not present and thus could not know about changes in the number of adults or children in a child's setting (e.g., while the child was in an extrafamilial setting), the parental information regarding children's social contexts was accurate.

Data Collection Procedures

As noted earlier, interviewers collected three types of daily routine information (caregiver, location, and social context for each hour of a child's typical day) while they were administering the Parent/Guardian Interview. The NRCs decided that whenever possible, to minimize the amount of recall required, the parent should be asked about the day immediately previous to the day of interview. To ensure that this would produce information about a typical weekday, the Parent/Guardian Interview was to be administered on Tuesday through to Friday. (In Belgium, where preschools are not open on Wednesday, interviewers administered the Parent/Guardian Interview on Tuesday, Wednesday, or Friday only.) If the parent indicated that the previous day had not been typical (e.g., if the child had been ill), then the interviewer was to ask for information for either the day *before* the previous day or for some other recent typical day.

Each NRC instructed the interviewers to use one of two recording procedures: (1) writing the information on the DR chart during the interview with the parent/guardian, or (2) writing the information on a running-record form and later transferring the data to the DR chart. Using either procedure, the interviewer produced a DR chart containing the three types of information described earlier.

Limitations

The DR chart information has several limitations that should be noted. First, the data refer only to a typical weekday and not to Saturday or Sunday. Second, the data refer only to a single day. Finally, only one set of information (the hour's most representative information) was recorded for each 1-hour period, even though the child may have changed caregiver, location, or social context within that hour. Within this 1-hour period, locations, or caregivers, or contexts of short duration are not specifically identified in the data set.

The Daily Routine Data

This examination of the data is limited to analyzing only the child's waking hours. Each NRC designated the 16-hour period that best represented the waking hours for 4-year-old children in their particular country, and this period was used for all children in that country, regardless of individual waking–sleeping patterns. Seven NRCs (in Belgium, China, Finland, Germany, Hong Kong, Nigeria, and the U.S.A.) selected 6:00 a.m. to 10:00 p.m. as the waking-hour period, while the NRCs from Portugal and Spain selected 8:00 a.m. to 12:00 midnight, and Thailand's NRC selected 5:00 a.m. to 9:00 p.m.

Caregivers

Table 6.1 lists, for 10 nations, the mean number of waking hours that 4-year-olds spend with each type of caregiver. The table shows that despite some differences from nation to nation, in every country the *mother* is the care provider for the greatest number of hours. Mothers in Belgium serve in this role for the shortest time each day, while mothers in the U.S.A. serve for the longest time. Belgium is the only nation with any caregiver having hours of supervision close to those of the mother (the *teacher/caregiver*). In all other countries, the mother's supervisory time is much longer than that of any other type of caregiver.

When the data are limited to types of caregivers who provide at least 1 hour of supervision, each country has three or four such caregivers. For

Table 6.1

Number of Waking Hours that 4-Year-Old Children Spend with Various Caregivers

Caregivers

Country/Territory	N	Mother mean (SD)	Two parents mean (SD)	Father mean (SD)	Sibling mean (SD)	Grand-parent mean (SD)	Other relative mean (SD)	Friend neighbor mean (SD)	Other adult mean (SD)	Teacher/caregiver mean (SD)	Nobody mean (SD)	Missing/no info. mean (SD)
Belgium (Fr.)	424	5.2 (3.8)	3.2 (3.3)	0.5 (1.2)	0.1 (0.4)	0.7 (1.8)	0.2 (0.9)	0.1 (0.6)	1.2 (1.3)	4.8 (1.6)	0.0 (0.2)	0.0
China (PRC)+	12,835	6.8 (4.7)	—	0.9 (2.2)	0.1 (0.9)	1.3 (3.2)	0.1 (1.0)	0.1 (0.8)	0.0 (0.5)	3.0 (4.0)	2.9 (4.2)	0.8 (0.0)
Finland	576	7.7 (5.1)	2.1 (3.2)	0.8 (1.7)	0.1 (0.8)	0.3 (1.5)	0.1 (0.7)	0.1 (0.5)	2.7 (3.9)	2.0 (3.5)	0.1 (0.4)	0.0
Germany (FRG)	509	10.0 (4.8)	1.9 (3.2)	0.6 (1.8)	0.1 (0.7)	0.9 (2.4)	0.1 (0.6)	0.2 (0.5)	0.2 (1.0)	1.9 (2.5)	0.1 (0.6)	0.0
Hong Kong+	947	7.5 (5.5)	0.8 (2.0)	0.1 (0.7)	0.0 (0.4)	1.4 (3.6)	0.3 (1.8)	0.1 (1.1)	0.6 (2.3)	3.3 (1.5)	0.0 (0.2)	1.9 (0.0)
Nigeria+	1,295	10.0 (5.0)	1.0 (2.5)	0.7 (1.1)	0.7 (1.5)	0.2 (1.6)	0.3 (1.2)	0.2 (0.9)	1.8 (3.0)	0.5 (1.9)	0.2 (0.9)	0.4 (0.0)
Portugal	581	8.2 (5.7)	1.6 (2.9)	0.4 (1.4)	0.2 (1.2)	1.9 (3.7)	0.5 (2.0)	0.0 (0.0)	0.8 (2.5)	2.3 (3.8)	0.1 (0.6)	0.0
Spain	480	7.6 (4.9)	2.3 (3.0)	0.3 (1.2)	0.2 (0.7)	0.7 (2.0)	0.1 (0.9)	0.1 (0.4)	0.3 (1.2)	4.3 (3.2)	0.1 (0.5)	0.0
Thailand	2,466	8.0 (5.9)	3.3 (4.2)	0.2 (1.3)	0.2 (1.3)	2.1 (4.3)	0.4 (1.9)	0.0 (0.7)	0.4 (1.8)	0.6 (2.0)	0.8 (2.1)	0.0
U.S.A.	432	10.7 (4.9)	0.9 (2.2)	0.7 (1.9)	0.1 (0.4)	0.5 (2.3)	0.2 (1.2)	0.1 (0.5)	1.0 (2.6)	1.8 (3.1)	0.0 (0.1)	0.0

The symbol + indicates that weighted data were used for analysis. A dash indicates that no data were available. Entries are in hours and total to 16.0.

example, *mother* meets this criterion in every country, and *teacher/caregiver* meets this criterion in 8 countries. The category of *two parents* meets the criterion in 7 countries, and the categories *grandparent* and *other adult* (e.g., family child care provider, baby sitter) meet it in 4 countries.

In recent decades, many countries have witnessed a growing interest in involving fathers in childrearing; so it is interesting to note in Table 6.1 that no country reported supervision by *father* exceeding 1 hour daily. There is, however, some variation from nation to nation in the amount of daily supervision by father. If the time that fathers serve as the primary caregivers for 4-year-old children is actually increasing in parts of the world, the increase may be occurring only for subpopulations of families, or the increase may be so small that it is not reflected in an aggregated data set with a 1-hour coding interval. Also, fathers may indeed be providing more care, but it may be in the presence of the mothers and thus recorded under the category *two parents* rather than the category *father*.

Locations

Table 6.2 presents, for 10 countries, the mean number of hours that 4-year-old children spend in various locations. In all nations, *home* is the location where children spend the greatest part of their waking hours. Belgium reported the least time in this location, while Nigeria reported the most time. In 8 nations, an organized facility (*school/center*) is where 4-year-old children spend the second-longest amount of time daily. The exceptions to this situation are Finland, where the time spent in a *child care home* is longer than the time spent in a school/center, and Nigeria, where the time spent in a *friend/neighbor home* is longer than the time spent in a school/center.

There are only 3 locations other than the family's own home (in 10 nations) and the school/center (in 9 nations) where children in any nation typically spend more than 1 hour a day. In Finland and the U.S.A. 4-year-old children average at least 1 hour a day in a child care home, and in Germany and Portugal they average at least 1 hour a day in a relative's home. In China and Spain at least 1 hour daily is spent in a play area.

Caregiver/Location Combinations

Figures 6.1–6.10 present the percentages of time that 4-year-old children in each nation experience various caregiver/location combinations. The findings reported in the figures were obtained using the following steps: First, the total number of waking child-hours was calculated for each country (e.g., for the U.S.A., 432 children × 16 hours = 6,912 child-hours). For each hour during the 16-hour waking period, the number of children experiencing each combination of caregiver/location was tallied (e.g., 7:00–8:00 a.m.: 378 children with mother in own home = 378 child-

Table 6.2
Number of Waking Hours that 4-Year-Old Children Spend in Various Locations

Country/Territory	N	Home mean (SD)	Relative's home mean (SD)	Friend/neighbor home mean (SD)	Child care home mean (SD)	School/center mean (SD)	Parent's workplace mean (SD)	Play area mean (SD)	Shops/stores mean (SD)	In transition mean (SD)	Missing/no info. mean (SD)
Belgium (Fr.)	424	8.6 (2.4)	0.9 (1.9)	0.1 (0.6)	0.0 (0.3)	6.0 (2.3)	0.0 (0.3)	0.1 (0.5)	0.0	0.3 (0.8)	0.0
China (PRC)+	12,835	8.7 (4.2)	0.3 (1.5)	0.6 (1.8)	0.4 (1.9)	3.0 (4.0)	0.4 (1.6)	1.4 (2.7)	0.2 (1.1)	0.3 (0.9)	0.7 (0.0)
Finland	576	10.1 (3.8)	0.3 (1.3)	0.2 (0.8)	2.4 (3.7)	2.1 (3.5)	0.0 (0.3)	0.7 (1.3)	0.2 (0.6)	0.0 (0.2)	0.0
Germany (FRG)	509	11.0 (3.4)	1.0 (2.4)	0.3 (1.0)	0.1 (0.8)	2.0 (2.4)	0.0	0.7 (1.4)	0.4 (0.9)	0.5 (1.2)	0.0
Hong Kong+	947	11.3 (3.6)	0.5 (2.3)	0.1 (1.1)	0.1 (0.7)	3.3 (1.5)	0.1 (0.8)	0.1 (0.4)	0.0 (0.1)	0.0	0.5 (0.0)
Nigeria+	1,295	13.0 (4.7)	0.5 (1.1)	0.8 (1.4)	0.1 (1.2)	0.6 (2.1)	0.3 (1.9)	0.2 (0.8)	0.0 (0.1)	0.0	0.5 (0.0)
Portugal	581	10.1 (4.5)	1.6 (3.4)	0.1 (0.7)	0.5 (2.2)	2.5 (3.9)	0.5 (1.7)	0.5 (1.6)	0.1 (0.6)	0.1 (0.4)	0.0
Spain	480	8.9 (3.0)	0.5 (1.5)	0.1 (0.5)	0.0 (0.3)	4.3 (3.1)	0.1 (0.9)	1.7 (1.6)	0.3 (0.8)	0.1 (0.4)	0.0
Thailand	2,466	12.6 (4.1)	0.9 (2.6)	0.8 (2.0)	0.1 (0.9)	1.0 (2.4)	0.2 (1.4)	0.3 (1.4)	0.0 (0.4)	0.1 (0.5)	0.0
U.S.A.	432	12.1 (3.7)	0.3 (1.0)	0.1 (0.7)	1.0 (2.6)	1.9 (3.1)	0.0 (0.4)	0.2 (0.6)	0.3 (0.8)	0.1 (0.4)	0.0

The symbol + indicates that weighted data were used for analysis. Entries are in hours and total to 16.0.

| | Caregiver | | | | | | | | | |
Location	Mother	Two Parents	Father	Sibling	Grand-Parent	Other Relative	Friend/ Neighbor	Other Adult	Teacher/ Caregiver	Nobody
Home	31	19	3							
Relative's home					4					
Friend/ neighbor home										
Child care home										
School/ center								7	30	
Parent's workplace										
Play area										
Shops/ stores										
In transition										

Total % for 16 hours = 100%. Total % in figure = 94%. Minimum % entered in figure = 2%.

Figure 6.1: Percentage of waking hours that 4-year-old children in Belgium experience various caregiver/location combinations ($N = 424$)

| | Caregiver | | | | | | | | | |
Location	Mother	Two Parents	Father	Sibling	Grand-Parent	Other Relative	Friend/ Neighbor	Other Adult	Teacher/ Caregiver	Nobody
Home	37		4		4					9
Relative's home										
Friend/ neighbor home										2
Child care home					2					
School/ center									19	
Parent's workplace	2									
Play area	2									5
Shops/ stores										
In transition										

Total % for 16 hours = 100%. Total % in figure = 86%. Minimum % entered in figure = 2%. Missing data = 4%.

Figure 6.2: Percentage of waking hours that 4-year-old children in China experience various caregiver/location combinations ($N = 12,835$)

	Caregiver									
Location	Mother	Two Parents	Father	Sibling	Grand-Parent	Other Relative	Friend/ Neighbor	Other Adult	Teacher/ Caregiver	Nobody
Home	44	13	4							
Relative's home										
Friend/ neighbor home										
Child care home								15		
School/ center									13	
Parent's workplace										
Play area	2									
Shops/ stores										
In transition										

Total % for 16 hours = 100%. Total % in figure = 91%. Minimum % entered in figure = 2%.

Figure 6.3: Percentage of waking hours that 4-year-old children in Finland experience various caregiver/location combinations ($N = 576$)

	Caregiver									
Location	Mother	Two Parents	Father	Sibling	Grand-Parent	Other Relative	Friend/ Neighbor	Other Adult	Teacher/ Caregiver	Nobody
Home	52	10	3							
Relative's home					4					
Friend/ neighbor home										
Child care home										
School/ center									11	
Parent's workplace										
Play area	3									
Shops/ stores	2									
In transition	2									

Total % for 16 hours = 100%. Total % in figure = 87%. Minimum % entered in figure = 2%.

Figure 6.4: Percentage of waking hours that 4-year-old children in Germany experience various caregiver/location combinations ($N = 509$)

	Caregiver									
Location	Mother	Two Parents	Father	Sibling	Grand-Parent	Other Relative	Friend/ Neighbor	Other Adult	Teacher/ Caregiver	Nobody
Home	46	5			7			3		
Relative's home					2					
Friend/ neighbor home										
Child care home										
School/ center									21	
Parent's workplace										
Play area										
Shops/ stores										
In transition										

Total % for 16 hours = 100%. Total % in figure = 84%. Minimum % entered in figure = 2%. Missing data = 11%.

Figure 6.5: Percentage of waking hours that 4-year-old children in Hong Kong experience various caregiver/location combinations ($N = 947$)

	Caregiver									
Location	Mother	Two Parents	Father	Sibling	Grand-Parent	Other Relative	Friend/ Neighbor	Other Adult	Teacher/ Caregiver	Nobody
Home	57	6	4	3				8		
Relative's home										
Friend/ neighbor home										
Child care home										
School/ center									3	
Parent's workplace	2									
Play area										
Shops/ stores										
In transition										

Total % for 16 hours = 100%. Total % in figure = 83%. Minimum % entered in figure = 2%. Missing data = 3%.

Figure 6.6: Percentage of waking hours that 4-year-old children in Nigeria experience various caregiver/location combinations ($N = 1,295$)

	Caregiver									
Location	Mother	Two Parents	Father	Sibling	Grand-Parent	Other Relative	Friend/ Neighbor	Other Adult	Teacher/ Caregiver	Nobody
Home	45	9	2		5					
Relative's home					6	2				
Friend/ neighbor home										
Child care home								3		
School/ center									14	
Parent's workplace	2									
Play area	2									
Shops/ stores										
In transition										

Total % for 16 hours = 100%. Total % in figure = 90%. Minimum % entered in figure = 2%.

Figure 6.7: Percentage of waking hours that 4-year-old children in Portugal experience various caregiver/location combinations (N = 581)

	Caregiver									
Location	Mother	Two Parents	Father	Sibling	Grand-Parent	Other Relative	Friend/ Neighbor	Other Adult	Teacher/ Caregiver	Nobody
Home	38	13			2					
Relative's home					2					
Friend/ neighbor home										
Child care home										
School/ center									27	
Parent's workplace										
Play area	7									
Shops/ stores										
In transition										

Total % for 16 hours = 100%. Total % in figure = 89%. Minimum % entered in figure = 2%.

Figure 6.8: Percentage of waking hours that 4-year-old children in Spain experience various caregiver/location combinations (N = 480)

| | Caregiver | | | | | | | | | |
Location	Mother	Two Parents	Father	Sibling	Grand-Parent	Other Relative	Friend/ Neighbor	Other Adult	Teacher/ Caregiver	Nobody
Home	45	19			9	2				
Relative's home					3					
Friend/ neighbor home	2									2
Child care home										
School/ center								2	4	
Parent's workplace										
Play area										
Shops/ stores										
In transition										

Total % for 16 hours = 100%. Total % in figure = 88%. Minimum % entered in figure = 2%.

Figure 6.9: Percentage of waking hours that 4-year-old children in Thailand experience various caregiver/location combinations ($N = 2,466$)

| | Caregiver | | | | | | | | | |
Location	Mother	Two Parents	Father	Sibling	Grand-Parent	Other Relative	Friend/ Neighbor	Other Adult	Teacher/ Caregiver	Nobody
Home	62	5	4		2					
Relative's home										
Friend/ neighbor home										
Child care home								5		
School/ center									12	
Parent's workplace										
Play area										
Shops/ stores	2									
In transition										

Total % for 16 hours = 100%. Total % in figure = 92%. Minimum % entered in figure = 2%.

Figure 6.10: Percentage of waking hours that 4-year-old children in the U.S.A. experience various caregiver/location combinations ($N = 432$)

hours in *mother/home* cell). Then, these cell-specific child-hours were aggregated across the 16-hour waking period (i.e., $378 + \ldots = 4{,}288$), and a percentage was calculated for the child-hours by dividing the child-hours in the *mother/home* cell by the total child-hours (e.g., $4{,}288/6{,}912 = 62\%$).

Figures 6.1–6.10 show that in most countries, *mother*, *father*, or *two parents* nearly always supervise the 4-year-olds at *home*. Only in Spain is any other single caregiver/location combination involving a parent experienced more than 5% of the time (Spanish children experience *mother/play area* 7% of waking time). In many countries *grandparent* supervision occurs in two different locations—in the child's home (the *grandparent/home* cell) and in the grandparent's home (the *grandparent/relative's home* cell). *Teacher/caregiver* supervision generally occurs in organized facilities (*teacher/ caregiver* in the *school/center*). In some countries (e.g., Belgium and Thailand) *other adult* supervision is in *schools/centers*, while in other countries (e.g., Finland and Portugal) it occurs in a *child care home*.

Across the 10 figures, the number of cells containing entries varies from 6 to 10, indicating that the total number of caregiver/location combinations that 4-year-old children encounter during a typical day is relatively small. In any one country, supervision by a given type of caregiver generally occurs in a single location. The exceptions to this include grandparent (who provides care in both the child's home and the relative's (grandparent's) home) and other adult (who provides care in the child care home and school/center).

Groupings of Caregivers and Locations

It is also possible to combine the information presented in Tables 6.1 and 6.2 with the data in Figures 6.1–6.10 to develop five general groupings of caregivers and locations. Table 6.3 presents the five groupings, with each defined by the nature of the relationship between the caregiver and the child as well as by the nature of the location:

(1) Parental care in all locations, which includes the caregiver categories of *mother*, *father*, and *two parents*. For this grouping, all locations in which parental supervision occurs (e.g., *home*, *play area*) are included.

(2) Relative care in all locations, which includes the caregiver categories of *sibling*, *grandparent*, and *other relative*. For this grouping, all locations in which relative supervision occurs (e.g., *home*, *play area*) are included.

(3) Nonfamilial care in informal locations, which includes the caregiver categories of *friend/neighbor*, *other adult*, and *teacher/caregiver*. For this grouping, all locations except *school/center* are included.

(4) Nonfamilial care in formal locations, which includes the caregiver

Table 6.3
Hours of Care of 4-Year-Old Children during Waking Hours by Various Caregivers in Various Locations

Country/Territory	N	Caregiver/Location Group					
		Parental, all locations	Relative, all locations	Nonfamilial, informal locations	Nonfamilial, formal locations	Nobody, all locations	Missing, no information
Belgium (Fr.)	424	8.9	1.0	0.1	6.0	0.0	0.0
China (PRC)[+]	12,835	7.7	1.5	0.1	3.0	2.9	0.8
Finland	576	10.6	0.5	2.8	2.0	0.1	0.0
Germany (FRG)	509	12.5	1.1	0.2	2.1	0.1	0.0
Hong Kong[+]	947	8.4	1.7	0.7	3.3	0.0	1.9
Nigeria[+]	1,295	11.7	1.2	2.0	0.5	0.2	0.4
Portugal	581	10.2	2.6	0.8	2.3	0.1	0.0
Spain	480	10.2	1.0	0.1	4.6	0.1	0.0
Thailand	2,466	11.5	2.7	0.0	1.0	0.8	0.0
U.S.A.	432	12.3	0.8	1.1	1.8	0.0	0.0

The symbol [+] indicates that weighted data were used for analysis. Entries are in hours and total to 16.0.

categories of *friend/neighbor*, *other adult* and *teacher/caregiver*. Only the *school/center* location is included in this grouping.

(5) Nobody caring for the child in all locations, which includes only the caregiver category of *nobody*. In this grouping, all locations are included.

The data for these five groupings, presented in Table 6.3, reveal the following.

Parental Care in all Locations

China reported the lowest number of hours of parental care, while Germany reported the highest. For 5 nations, parents are the caregivers for 10–12 hours of the child's waking time. In Belgium, China, and Hong Kong, parental care covers less than 10 hours; in Germany and the U.S.A., it covers more than 12 hours.

Relative Care in all Locations

In most countries, supervision of 4-year-old children by relatives typically occurs for only a short time each day. In 8 of the 10 countries, relatives supervise for periods ranging from 0.5 hour to 1.7 hours. Only in Portugal and Thailand do relatives supervise young children for more than 2 hours a day.

Nonfamilial Care in Informal Locations

Only 3 nations reported more than 1 hour per day for this caregiver and location grouping. In 2 of these 3 countries (Finland and the U.S.A.), the care usually involves a caregiver in a child care home. In the third country (Nigeria, 2.0 hours), the care is generally provided by a maid or childminder in the child's own home.

Nonfamilial Care in Formal Locations

Nigeria reported the least time in this type of care (0.5 hour), while Belgium reported the most time (6.0 hours). In the remaining nations, 4-year-old children experience from 1.0 to 4.6 hours of this type of supervision in formal locations.

Nobody Caring for the Child in all Locations

China is the only nation reporting more than 0.8 hour in this grouping. *Nobody* as a caregiver occurs primarily in the rural areas of China (80% of the country), where it is commonly considered safe to leave a 4-year-old child playing unattended near the family's home without direct adult supervision while the parents are away for several hours, working in the fields.

On the basis of these five groupings, it is possible to identify some countries where children typically experience similar daily patterns of caregivers and location. For example, young children in Belgium and Spain have several hours of nonfamilial care in formal locations and parental supervision for most of their remaining waking hours. Children in Germany and the U.S.A. spend a great amount of time under parental supervision, with their remaining waking hours divided between relative care and nonfamilial care in both informal and formal locations. Finally, children in Portugal and Thailand share a pattern that includes more than 2 hours of relative care daily.

Patterns of Caregivers and Locations

Behind the general descriptions just presented, it is useful to look for groups of children within each nation who have similar patterns of caregivers and locations during their waking hours. Researchers applied cluster analysis procedures (BMDP, k-means clustering) using 19 variables (10 caregivers, 9 locations) to each set of national data to identify the groups of children who share common patterns. For the countries in which weighted data were used for the analysis, a Fortran program was additionally prepared to produce weighted cluster analysis results. A standard procedure was followed to determine the number of clusters to represent the patterns in each nation, and the largest number of clusters in which the smallest cluster contained at least 5% of the sample children was selected.

Tables 6.4–6.13 present detailed information for each pattern identified from the sets of national data. The tables give, for each country, the number and percentage of children in each cluster (immediately under the column head) as well as the average number of hours children spend with each type of caregiver and in each location. The data for those variables deemed to characterize the cluster are indicated in bold type.[2] In each

---

[2]The column headings in Tables 6.4–6.13 describe the various clusters by listing the major caregivers and major locations of children in each cluster. The boldfacing of data within each column of the table highlights what is *unique* to a given cluster—what sets it apart from the other clusters of that country. In general, each column heading comprehensively includes (1) any caregivers and locations utilized for several hours a day and (2) any unique elements of the cluster.

Examples of how the above guidelines were followed can be seen in Table 6.4 (Belgium). The *teacher/caregiver*, who supervises the child for at least 1 hour in every cluster, is only included in the headings of the first four clusters (i.e., the clusters with longer periods of *teacher/caregiver* time). Even though *teacher/caregiver* is in the heading of the third cluster, it does not have highlighted data in that cluster, since the *teacher/caregiver* category appears in all clusters and thus is not unique to the third cluster. In the fifth cluster, the *teacher/caregiver* supervises for only a short period of time, so *teacher/caregiver* does not appear in the heading nor does it have highlighted data.

Continued

figure, the clusters for that country are ordered according to the number of children in each, in decreasing order.

As already mentioned, the findings presented in Figures 6.1–6.10 indicate that most caregivers provide supervision in a single location. Consequently, Figures 6.11–6.20 depict just the caregiver portions of each nation's cluster information (from Tables 6.4–6.13). The width of each bar represents the percentage of the sample (N) included in the cluster (i.e., a wide bar represents a large percentage of the sample, whereas a narrow bar indicates a small percentage).

A cluster found in most countries is a combination *mother-teacher/ caregiver* cluster, defined by a minimum of 12 hours of supervision provided by these caregivers. The pattern is present in 8 of 10 countries and is generally one of the larger groupings of children. Only Nigeria and Thailand do not have such a cluster. In some countries there are 2 or 3 *mother-teacher/caregiver* clusters that are differentiated by the addition of one other category (e.g., *grandparent* in Spain's fourth cluster). Also, the groupings vary in the proportion of time that mothers or teachers/caregivers serve as supervisors for the children.

Another cluster found in 8 of the 10 nations is a *mother-only* pattern, that is, a group of children for whom the mother serves as the only caregiver for nearly the entire waking period. In most countries, this cluster contains the highest or the second-highest percentage of children, and most of the mother's supervision takes place in the family *home*. Only Belgium and Hong Kong do not have this pattern. Nigeria has two mother groupings, one characterized by mother care in the home and another characterized by mother care in two locations, the *workplace* (e.g., the marketplace) and the *home*. Portugal also has 2 mother groupings, 1 cluster characterized by mother care in the *home* and another cluster characterized by mother care in the *workplace* and *play area* as well in the home.

Six countries have a *grandparent* cluster, that is, a grouping in which a grandparent typically supervises the child for a minimum of 5 hours a day. This cluster often contains only a small percentage of children (i.e., 8–15%), but the proportion of the child's waking hours that the grandparent

---

Continued

By scanning Belgium's clusters and looking at the highlighted data, it is possible to see how the 5 Belgian clusters differ from one another. For example, in 2 clusters, the category *mother* is highlighted, while in 2 others, the category *two parents* is highlighted. In the fourth cluster, only *grandparent* and *teacher/caregiver* data are highlighted, even though there are short periods during which the *mother* and *two parents* supervise the child. The combination of *grandparent* and *teacher/caregiver* is what makes this cluster unique among Belgium's clusters.

Table 6.4
Hours of Caregivers and Locations for 4-Year-Old Children in Belgium (*N* = 424)

	Pattern (Cluster)				
	1	2	3	4	5
Category	Mother in home; T/C, OA in S/C *n* = 157; 37% of *N*	2 Parents in home; T/C, OA in S/C *n* = 153; 36% of *N*	Mother in home; T/C in S/C *n* = 54; 13% of *N*	GP in GP home; T/C in S/C *n* = 41; 9% of *N*	2 Parents in home *n* = 19; 5% of *N*
Caregiver					
Mother	**7.4**	2.2	**10.9**	2.5	1.3
Father	0.4	0.5	0.4	0.6	1.1
2 Parents	0.6	**5.7**	1.2	2.6	**10.4**
Sibling	0.1	0.0	0.1	0.0	0.1
Grandparent(GP)	0.3	0.2	0.4	**5.0**	0.2
Other relative(OR)	0.1	0.1	0.2	0.3	1.3
Friend/neighbor(F/N)	0.2	0.1	0.0	0.0	0.0
Other adult(OA)	**1.5**	1.7	0.0	0.3	0.0
Teacher/caregiver(T/C)	**5.4**	5.5	2.7	4.7	1.3
Nobody	0.0	0.0	0.0	0.0	0.3
Location					
Home	**8.3**	**8.2**	**12.1**	5.6	**10.9**
Relative's home	0.4	0.2	0.4	**5.1**	1.8
F/N Home	0.1	0.1	0.1	0.0	0.0
Child care home(CCH)	0.0	0.1	0.0	0.0	0.1
School/center(S/C)	**6.8**	**7.1**	2.7	**5.0**	1.3
Workplace(WP)	0.0	0.0	0.0	0.0	0.2
Play area(PA)	0.1	0.1	0.1	0.0	0.4
Shops/stores	0.0	0.0	0.0	0.0	0.0
In transition	0.2	0.2	0.5	0.3	1.3

Guidelines for interpreting table: (1) The smallest cluster contains at least 4.5% (≈5%) of the sample children. (2) Entries are in hours and total 16.0. (3) All times greater than 1.0 hour are listed in left column under cluster. (4) All times less than 1.0 hour are listed in right column under cluster. (5) The numbers critical to understanding the uniqueness of the cluster are boldfaced.

Table 6.5

Hours of Caregivers and Locations for 4-Year-Old Children in China (N = 12,835)

	Pattern (Cluster)							
	1	2	3	4	5	6	7	8
Category	T/C in S/C; Mother in home n = 2,567 20% of N	T/C in S/C; Father in home n = 2,181 17% of N	Mother in home n = 1,669 13% of N	Nobody or mother in home or PA n = 1,540 12% of N	Mother in home, PA, or WP n = 1,412 11% of N	Nobody or mother in home n = 1,284 10% of N	GP or mother in home n = 1,155 9% of N	Father in home n = 1,027 8% of N
Caregiver								
Mother	7.1	3.1	**14.4**	4.4	**12.6**	4.6	4.0	3.6
Father	0.4	**1.5**	0.4	0.5	0.4	0.6	0.4	**4.3**
2 Parents	–	–	–	–	–	–	–	–
Sibling	0.0	0.0	0.1	0.1	0.1	0.2	0.0	0.7
Grandparent(GP)	0.3	0.6	0.2	0.4	0.3	0.4	**10.2**	0.3
Other relative(OR)	0.0	0.1	0.1	0.1	0.1	0.1	0.0	**1.1**
Friend/neighbor(F/N)	0.0	0.0	0.1	0.0	0.2	0.1	0.1	0.7
Other adult(OA)	0.1	0.1	0.0	0.0	0.0	0.0	0.0	0.1
Teacher/caregiver(T/C)	**7.1**	**8.9**	0.1	0.1	0.1	0.2	0.2	0.2
Nobody	0.7	1.4	0.5	**10.1**	1.5	**9.8**	0.8	0.9
Location								
Home	7.4	**5.2**	**14.8**	**6.7**	**8.2**	**13.1**	**9.3**	**7.0**
Relative's home	0.1	0.3	0.1	1.5	1.2	0.2	1.0	1.4
F/N Home	0.2	0.1	0.4	0.3	0.1	0.7	0.7	0.4
Child care home(CCH)	0.0	0.2	0.0	0.2	0.1	0.0	2.8	0.5
School/center(S/C)	**7.3**	**9.1**	0.1	0.4		0.3	0.2	0.8
Workplace(WP)	0.1	0.0	0.1		**2.1**	0.3	0.2	
Play area(PA)	0.3	0.4	0.3	**5.4**	**2.9**	0.8	1.4	1.4
Shops/stores	0.0	0.0	0.1	0.5	0.3	0.3	0.1	0.6
In transition	0.5	0.4	0.1	0.4	0.3	0.2	0.2	0.3

A dash indicates no data were available. Guidelines for interpreting table: (1) The smallest cluster contains at least 4.5% (≈5%) of the sample children. (2) Entries are in hours and total 16.0. (3) All times greater than 1.0 hour are listed in left column under cluster. (4) All times less than 1.0 hour are listed in right column under cluster. (5) The numbers critical to understanding the uniqueness of the cluster are boldfaced.

Table 6.6
Hours of Caregivers and Locations for 4-Year-Old Children in Finland (N = 576)

	Pattern (Cluster)						
	1	2	3	4	5	6	7
Category	Mother in home; n = 134; 23% of N	T/C in S/C; Mother in home; n = 123; 21% of N	OA in CCH; Mother in home; n = 118; 20% of N	Mother or 2 parents in home; n = 76; 13% of N	OA in CCH; 2 parents in home; n = 54; 10% of N	Mother in home; T/C in S/C; GP in GP home; n = 46; 8% of N	2 parents in home; GP in GP home; n = 25; 5% of N
Caregiver							
Mother	**15.0**	4.2	6.9	**7.9**	0.8	**9.5**	1.0
Father	0.4	0.7	0.5	1.5	1.2	1.0	1.4
2 Parents	0.2	2.4	0.1	**4.3**	**5.4**	0.5	**9.4**
Sibling	0.0	0.0	0.1	0.5	0.0	0.3	0.3
Grandparent(GP)	0.1	0.0	0.0	0.6	0.0	**1.5**	**2.2**
Other relative(OR)	0.0	0.0	0.0	0.0	0.0	0.2	0.2
Friend/neighbor(F/N)	0.1	0.1	0.0	0.0	0.0	0.8	0.1
Other adult(OA)	0.0	0.1	**8.2**	0.8	**8.6**	0.2	
Teacher/caregiver(T/C)	0.2	**8.4**	0.1	0.3	0.0	**1.8**	1.0
Nobody	0.0	0.1	0.0	0.1	0.0	0.2	0.3
Location							
Home	**14.1**	7.0	7.2	**14.2**	7.2	9.2	**13.0**
Relative's home	0.1	0.0	0.0	0.0	0.0	**2.6**	**1.1**
F/N Home	0.3	0.0	0.1	0.1	0.0	0.5	0.1
Child care home(CCH)	0.0	0.0	**7.7**	0.1	**8.2**	0.2	0.2
School/center (S/C)	0.2	**8.4**	0.1	0.4	0.2	**2.2**	0.3
Workplace(WP)	0.0	0.0	0.0	0.1	0.0	0.0	0.2
Play area(PA)	0.9	0.3	0.6	0.8	0.2	0.9	0.8
Shops/stores	0.3	0.1	0.2	0.3	0.1	0.3	0.2
In transition	0.0	0.0	0.1	0.0	0.0	0.1	0.0

Guidelines for interpreting table: (1) The smallest cluster contains at least 4.5% (≈5%) of the sample children. (2) Entries are in hours and total 16.0. (3) All times greater than 1.0 hours are listed in left column under cluster. (4) All times less than 1.0 hours are listed in right column under cluster. (5) The numbers critical to understanding the uniqueness of the cluster are boldfaced.

Table 6.7
Hours of Caregivers and Locations for 4-Year-Old Children in Germany (N = 509)

	Pattern (Cluster)			
	1	2	3	4
	Mother in home	Mother in home T/C in S/C	2 Parents/home; T/C in S/C	GP in GP home; Mother in home
Category	n = 255; 50% of N	n = 167; 33% of N	n = 45; 9% of N	n = 42; 8% of N
Caregiver				
Mother	**13.5**	8.1	1.8	4.5
Father	0.3	0.7	1.6	0.6
2 Parents	0.9	1.5	**8.9**	1.6
Sibling	0.1	0.1	0.2	0.0
Grandparent(GP)	0.5	0.3	0.5	**6.2**
Other relative(OR)	0.1	0.1	0.2	0.3
Friend/neighbor(F/N)	0.1	0.4	0.4	0.0
Other adult(OA)	0.1	0.2	0.6	0.0
Teacher/caregiver(T/C)	0.4	4.4	1.7	0.5
Nobody	0.0	0.2	0.1	0.0
Location				
Home	**13.0**	9.3	11.0	5.5
Relative's home	0.4	0.4	0.6	**6.6**
F/N Home	0.2	0.4	0.3	0.0
Child care home(CCH)	0.0	0.1	0.2	0.0
School/center(S/C)	0.6	4.4	1.8	0.6
Workplace(WP)	0.0	0.0	0.0	0.0
Play area(PA)	0.8	0.6	0.8	0.4
Shops/Stores	0.5	0.2	0.3	0.4
In transition	0.5	0.5	0.9	0.2

Guidelines for interpreting table: (1) The smallest cluster contains at least 4.5% (≈5%) of the sample children. (2) Entries are in hours and total 16.0. (3) All times greater than 1.0 hour are listed in left column under cluster. (4) All times less than 1.0 hour are listed in right column under cluster. (5) The numbers critical to understanding the uniqueness of the cluster are boldfaced.

Table 6.8
Hours of Caregivers and Locations for 4-Year-Old Children in Hong Kong (N = 947)

| | Pattern (Cluster) | | | | |
Category	1 — Mother in home; T/C in S/C; n = 511; 54% of N	2 — T/C in S/C; 2 Parents in home; n = 180; 19% of N	3 — GP in multiple home settings; T/C in S/C; n = 133; 14% of N	4[a] — OR, F/N,OA in multiple home settings; T/C in S/C; n = 66; 7% of N	5 — OA in home; T/C in S/C; n = 57; 6% of N
Caregiver					
Mother	**12.2**	2.9	1.3	1.2	1.5
Father	0.0	0.3	0.1	0.1	0.0
2 Parents	0.4	**2.5**	0.7	0.5	0.6
Sibling	0.0	0.1	0.0	0.0	0.0
Grandparent(GP)	0.0	0.1	**9.8**	0.2	0.0
Other relative(OR)	0.0	0.4	0.0	3.2	0.0
Friend/neighbor(F/N)	0.0	0.0	0.0	1.7	0.0
Other adult(OA)		0.1	0.0	1.5	**8.1**
Teacher/caregiver(T/C)	3.1	4.9	3.0	2.2	3.1
Nobody	0.0	0.0	0.0	0.0	0.0
Location					
Home	**12.7**	**10.6**	**10.9**	1.8	**12.7**
Relative's home	0.0	0.0	**2.0**	3.2	0.0
F/N Home	0.0	0.0	0.0	1.5	0.0
Child care home(CCH)	0.0	0.0	0.0	0.6	0.2
School/center(S/C)	3.1	4.9	3.0	2.2	3.1
Workplace(WP)	0.1	0.3	0.0	0.0	0.0
Play area(PA)	0.1	0.1	0.1	0.0	0.0
Shops/stores	0.0	0.1	0.0	0.0	0.0
In transition	0.0	0.0	0.0	0.0	0.0

Guidelines for interpreting table: (1) The smallest cluster contains at least 4.5% (≈5%) of the sample children. (2) Entries are in hours and total 16.0. (3) All times greater than 1.0 hour are listed in left column under cluster. (4) All times less than 1.0 hour are listed in right column under cluster. (5) The numbers critical to understanding the uniqueness of the cluster are boldfaced.

[a]Because of the large amount of missing data, no entries are boldfaced.

Table 6.9
Hours of Caregivers and Locations for 4-Year-Old Children in Nigeria (N = 1,251)

	Pattern (Cluster)							
	1		2		3		4	
Category	Mother in home n = 587; 47% of N		Mother, 2 parents, or sibling in home; T/C in S/C n = 356; 28% of N		Mother or OA in home n = 249; 20% of N		Mother in home or WP n = 59; 5% of N	
Caregiver								
Mother	**14.2**		**5.5**		**5.9**		**13.7**	
Father		0.5		0.8		0.7		0.4
2 Parents		0.3	**2.7**			0.4		0.5
Sibling		0.2	**1.6**			0.6		0.5
Grandparent(GP)		0.0		0.8		0.0		0.0
Other relative(OR)		0.1		0.9		0.1		0.0
Friend/neighbor(F/N)		0.0		0.5		0.0		0.2
Other adult(OA)		0.2		0.3	**8.2**			0.0
Teacher/caregiver(T/C)		0.1	**1.6**			0.0		0.2
Nobody		0.1		0.4		0.0		0.5
Location								
Home	**14.8**		**10.4**		**13.9**		**6.6**	
Relative's home		0.3		0.7		0.7		0.0
F/N Home		0.4	**1.2**			0.9		0.7
Child care home(CCH)		0.0		0.4		0.1		0.1
School/center(S/C)		0.2	**1.8**			0.1		0.1
Workplace(WP)		0.0		0.2		0.0	**6.0**	
Play area(PA)		0.1		0.4		0.2		0.9
Shops/stores		0.0		0.0		0.1		0.0
In transition		0.0		0.0		0.0		0.0

Guidelines for interpreting table: (1) The smallest cluster contains at least 4.5% (≈5%) of the sample children. (2) Entries are in hours and total 16.0. (3) All times greater than 1.0 hour are listed in left column under cluster. (4) All times less than 1.0 hour are listed in right column under cluster. (5) The numbers critical to understanding the uniqueness of the cluster are boldfaced.

Table 6.10
Hours of Caregivers and Locations for 4-Year-Old Children in Portugal ($N = 581$)

Category	Pattern (Cluster)					
	1 — Mother in home $n = 174$; 30% of N	2 — T/C in S/C; mother in home $n = 160$; 28% of N	3 — GP in multiple home settings $n = 87$; 15% of N	4 — 2 Parents, mother, OR, sibling in multiple home settings $n = 70$; 12% of N	5 — Mother in home, WP, PA $n = 58$; 10% of N	6 — OA in CCH $n = 32$; 5% of N
Caregiver						
Mother	**14.0**	4.5	3.7	4.0	**15.2**	3.4
Father	0.2	0.3	0.5	1.2	0.0	0.5
2 Parents	0.7	1.8	1.5	**4.4**	0.2	1.9
Sibling	0.2	0.1	0.1	1.1	0.0	0.1
Grandparent(GP)	0.5	0.6	**9.9**	0.7	0.1	0.1
Other relative(OR)	0.1	0.1	0.1	**3.0**	0.1	0.0
Friend/neighbor(F/N)	0.1	0.0	0.0	0.1	0.0	0.0
Other adult(OA)	0.1	0.5	0.0	0.3	0.3	**9.7**
Teacher/caregiver(T/C)	0.1	**8.1**	0.2	0.2	0.0	0.2
Nobody	0.0	0.0	0.0	0.3	0.1	0.1
Location						
Home	**14.9**	6.6	9.0	**10.3**	9.2	6.3
Relative's home	0.3	0.4	**6.0**	**2.9**	0.8	0.0
F/N Home	0.0	0.0	0.2	0.1	0.1	0.0
Child care home(CCH)	0.0	0.0	0.0	0.1	0.1	**9.3**
School/center(S/C)	0.1	**8.4**	0.2	0.2	0.2	0.2
Workplace(WP)	0.1	0.2	0.1	0.5	**2.9**	0.0
Play area(PA)	0.3	0.1	0.2	1.1	**2.2**	0.2
Shops/stores	0.2	0.0	0.1	0.1	0.3	0.0
In transition	0.1	0.2	0.0	0.0	0.1	0.0

Guidelines for interpreting table: (1) The smallest cluster contains at least 4.5% (≈5%) of the sample children. (2) Entries are in hours and total 16.0. (3) All times greater than 1.0 hour are listed in left column under cluster. (4) All times less than 1.0 hour are listed in right column under cluster. (5) The numbers critical to understanding the uniqueness of the cluster are boldfaced.

Table 6.11

Hours of Caregivers and Locations for 4-Year-Old Children in Spain (N = 480)

	Pattern (Cluster)				
	1	2	3	4	5
Category	Mother in home; T/C in S/C; n=129; 27% of N	T/C in S/C; 2 parents in home; n=123; 26% of N	Mother in home or PA; n=97; 20% of N	T/C in S/C; mother or GP in home; n=77; 16% of N	Mother in home or PA; 2 parents in home; GP in multiple home settings; n=54; 11% of N
Caregiver					
Mother	**9.5**	2.5	**14.7**	5.2	**5.8**
Father	0.1	0.4	0.0	0.1	1.1
2 Parents	0.4	**5.9**	0.2	0.5	**5.0**
Sibling	0.1	0.2	0.3	0.3	0.0
Grandparent(GP)	0.3	0.2	0.2	0.1	**2.3**
Other relative(OR)	0.1	0.0	0.1	0.1	0.5
Friend/neighbor(F/N)	0.1	0.0	0.2	0.1	0.2
Other adult(OA)	0.1	0.5	0.1	0.1	0.8
Teacher/caregiver(T/C)	**5.3**	**6.3**	0.1	**7.8**	0.2
Nobody	0.0	0.0	0.1	0.1	0.1
Location					
Home	**8.8**	**7.3**	**12.3**	**6.0**	**11.0**
Relative's home	0.3	0.2	0.5	0.9	**1.0**
F/N Home	0.0	0.0	0.1	0.0	0.3
Child care home(CCH)	0.0	0.0	0.0	0.0	0.1
School/center(S/C)	**5.3**	**6.3**	0.1	**7.7**	0.2
Workplace(WP)	0.1	0.0	0.3	0.1	0.3
Play area(PA)	1.4	1.9	**2.1**	1.1	**2.4**
Shops/stores	0.1	0.1	0.6	0.1	0.7
In transition	0.0	0.2	0.0	0.1	0.0

Guidelines for interpreting table: (1) The smallest cluster contains at least 4.5% (≈5%) of the sample children. (2) Entries are in hours and total 16.0. (3) All times greater than 1.0 hour are listed in left column under cluster. (4) All times less than 1.0 hour are listed in right column under cluster. (5) The numbers critical to understanding the uniqueness of the cluster are boldfaced.

Table 6.12
Hours of Caregivers and Locations for 4-Year-Old Children in Thailand (*N* = 2,466)

	Pattern (Cluster)							
	1	2	3	4	5	6	7	8
Category	Mother in home *n*=593; 24% of *N*	Mother or 2 parents in home *n*=481; 20% of *N*	T/C or OA in S/C; mother or 2 parents in home *n*=317; 13% of *N*	GP in home *n*=251; 10% of *N*	Mother in multiple home settings or WP *n*=250; 10% of *N*	Nobody, mother, 2 parents, OR in multiple home settings or PA *n*=225; 9% of *N*	2 Parents in home or WP *n*=196; 8% of *N*	GP or 2 Parents in multiple home settings *n*=153; 6% of *N*
Caregiver								
Mother	**15.2**	8.5	4.2	1.8	**13.1**	4.4	0.8	2.2
Father	0.0	0.4	0.2	0.0	0.1	0.7	0.3	0.1
2 parents	0.3	**5.5**	2.5	1.5	1.3	2.0	**13.7**	3.4
Sibling	0.0	0.4	0.1	0.0	0.1	0.4	0.6	0.3
Grandparent(GP)	0.2	0.3	0.8	**12.2**	0.5	0.7	0.3	**8.5**
Other relative(OR)	0.0	0.5	0.3	0.2	0.1	**1.6**	0.2	0.9
Friend/neighbor(F/N)	0.0	0.0	0.1	0.0	0.0	0.1	0.0	0.0
Other adult(OA)	0.0	0.1	**3.1**	0.0	0.0	0.1	0.0	0.1
Teacher/caregiver(T/C)	0.0	0.0	**4.4**	0.0	0.0	0.0	0.0	0.1
Nobody	0.1	0.3	0.2	0.2	0.8	**5.8**	0.1	0.3
Location								
Home	**15.7**	**15.4**	7.5	14.7	**9.3**	9.9	14.3	5.5
Relative's home	0.1	0.2	0.2	0.2	1.0	0.7	0.2	**9.5**
F/N Home	0.1	0.3	0.1	0.9	**3.4**	2.7	0.1	
Child care home(CCH)	0.0	0.0	0.3	0.0	0.1	0.1	0.0	0.4
School/center(S/C)	0.0	0.0	**7.0**	0.0	0.0	0.0	0.0	0.2
Workplace(WP)	0.0	0.0	0.1	0.0	1.0	0.2	**1.2**	0.2
Play area(PA)	0.0	0.1	0.1	0.1	0.9	**2.0**	0.1	0.0
Shops/stores	0.0	0.0	0.0	0.0	0.1	0.2	0.0	0.0
In transition	0.0	0.0	0.7	0.0		0.0	0.1	0.2

Guidelines for interpreting table: (1) The smallest cluster contains at least 4.5% (≈5%) of the sample children. (2) Entries are in hours and total 16.0. (3) All times greater than 1.0 hour are listed in left column under cluster. (4) All times less than 1.0 hour are listed in right column under cluster. (5) The numbers critical to understanding the uniqueness of the cluster are boldfaced.

Table 6.13
Hours of Caregivers and Locations for 4-Year-Old Children in the U.S.A. (*N* = 428)

Category	Pattern (Cluster)		
	1 Mother in home *n*=252; 59% of *N*	2 Parents or GP in home; OA in CCH *n*=95; 22% of *N*	3 T/C in S/C; mother in home *n*=81; 19% of *N*
Caregiver			
Mother	**14.1**	5.3	6.2
Father	0.5	1.3	0.7
2 Parents	0.6	1.7	1.0
Sibling	0.0	0.1	0.1
Grandparent(GP)	0.1	**1.9**	0.1
Other relative(OR)	0.0	0.8	0.0
Friend/neighbor(F/N)	0.1	0.2	0.0
Other adult(OA)	0.1	**4.1**	0.2
Teacher/caregiver(T/C)	0.5	0.6	**7.7**
Nobody	0.0	0.0	0.0
Location			
Home	**14.4**	9.7	7.7
Relative's home	0.2	0.5	0.1
F/N Home	0.1	0.2	0.0
Child care home(CCH)	0.0	**4.2**	0.1
School/center(S/C)	0.5	0.7	**7.7**
Workplace(WP)	0.0	0.0	0.0
Play area(PA)	0.3	0.2	0.1
Shops/stores	0.4	0.3	0.1
In transition	0.1	0.1	0.2

Guidelines for interpreting table: (1) The smallest cluster contains at least 4.5% (≈5%) of the sample children. (2) Entries are in hours and total 16.0. (3) All times greater than 1.0 hour are listed in left column under cluster. (4) All times less than 1.0 hour are listed in right column under cluster. (5) The numbers critical to understanding the uniqueness of the cluster are boldfaced.

Belgium (*N* = 424)

Figure 6.11: Patterns of time spent with different caregivers between
6:00 a.m. and 10:00 p.m.

China (*N* = 12,835)

Figure 6.12: Patterns of time spent with different caregivers between 6:00 a.m.
and 10:00 p.m.

Finland (*N* = 576)

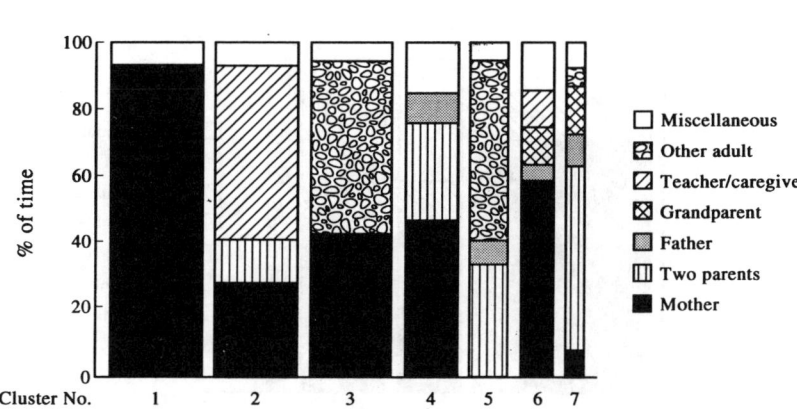

Figure 6.13: Patterns of time spent with different caregivers between 6:00 a.m. and 10:00 p.m.

Germany (*N* = 509)

Figure 6.14: Patterns of time spent with different caregivers between 6:00 a.m. and 10:00 p.m.

Figure 6.15: Patterns of time spent with different caregivers between 6:00 a.m. and 10:00 p.m.

Figure 6.16: Patterns of time spent with different caregivers between 6:00 a.m. and 10:00 p.m.

Portugal (*N* = 581)

Figure 6.17: Patterns of time spent with different caregivers between 8:00 a.m. and 12:00 midnight

Spain (*N* = 480)

Figure 6.18: Patterns of time spent with different caregivers between 8:00 a.m. and 12:00 midnight

Figure 6.19: Patterns of time spent with different caregivers between 5:00 a.m. and 9:00 p.m.

Figure 6.20: Patterns of time spent with different caregivers between 6:00 a.m. and 10:00 p.m.

serves as caregiver is generally very large (more than 60% in 4 of the 6 countries).

A *mother/other adult* cluster is found in 3 countries. In 2 of these countries (Finland and the U.S.A.) many families use *child care homes* for their 4-year-old children, whereas in Nigeria many families have a maid or childminder come into their homes to supervise the preschool-aged children during the day.

Although there are similarities among countries in the types of clusters found, each country presents a distinct pattern of clusters with regard to the percentage of children represented by each cluster, the combinations of caregivers and locations included in each cluster, and the presence of unique clusters. For example, even among the countries that have a *mother* cluster, the percentages of children represented by this cluster range from 13% (in China) to 59% (in the U.S.A.). Also, Germany and Portugal each have a *grandparent* cluster, but this cluster in Portugal includes 15% of the children, while the same cluster in Germany includes 8% of the children.

In some countries (e.g., Belgium, Hong Kong) nearly all clusters include a *teacher/caregiver* category, whereas in other countries (e.g., Nigeria, Portugal) only a single cluster includes this category. Also, in some nations (e.g., Belgium, Thailand) the category *two parents* appears in nearly all clusters, while in others (e.g., Hong Kong, Nigeria) it appears in only a single cluster.

Perhaps the most unusual clusters among the 10 countries are those that include *nobody* as a caregiver. When the NRCs were developing the categories of caregivers, some of the directors from industrialized nations questioned the usefulness of including this category, noting that parents might be reluctant to report that nobody was supervising their child, even when this was the case. However, NRCs from other nations considered this to be a realistic category and thought that parents in their countries would report it accurately. The category of *nobody* as a caregiver (for at least 1 hour) does indeed appear in Thailand's sixth cluster and in China's second, fourth, fifth, and sixth clusters. Another unusual type of cluster includes the *sibling* as caregiver—Nigeria's second cluster and Portugal's fourth cluster are examples of this type.

Summary—The Daily Routine Data in a Weekly Context

Are the daily routine findings congruent with the findings reported in previous chapters? To answer this question, this section will briefly examine each country's daily routine clusters in relationship to findings presented earlier about that country's sample characteristics (e.g., the percentage of mothers active in the labor force) and families' weekly use of various types of early childhood services.

Belgium (Fr.)

As the findings in Chapter 4 indicated, nearly all of Belgium's sample children attended an extraparental care or education setting, with most attending an organized facility. Forty-one percent of sample children attended at least a second setting, with about two-thirds of second settings being organized facilities (schools/centers) and the rest home settings.

Belgium's cluster findings indicate that, as expected, school/center as a location (for at least 1 hour a day) occurs in all 5 clusters. In the 2 largest clusters, children remain in an organized facility for additional hours in the care of some other adult. Belgium's fourth cluster includes grandparent care in the grandparent's home, indicating that the second setting is a home setting. As noted in Table 6.4, care in the child's own home is provided mainly by the mother or the two parents.

China (PRC)

According to earlier chapters, in China, almost half of 4-year-old children attend an extraparental setting, with most of those enrolled in an organized facility; the rest are divided nearly equally between own-home settings and other-home settings, where the care is provided almost entirely by relatives. While nearly all mothers of 4-year-olds are active in the labor force, over half work in agriculture and consequently may be able to care for their own children during at least part of their working day.

Table 6.5 and Figure 6.12 show that children attending schools/centers are included in the first and second clusters, and that these children are in schools/centers 7–9 hours a day; their remaining waking hours are spent in the care of one or both parents at home. Five clusters contain children in a parental-care-only category; these clusters include 2 that are primarily mother care and that are differentiated by the location in which the mother care occurs (home in the third cluster and home, workplace, and play area in the fifth cluster). The eighth cluster includes care mainly by the mother or father in several locations. The 2 remaining clusters (the fourth and sixth) are the nobody clusters, and each includes approximately 10 hours when 'nobody' cares for the child, with supervision provided by the mother for the remaining waking hours. China's final cluster represents extraparental care in a home setting, with grandparents providing supervision.

Finland

The findings reported in previous chapters were that approximately 25% of 4-year-old Finnish children are cared for exclusively by their parents, while the other 75% participate in extraparental settings, mainly other-home settings and organized facilities. When an other-home setting is selected by parents, the care is nearly always provided by a nonrelative (e.g., by some other adult).

In view of this information, it is not surprising that of Finland's 7 clusters, 2 are organized facility clusters, 2 are other-home clusters, 2 are parental-care-only clusters, and the smallest cluster includes relative care in a home setting. The first and fourth clusters contain children in parental care and are differentiated by which parent is the caregiver (the mother in the first cluster, and the mother, father, or both parents in the fourth cluster). The second and sixth clusters include children attending a school/center as well as being cared for in-home by different combinations of parents and relatives. The third and fifth clusters are characterized by other-home care, with children spending approximately 8 hours a day in home-based settings.

Germany (FRG)

Chapter 4 related that only 18% of Germany's total sample of 4-year-olds were cared for exclusively by parents, while most attended at least one extraparental setting, nearly half in organized facilities. Slightly over half of the sample children attended more than one setting, and their second setting was usually the family home or some other home. As Table A.1 (Appendix A, p. 198) indicates, when a child's first setting was either an own-home or other-home setting, the caregiver was usually a relative. This was also likely to be the case when a home setting was the child's second, third, or fourth setting.

Of Germany's 4 daily routine clusters, 2 (the first and third) are characterized by either mother or two-parent care in the child's home. Two other clusters (the second and third) include care by teachers/caregivers in schools/centers, and a very small amount of time in school/centers is noted in the remaining 2 clusters (0.4 and 0.5 hour). Grandparent care predominates in the fourth cluster, supporting the information provided by parents about relative care in either own-home or other-home settings.

Hong Kong

As noted in Chapter 2, since nearly all 4-year-olds in Hong Kong attend organized facilities, the sample children were selected from these settings. One would therefore expect each of Hong Kong's clusters to include at least a few hours in schools or centers. In fact, all 5 clusters do indicate that children spend time in such settings, with the minimum time being 2.2 hours daily (in the fourth cluster). When children are not in schools or centers, in all but one cluster, they are generally in home settings being cared for mainly by one or more of the following: mother, two parents, a grandparent. In the fifth cluster, some other adult (e.g., a maid) provides supervision in the child's home.

Nigeria

Nigeria reported the lowest percentages of children cared for in extraparental settings (33%); this included 22% cared for at home by someone other than a parent (see Table A.1, Appendix A, p. 198). Also in Nigeria, although two-thirds of mothers of the sample children were active in the labor force, one-third worked in agriculture and consequently might have been able to have their children with them during working hours.

Nigeria's daily routine clusters are in close agreement with the findings just reviewed. There are two mother-care clusters, one characterized by home as the location and one characterized by two locations—home and the parent's workplace. Another cluster includes a large amount of time (8.2 hours) during which some other adult cares for the preschool-aged child in the child's own home. Still another cluster includes care by mother, two parents, and sibling in various home settings, as well as a small amount of time spent in schools/centers.

Portugal

Earlier chapters related that 29% of Portugal's 4-year-olds are cared for exclusively by their parents, while the remainder attend extraparental settings, over half in either other-home settings or organized facilities. As noted in Table A.1 (Appendix A, p. 198) the care in own-home extraparental settings is provided primarily by relatives, while the care in other-home settings is sometimes provided by nonrelatives.

Portugal's daily routine clusters include 2 parental care clusters; the home is the primary location in the first cluster, whereas the home, parental workplace, and play areas are the locations in the fifth cluster. Children attending school/centers are represented in the second cluster, with children in mother care or two-parent care at home making up the remainder of the child's time. Relative care is included in the third and fourth clusters; grandparents provide the majority of this care, either in the child's home or in their home. The final, sixth, cluster includes the small percentage of children cared for in other-home settings by nonrelatives.

Spain

There is almost perfect agreement between Spain's daily routine clusters and the findings reported earlier for the weekly use of early childhood services in Spain. For example, Chapter 4 indicated that approximately 20% of Spain's sample children were cared for exclusively by their parents, and these children are represented in Spain's third cluster. Also, approximately 69% of the total sample of families reported that their children attended organized facilities, and these children are represented in Spain's first, second, and fourth clusters. Finally, approximately 10% of Spain's 4-year-olds are served by extraparental home-based caregivers, either in own-home settings or in other-home settings. The country's fifth cluster includes these children, with grandparents providing the extraparental supervision in either the child's home or their own home.

Thailand

In Thailand, 36% of sample families reported that their 4-year-old children attended extraparental care or education settings, in own-home, other-home, or organized facilities. For children participating in home-based settings, Table A.1 (Appendix A, p. 198) indicates that the supervision was nearly always provided by relatives. Slightly over half of the mothers in the sample were active in the labor force, but 60% of those mothers worked in agriculture and may have been able to supervise their young children during at least some of their working hours. This would suggest that Thailand's daily routine clusters might include large amounts of supervision by parents and relatives.

Of Thailand's 8 national clusters, 4 are predominantly parental clusters. The first 2 clusters include parental supervision primarily in the child's home, with the mother serving as care provider in the first cluster and the mother and both parents sharing these responsibilities in the second cluster. The fifth and seventh clusters are characterized by parental supervision in the home, the workplace, and other-home settings; the mother is supervisor in the fifth cluster, and both parents provide care in the seventh cluster.

The fourth and eighth clusters contain children in relative care; grandparents provide nearly all of this care in either the child's home or their own home. The third cluster includes the small percentage of 4-year-olds who attend a school/center. Finally, the sixth cluster is characterized by children who have nobody supervising them for approximately 6 hours a day.

The U.S.A.

Chapter 4 reported that 39% of the U.S.A. sample children were cared for exclusively by parents, 35% attended schools/centers, 17% were cared for in other homes, and 9% were cared for by others in the child's own home. Twenty-nine percent of the sample attended two or more settings, and these additional settings were either own-home, other-home, or organized facility settings.

The U.S. daily routine data yielded 3 national clusters. Not surprisingly, the first, or largest, cluster is predominantly mother care in the child's home. The number of children included in this first cluster is larger than expected. However, considering that the cluster includes 0.5 hour of school/center time, it is possible to conclude that it may contain some children who attend organized facilities for a short time each week (e.g., a 2-hour preschool program, 2–3 days a week). The second U.S.A. cluster contains the children who attend child care homes for approximately one-half day as well as those children cared for by grandparents in their own homes for a few hours a day. The final, third, cluster consists of children who attend schools or centers, usually for the entire day.

In nearly every country researchers discovered a good correspondence between the information reported by parents/guardians about their weekly use of early childhood services and the information reported in the daily routine section of the household survey. Each set of information provides a different perspective from which to look at the lives of young children in various nations.

7

A Nation-by-Nation Look at the Findings

PATRICIA P. OLMSTED AND MARGE MELIN SENNINGER

Previous chapters—on families' use of services, on use of organized facilities, and on children's daily routines—have looked at data cross-nationally. This chapter considers the findings in another way, summarizing each nation's findings individually and comparing those national findings to the information that the National Research Coordinators (NRCs) provided at the outset of the study, in *How Nations Serve Young Children: Profiles of Child Care and Education in 14 Countries* (Olmsted & Weikart, 1989). Much of what is presented here corroborates and clarifies the initial profile that each nation provided in 1989, based on statistics available at that time. In some cases, the IEA data for a particular country enable us to update or supplement the earlier profile, or even to refute some part of it. This chapter also provides an opportunity to describe findings for subregions or subpopulations within an individual country, whenever such findings are of interest.

Belgium(Fr.)—Part-Day Services and Full-Day Needs

Background Information

The Belgian profile (Delhaxhe, 1989) described a country where (at the time of writing) a majority (66%) of mothers of children under age 10 were "economically active," meaning employed full-time, employed part-time, or actively seeking employment. Reflective of this economic picture is Belgium's explicit family policy of maternity leave, child care leave, and subsidization and supervision of day care for children under age 2½. Furthermore, since 1969, children aged 2½–6 years have been able to attend nursery schools that are subsidized, regulated, and supervised by the National Ministry of Education.

With the rare exception of a handful of schools that charge for admission, Belgian nursery schools are free, and almost 100% of 4-year-olds

137

attend them. Rather than being a consequence of the extensive maternal employment, however, this high level of nursery school attendance is explained by the educational character of the nursery schools. As long ago as the early 1950s, official recommendations were advising Belgian mothers to entrust their preschool-aged children to educational professionals.

The Ministry of Education is responsible for planning the programs and for regulating the establishment and functioning of nursery schools. Of the approximately 2,000 nursery schools in the French-speaking part of Belgium, about half are local-authority schools, about a third are private (mainly Roman Catholic schools), and the rest are French-speaking Community schools.

Every nursery school, whether local-authority, Roman Catholic, or Community, observes the same equipment norms, salary schedule, student–teacher ratios, timetable, and so on. Nursery school teachers must undergo 3 years of study in a vocational school (the *institut supérieur pédagogique*).The nursery schools are often annexed to the primary school, and they have the same operating hours: 8:30–12:00 in the morning, and 1:30–3:00 in the afternoon for 5 days a week during the school year (with the exception that schools are closed on Wednesday afternoons). Most 4-year-olds attend for the full day.

Delhaxhe's (1989) initial description of early childhood services in Belgium revealed a situation in which nursery school services are available to and used by nearly all families; nevertheless, for many families—especially those in which all adults are "economically active"—there would appear to be a mismatch between when services are available and when they are needed. For this reason, many families typically seek out additional care/education services for their 4-year-olds each week. This summary of Belgium's IEA/PPP Phase 1 study methods and findings looks at the family survey results to see (1) how they compare with Delhaxhe's 1989 description and (2) how families address any disparity between services offered and services needed.

The Findings about Belgium's Preprimary Care/Education

The IEA family survey generally confirmed the information in the 1989 profile by Delhaxhe. Survey findings were these: (1) of sample children, nearly all attended organized facilities (nursery schools); (2) very few parents paid for these services; and (3) the majority of families typically used two or more care/education settings for their 4-year-olds each week. Of sample families, 98% reported using extraparental care/education services—95% making use of nursery schools and 3% utilizing home-based settings as the *first setting*. Of the 73% of families who used a *second setting*, this included 51% using an organized facility (usually care services provided in the nursery school building) and the remainder using a home-based setting (generally care by a relative in the relative's home or in the child's own home).

The IEA family survey found that Belgian 4-year-olds average 34 hours per week in care/education settings, a figure that is very close to the length of time that mothers typically spend away from their children each week but much less than the length of time fathers spend away. These findings support those of earlier research reported by Delhaxhe (1989):

> A research study by V. Pieltain shows that the time spent outside the home by a child correlates with the time spent outside the home by the mother. The daily schedule for the father does not influence that of the child (p. 32).

In the information presented in Chapter 5 about the organized facilities used by families in various countries, all organized facilities used by Belgian parents were categorized as *educational*, which would be consistent with Delhaxhe's 1989 characterization of the prevailing services.

The IEA household survey found that while all nursery schools are sponsored by the government, half of them are also sponsored by local authorities and 41% are additionally sponsored by the Roman Catholic church—findings very much in agreement with the 1989 profile's breakdown of 53% and 37%, respectively, which was based on national statistics.

One finding of the family survey, in particular, runs contrary to what one would anticipate from the information provided in Delhaxhe's 1989 profile. When sample parents were asked about the problems they experienced with the nursery schools, very few identified any problem at all. The low percentage of parents citing *hours of operation* is surprising, since both Delhaxhe's 1989 profile and family survey results seem to indicate a need for weekly care/education services over and above those offered by nursery schools. Possibly parents do not consider it to be the role of the nursery school to provide all the service needs they have. Rather, they may see the nursery school as focusing on one or more particular aspects of their children's development, and they may believe that other solutions need to be found to meet the need for any additional hours of supervision for their children.

If nursery schools operate for only the limited hours indicated in Delhaxhe's 1989 profile, looking at the caregivers for 4-year-olds during the nursery school lunch-break and during the late afternoon hours should provide information about the solutions parents have found to supplement nursery school services. A report of Belgian IEA Preprimary Project findings prepared by Delhaxhe and Hindryckx (1991) provided this information: Between 12:00 noon and 1:00 p.m., 49% of sample children were with caregivers (at school), 34% were with parents, and 10% were with grandparents. Between 4:00 and 5:00 p.m., 65% of children were with their parents, 13% were with extrafamilial caregivers (either at the school or at another location), and 13% were with their grandparents. Thus, it would seem that for 4-year-olds from homes in which parents are not available at noon and after nursery school, there are two major groups of supervisors—grandparents and caregivers at the nursery schools. Delhaxhe and Hindryckx examined the relationship between family characteristics and the child's daily pattern of caregivers and noted the following:

> The socio-economic status of the family is related to the child's daily routine: children who are cared for by relatives [generally grandparents] belong to families with lower income, where fathers have a lower professional level . . . . Children who attend care services [either at school or in another location] belong to families with higher income . . . (p. 61).

As Delhaxhe noted in her 1989 profile, a major concern in Belgium is the *quality* of the services provided for children who remain at the nursery school outside of official curriculum hours:

> There is no overall care policy for these children to date (regarding caregivers, activities, child–adult ratio, quality of care, and organization of meals) . . . . Thus, at the end of the 20th century, we find in the child care services organized during the extracurricular time some characteristics reminiscent of the first preschool setting that sheltered young children in the 19th century—low wages for staff, unqualified staff, excessive noise, inadequate facilities, and grouping together of children of different ages (p. 34).

Having derived from the IEA survey a sense of how great the need is, early childhood professionals and policymakers in Belgium eventually hope to work on improving the services outside of nursery school hours. Their goal will be to provide a high-quality environment for 4-year-olds whenever it is needed by Belgium's families. From the results of future phases of the IEA Preprimary Project, Belgium hopes to be able to assess the variability between practices adults use with children—both in and out of nursery school—and the consequences for child development.

China (PRC)—Striving for Modernization

Background Information

The founding of the People's Republic in 1949 brought on a period of extensive and rapid growth in early childhood institutions. Throughout the 1950s a series of government decrees defined, guided, and set requirements for kindergarten (for children aged 3–6 years), which were to "foster healthy development in children before primary school" and "lighten mothers' child care burdens so that they could take part in political, productive, cultural, and educational activities."

Between 1949 and 1985, the number of kindergartens in China grew from approximately 1,300 to approximately 170,000. About three quarters were rural kindergartens, a fact that reflects not only the agricultural nature of the country but also the increasing attention being paid to the collective care and education of young children in rural areas.

Chinese kindergartens do try to meet the needs of working parents. The hours of operation vary, with four general types of kindergarten being offered: daytime service (usually from 7:00 a.m. to 6:00 p.m.); boarding service (the whole week, day and night, except for Sunday); half-day service; and temporary service (covering just a season or certain hours, according to the needs of various kinds of workers).

The issues China faces are those expected for a care and education system that has grown so far so fast; Teacher training lags behind the need for qualified teachers, and research lags behind educational practice and policymaking. Participation in the IEA Preprimary Project comes at a time when planning activities for China's early childhood services have just been decentralized, shifting principal program-planning responsibility from the State Education Commission to committees at the provincial level.

In the People's Republic of China, the IEA Preprimary Project has been the first large-scale survey study in many years involving families with preschool-aged children. These words from a 1990 speech delivered in Beijing by Professor Shi Hui Zhong, the NRC of the IEA Preprimary Project in China, convey how important the study is to China's overall progress as a nation:

> In a country with a population of 1.1 billion and a territory of 9.6 million square kilometers, one of the urgent tasks is to enhance the quality of the nation. Therefore, it is an important objective for us early childhood educators to lay a good foundation for this cause . . . . [The IEA Preprimary Project] has enabled us to get a clear understanding of the care and educational situation of young children of the country and to provide our policy makers with a scientific basis for the reform of our early childhood education (p. 1).

Chinese researchers looked at the IEA study not only as an opportunity to cooperate with other nations in a cross-national project but also as a chance to collect needed information for planning future policies and programs for China's children and families. This summary of China's Phase 1 findings presents basic data of cross-national interest and also highlights those findings that were of particular interest nationally.

The Families Surveyed in China

The details of the sampling methodology are discussed in Chapter 2. To ensure that the household survey would include even very remote rural families, interviewers were required to collect data from any family selected that was within a 24-hour walking distance. The result of this unusual effort has been that this study may be the first in recent times to include those Chinese families living in very primitive conditions in mountainous regions.

The Findings about China's Preprimary Care/Education

According to Shi (1989), by 1985 there were only enough kindergartens to accommodate approximately 20% of China's preschool-aged children. Updating this 20% statistic are the findings from the IEA Phase 1 survey, which indicate that 43% of Chinese families with 4-year-old children use extraparental care/education services each week—including 33% using the services provided by an organized facility (kindergarten). Since the sample families were representative of the nation's population, the findings suggest that since 1985, fairly rapid growth of kindergartens has continued, so organized settings are now available for a considerably larger percentage of China's children.

Response to the household survey indicated that most of the sample children who were service-users typically attended only one setting each week, while a small number attended two or more settings. Children's second and third settings were always home settings. Children attending extraparental settings did so for an average of 55–56 hours per week; this care time agrees with the length of time that parents were typically away from the child. Sample parents were generally satisfied with their children's care/education settings, and the problems they identified were those one would expect to find in a nation that is rapidly increasing the availability of services.

Taking only those sample children in China who attended organized facilities, the average weekly time children spent in such settings was 47 hours, with the maximum weekly time being 163 hours. This maximum refers to a small number of 4-year-olds, mostly in urban areas, who attended boarding, or residential, kindergartens for 24 hours a day, 5 or 6 days each week.

Because China's urban and rural areas involve considerable contrast, Table 7.1 presents the sample's family and household characteristics separately for the two kinds of areas. Survey results reveal further urban-rural contrasts. As Table A.2 (Appendix A, p. 199) indicates, a much higher proportion of rural families than urban families reported caring for their young children by themselves. However, a closer look at the actual care situations for rural children (Shi & Xiang, 1990) reveals that a fairly large proportion of parents in rural areas reported that their preschool-aged children spent several hours a day without direct adult supervision. This situation is considered safe in rural areas, where there are thought to be few dangers (such as traffic, or adults who abduct children). A larger percentage of urban families (67%) than rural families (19%) reported using organized

Table 7.1
China's Urban/Rural Information for Selected Family
and Household Characteristics

Characteristic	Total sample		Urban sample		Rural sample	
	N	Mean	*N*	Mean	*N*	Mean
Mother's yr of education	12,363	6.9	3,884	9.4	8,483	6.0
Father's yr of education	12,370	8.1	3,872	9.7	8,499	7.5
Mother's hr away	9,255	52.2	3,513	57.3	5,833	49.6
Father's hr away	10,428	65.1	3,636	63.0	6,848	66.0
Number of children	–	–	4,000	1.2	8,835	1.8
	N	%	*N*	%	*N*	%
Mother works for pay	12,835	98	4,000	98	8,835	97
Father works for pay	12,835	98	4,000	99	8,835	98
Indoor water	12,835	35	4,000	81	8,835	17
Television	12,835	56	4,000	88	8,835	43

A dash indicates that no data were available.

facilities for their children, but equal percentages in the two areas utilized home-based settings (10%).

Because Chinese IEA researchers were interested in gathering information about parents' educational perceptions and practices, they included a set of interview questions covering these topics: (1) parents' expectations concerning the child's level of education and future occupation; (2) parents' views of their children's strong points; (3) parental praise of children (frequency and reasons); and (4) educational activities that parents engage in with their children. The researchers were surprised and disquieted by the types of parental responses, especially in rural areas. As a result, the government decided to develop a widespread training program involving parent-education classes to be held in various areas of the country for parents of young children. Shi and Xiang (1990) stressed the importance China places on the cooperative effort of families, early childhood educators, and society:

> The views and practices of parents are an important factor which will exert a great influence on the development of the child. Early childhood educators should realize that parent education is an indispensable part of their work and worth their great effort on it. On the other side, the parents should be aware of their responsibility . . . . Only when the family, early childhood educators, and the whole society are united, will there become a better environment for our child development (p. 1).

In the speech referred to at the beginning of this summary, Shi (1990) explained how the data from Phase 1 of the IEA Preprimary Project should expand her country's thinking about *early childhood care and education*. Rather than being merely synonymous with *kindergarten*, the phrase also refers to the many children being cared for exclusively by their parents and to those receiving extraparental care in "other-home" settings. Shi called for a broadening of the curriculum of teacher-training institutions to increase awareness of and training in several types of early childhood care and education, including parent education.

Finland—Aiming at Integrated National Policies

Background Information

By the end of the 1960s, the rapid industrialization and urbanization that occurred in Finland after World War II brought about national discussion of families' critical day care needs (by 1970 about three-fifths of women were employed outside the home). The discussion, which involved controversy over the merits of "home care" versus "day care," culminated in a reorganization of early childhood services under the 1973 Children's Day Care Law. This law has required each municipality to provide public or publicly supervised private care services as needed. Enrollment priority is given to children whose parents are employed, ill, in school, or otherwise unable to care for their children. Also, some children with special needs—minorities, returning emigrants, the handicapped, and those in children's homes—receive special consideration.

With enactment of the law, what had been kindergartens became *day care centers*, and a new form of institutionalized care, *family day care*, came into being. Both forms of care can be either public or private, are subject to supervision of social welfare boards, and (except for private family day care) can receive state subsidies. Both forms can serve, in principle, children aged 0 to 6 (school-entry age is 7). However, in practice, family day care, which is small-group care in the child's or another's home, is preferred for infants and toddlers. In 1983 about one-fifth of 4-year-olds were in day care centers, and one-sixth were in family day care. Though part-time care is an option, both in centers and in homes, the majority of children were in full-time care.

A slowdown in its population growth and prospects of population decline have led Finland to institute quite extensive family policy, including maternity allowance, maternity and paternity leave, maternity and child health care, child benefits, housing subsidies, and so on. In line with this is the government involvement—both supervisory and financial—that one finds in early childhood services. In 1983, because of national and municipal government subsidies, Finnish parents paid (on a sliding-scale basis) less than a fifth of the costs of day care for their children.

The day care system set up in the 1973 law has demanded continuing development. By 1983 the number of mothers employed outside of the home had increased such that only three-fifths of Finnish children needing care could be served by the day care system. To meet this increasing demand for services, Finland set a goal of creating 7,000 new day care places per year for 1986–1990, envisioning that supply will have balanced demand by the mid-1990s. Along with this quantitative improvement, qualitative improvement is also called for. Important "reform" issues are increasing the number of trained personnel, coordinating personnel training and graduate and continuing education, promoting development of curriculum, and conducting basic research (like the IEA study), so reform can be based on "scientific rather than pragmatic ideas."

Finland is another country with considerable urban–rural contrast. Most of the population is concentrated in the South, where the climate is relatively mild, while the rest of the population is sparsely distributed throughout the North. Finland's urban–rural contrasts are reflected in its IEA Preprimary Project data, as will be explained in this summary of Phase 1 findings. In addition to presenting a general picture of findings from the household survey, Finland's current efforts at integrating national policies affecting families, employment, and education will be described.

The Findings about Finland's Preprimary Care/Education

When questioned about the weekly use of care/education services for their 4-year-olds, 75% of Finnish parents indicated that their children were in some kind of extraparental care, the majority was divided equally between those whose children were cared for in another person's home, and whose children attended organized facilities. Only a small number of families reported that their children attended two or three settings, and of those using two or more settings, about half selected an organized facility for the second setting, and half selected home settings. Very little of the home-based extraparental care in Finland was provided by relatives. Reporting few problems, parents were generally satisfied with the care/education services their children received.

When Finnish parents were asked to state the major reason for their use of extraparental care/education services, 76% said that *parental employment* was the major reason, while 14% said that they considered the services to be important for *the child's social–emotional development*. A more detailed analysis of these findings by Ojala (1990) indicated that compared with families using home-based settings, a higher percentage of organized facility users gave a reason related to the child's social–emotional development.

One interesting finding about Finnish children, compared with sample children in the other participating nations, was the high percentage receiving various types of health examinations during the year prior to the survey. The data in Table 5.7 suggests that these examinations were not connected to early childhood services, since only 21% of Finnish families reported that health services were available at their children's organized facilities.

A striking feature of organized facility care in Finland was the diversity and amount of home-setting contact. Over half of sample parents reported having four different types of home-setting contact during the past 3 months, and many families had more than one type of contact weekly or monthly.

In his 1990 report on the Finnish IEA Preprimary Project, Ojala examined the relationship between the use of extraparental care/education services and family-background variables. He found that the use of extraparental services is related to the level of education of both mother and father. Families in which parents have fewer years of education are less likely to use extraparental care/education services for their child. Also, the number of care/education settings used is related to the father's years of education: a family in which the father has a higher level of education is more likely to use multiple care/education settings for their child.

Table 7.2 compares data for selected family and household characteristics for urban and rural areas. Table A.2 (Appendix A, p. 199) which presents urban–rural information on the use or nonuse of extraparental services, indicates that rural families are less likely than urban families to use such services. Also, urban families are more likely to use organized facilities than other-home settings, while for rural families, the reverse is

Table 7.2
Finland's Urban/Rural Information for Selected Family and Household Characteristics

Characteristic	Total sample		Urban sample		Rural sample	
	N	Mean	N	Mean	N	Mean
Mother's yr of education	568	12.4	341	12.7	227	12.0
Father's yr of education	527	12.1	311	12.8	216	11.1
Mother's hr away	457	33.9	288	35.6	169	31.1
Father's hr away	491	47.2	289	46.9	202	47.7
	N	%	N	%	N	%
Mother works for pay	576	75	344	79	228	69
Father works for pay	576	98	317	99	223	96

For 4 of the 6 characteristics in this table, urban/rural differences, when tested by t test or chi square, were significant at $p < .05$ (*father's hr away* and *father works for pay* were the 2 exceptions).

true. The data presented in Table A.2 are consistent with statements made in the 1989 profile by Ojala.

In discussing early childhood issues for the 1990s, Ojala's 1989 profile mentioned needing to improve availability of services as well as provide more trained care/education staff, which are issues echoed by many of the participating countries. Ojala summarized some of the efforts under way in Finland to integrate the national policies for early childhood services, families, employment, and education. For example, Finland's government is studying the relationships between family policies (e.g., extended maternity leave, home care benefits, the assured right to return to work) and provision of early childhood services. Also, measures concerning flexible working hours for parents with preschool-aged children are gaining support; such measures would, of course, affect parents' needs for early childhood services. Finally, the nature of the preschool training that some Finnish 6-year-olds currently receive may eventually lead to lowering the country's school-entry age to 6 years, leaving early childhood settings to serve predominantly 3 to 5-year-old children. Since Finland is at the forefront of nations working to integrate all the various aspects of social policy, other nations developing early childhood policies would do well to stay informed of developments in Finland.

Germany(FRG)—Meeting the Needs of a Changing Population and a Changing Nation

Background Information

In 1970, in the process of fundamental reform of the entire education system to better meet the needs of a developed industrial nation, the German Council on Education coined the term *Elementarbereich* (elementary level) to describe the kindergarten stage of education for 3 to 5-year-olds. The result was a rapid expansion of kindergarten places, so that by 1977 well over half of German 3 to 5-year-olds were enrolled. Though kindergarten was not to be compulsory, the goal was to reach all children by providing an ample supply of places.

Perhaps as a result of the social welfare origins of Germany's pre-schools (their early protection and custody role), the present-day kindergarten, though a stage of the educational system, is administered by the youth welfare offices and is often provided by an independent agency, such as a parish or some type of welfare agency. Only when such authorities fail to provide kindergartens is the public authority required to be the provider (about one-third are publicly provided). Kindergartens are parent-, agency-, community-, and state-subsidized; only low-income families are exempt from paying kindergarten fees.

Statistics from 1986 reveal that about two-fifths of 3-year-olds and two-thirds of 4-year-olds attend kindergarten. Kindergarten programs operate from 8:00 a.m. to midday, close at midday for 2 hours, and many offer 2 or 3 hours of afternoon care. Most children who attend kindergarten receive only a half-day program, with a smaller number returning for care during the afternoon hours.

The social context for Germany's early childhood provision is much like that of other industrialized countries: rising educational levels among women, a rising divorce rate, a rising female-employment rate, and decreasing rates of childbirth and three-generation households (meaning that for households where a single parent or both parents work outside the home, the alternative of "grandparent care" for their children is becoming more problematic, and multiple care arrangements are more common). Germany's female-employment rate is not as high as those in some other industrialized countries. Over a third of employed mothers with preschool-aged children work 40 or more hours a week, but all-day places are available for only half of their children.

Thus, after the increase in quality and quantity that occurred in kindergartens in the 1970s, when they became a part of the educational system, Germany is again looking to expand both the quantity and quality of its early childhood provisions in ways that respect the needs of modern families and children.

The 1989 profile of early childhood services in the Federal Republic of Germany, by Tietze, Rossbach, and Ufermann, described the situation at the time this way:

> Most recently, kindergarten has again been brought to public notice. Changes in the structure of the family, the increase in single-parent families, the improvement in the standard of education of young mothers and their desire for employment outside the family, as well as the remaking of woman's image that has resulted from the feminist movement, all appear to be causes for the appeal for institutions that are more capable of responding to the changing needs and lifestyles of families and children (p. 51).

This response to changing needs and lifestyles may involve expanding early childhood services in many geographic regions of Germany and providing more flexible hours of operation—both efforts aimed at increasing the supply, based on an accurate assessment of the demand. This summary attempts to clarify current demand by comparing Phase 1 findings from the IEA Preprimary Project as it was conducted in the Federal Republic of Germany with information presented in that country's 1989 profile. It also discusses recent changes in Germany that will be placing extra demands on its early childhood education/care system.

The Families Surveyed in Germany

Interviewers in Germany's IEA Preprimary Project research team included a household in the study if (1) it was maintained by a German-surnamed householder and (2) it contained the child's genetic or social mother. Consequently, the study did not include any household of foreign nationals living and working in the country, even if the household contained children in the appropriate age-range.

The Findings about Germany's Preprimary Care/Education

Phase 1 results indicate that four-fifths of families in the survey typically use early childhood education/care services each week, with nearly half enrolling their children in an organized facility (kindergarten) and a third utilizing home-based services. Since families with both 3- and 4-year-old children were included in the study, the percentage enrolled in kindergartens can be compared with the kindergarten enrollment rates reported in the 1989 profile for 3-year-olds (38%) and 4-year-olds (71%); the two sets of figures (the Phase 1 percentages and the 1989 percentages) are indeed similar.

In the Federal Republic, 39% of 3- and 4-year-olds typically attend one extraparental care/education setting each week, and 43% attend two or more such settings. Among the 11 nations participating in Phase 1, Germany was found to have the second-highest percentage of young children in multiple early childhood care/education settings. Data consistent with this IEA Project finding come from a special study (Rossbach, 1988) of the daily and weekly routines of young children in the Federal Republic. Rossbach found that on average, a child typically experiences 2.5 changes in caregivers/teachers in a day.

When other organized facility data from Germany's Phase 1 findings are examined, it emerges that 60% of facilities were sponsored by religious organizations; 29% by government (public) agencies; and 10% by voluntary or other organizations. These findings are very similar to those presented in the 1989 profile.

The IEA Phase 1 researchers found that on average, young children in Germany spend 20 hours per week in kindergartens, with 11% of the children in such settings for 30 hours or more each week. The 1989 profile essentially concurred with this latter figure in noting that "only 12% of kindergarten children are cared for over and beyond midday" (p. 72). When IEA interviewers asked parents to cite any problems they encountered with kindergartens, the problem identified by the highest percentage of parents (13%) was *hours of operation*; the problem identified by the second-highest percentage of parents (5%) was *cost*. Thus, the Phase 1 findings summarized here would seem to support the contention that Germany needs to better fit services—both the availability and the cost—to the needs of families with young children.

As noted at the beginning of this summary, during recent years, the Federal Republic of Germany has been experiencing the types of family and societal changes that have occurred in many industrialized nations (e.g., changes in family structure, in employment of mothers with young children). In addition, 1990 brought a major change—the unification of the Federal Republic of Germany and the German Democratic Republic and the subsequent immigration of large numbers of Eastern Europeans to unified Germany. Besides introducing new issues of assimilation as well as new quantitative demands on educational systems already in place, unification also juxtaposed two early childhood systems (from former West and East Germany) that to this day continue to have strong differences.

At the time of unification, the former West Germany had kindergarten places for barely 70% of children aged 3 and older and *krippe* (day care center) places for fewer than 2% of children under age 3. By comparison, the former East Germany provided places for 95% of children aged 3 and older and for 56% of children under age 3. Moreover, *all* early childhood services in the former East Germany are usually available for the entire day (10–12 hours); in the former West Germany, this is true of *krippen*, but not of most kindergartens (only 14% are full-day). Sponsorship also differs: in the former West Germany, early childhood programs are mostly operated by churches or other voluntary organizations, with a few operated by municipalities; former East German programs are operated almost entirely by municipalities.

This dichotomous situation is expected to change eventually. For example, spreading unemployment among women in the former East Germany could lead to *krippen* services there decreasing to approach the under-age-3 service situation now prevalent in the western part of Germany. For children aged 3 and older (including immigrant children in this age-range), a new law of the unified Germany now guarantees universal kindergarten coverage by the year 1996. This will provide for all children aged 3 and older a service that children in former East Germany have had available for many years.

Hong Kong—Adding Quality to Quantity

Background Information

Sylvia Opper's 1989 profile of Hong Kong describes a situation of almost universal preprimary coverage by two kinds of privately offered services—*kindergartens* and *child care centers*. About 90% of the 3-, 4-, and 5-year-old children attending are in kindergartens, and 10% are in child care centers.

The backdrop for this "almost universal" coverage by private services must be understood: First of all, in Hong Kong, formal education is an important avenue to social and economic mobility, since it has the potential to lead to a much-sought-after university education available to less than 2% of the population. What is surprising is that although the majority of Hong Kong's compulsory 6-year primary schools and 6-year secondary schools (3 years of which are compulsory) are government or government-aided, the preschool sector is almost entirely in the hands of private sponsors, although government does play a role in preschool education and care.

After World War II, and as Hong Kong residents became aware of the benefits of early education and affluent enough to afford it, the number of privately run, profit-making kindergartens grew dramatically. Unfortunately, because of their extremely rapid growth and because of only minimal government involvement, the kindergartens were overcrowded (often set up in residential flats) and understaffed. By 1971, the kindergarten teacher–child ratio was 1:35, and with teacher-training programs stretched beyond their limits, only about a fifth of teachers were trained. In 1953, the government set up a Kindergarten Section within the Education Department to help with program planning and implementation and to run training courses for teachers.

In the later postwar years (from 1975 on), professional bodies and the public began to ask for more government involvement in the preprimary sector. One result was a 1981 White Paper that, for the first time, set out government policy on early education and care. The paper dealt with the need for improved teacher training and for a fee-assistance scheme for low-income families, and it contained facility and equipment recommendations as well as suggestions for improving curriculum.

Unfortunately, a serious economic recession during the 1980s caused the postponement of many of the measures suggested in the 1981 White Paper. A fee-assistance scheme for low-income parents was instituted, however, within the Social Welfare Department. As of 1989, the White Paper's percentage goals for kindergarten teachers' inservice training had been only partially met. Other kindergarten-upgrade recommendations— for a better teacher–child ratio and unified standards for the two preprimary sectors—were made in 1986 by a group of eminent business persons and educators, the Education Commission.

The government's role in the child care sector increased with its adoption in 1975–1976 of ordinances and regulations for child care centers. Adoption of the legislation was followed by intense training efforts that resulted in the majority of child care workers being trained by 1983.

Despite the nearly universal service provision for preschool-aged children, and despite the somewhat increased government involvement of the 1970s and 1980s, Hong Kong is left with a dual early childhood provision system. One sector (kindergartens) is controlled largely by commercial interests and the other sector (child care) is controlled largely by voluntary agencies. The two sectors are regulated by different government departments, have different teacher-training requirements, and have different curriculums (parents perceive the more formal approach of the kindergarten as "education" and the learning-through-play approach of the child care centers as only "care"). Whereas most child care centers operate full-day programs, kindergartens, which are the parental choice for 90% of preschool placements, provide only a half-day program. Thus, employed parents must resort to other informal care arrangements for the remainder of the day—care by household maids, relatives, friends, or neighbors. Overcrowding, unsuitable teacher–pupil ratios, and a large percentage of untrained teaching staff still plague the kindergartens, in particular. Both sectors need improved teacher training, more extensive curriculum development, and unified standards.

Concluding that "the distinction between kindergartens and child care centers results in anomalies and discrepancies in the delivery of services to young children," the profile of Hong Kong's early childhood services ended with a plea for "an overall policy" on the part of government for the field of early education and care. Data from the IEA Preprimary Project could be valuable in the formulation of such a policy.

The Findings about Hong Kong's Preprimary Care/Education

Study results indicated that 96% of sample children attended kindergartens (educational organized facilities) and 4% attended nurseries (care-oriented organized facilities). These findings roughly agree with the percentages given in the 1989 profile. The study further found that sample children spent an average of 17 hours per week, or approximately 3.5 hours per day, in their extraparental settings. The settings were close to families' homes, so that 81% of children traveled only 15 minutes or less to reach them, and 64% of children were able to walk to their kindergartens or nurseries.

When families were asked to give their major reason for using early childhood services, their replies were predominantly child-related. Of the more than 800 parents who responded, two-thirds said that *social–emotional development of the child* was the major reason, while the remaining third gave *educational development of the child* as the major reason. In discussion of the Hong Kong IEA Preprimary Project findings, Opper (1990) wrote,

> It is clear that the majority of parents feel that preschool, even for only half a day, is an essential component of the life of young children in Hong Kong. This is substantiated by the large number of nonworking mothers who do not require care for their children during the day, [but] nevertheless voluntarily

choose to send their children to preschool. The majority of preschools in Hong Kong do not appear to fulfil a need for day care but are serving some other function for young children and their families (pp. 22–23).

The Phase 1 study found that of the care/education settings identified by sample families, 28% were sponsored by private organizations, 60% were sponsored by religious organizations, and 11% were sponsored by voluntary agencies. Educational institutions sponsored 1% of the settings, and no setting was sponsored by the government. This information corroborates the 1989 profile's contention that private and voluntary organizations are the primary sponsors of organized settings for young children.

In discussing the early childhood services in Hong Kong, Opper's 1989 profile noted the following pressing needs: improved facilities and equipment, improved teacher training, curriculum improvement, and an expanded program of fee assistance for low-income families. One might have expected most parents interviewed in the Phase 1 study to mention similar needs, but this was not the case. When Phase 1 researchers asked parents about problems they had encountered with their children's services, only a minority answered by citing one or more specific problems. However, among this minority of parents, the most cited problems did support the needs listed earlier by Opper: equipment and facilities, the academic orientation (i.e., the philosophy) of the setting, and cost. Despite the specific problems they cited, those parents who responded to the satisfaction item seemed to be generally satisfied with the settings they had selected.

In her 1990 report on Hong Kong's Phase 1 findings, Opper suggested that the high degree of satisfaction and the small percentage of parents citing problems may be due either to parents' relatively low expectations of teachers/caregivers or to parents' limited contact with settings and their consequent lack of awareness of what actually happens in the settings. Regarding parents' limited contact with settings, information is presented in Chapter 5 of this volume. There, the cross-national data about various types of home-setting contacts do indeed show very limited *in-person* or *within-setting* contact between Hong Kong parents and their children's caregivers/teachers.

However, one type of home-setting contact that is not included in the Chapter 5 data needs to be mentioned here to provide a more complete picture of the parental role in Hong Kong. Nearly all of the Territory's kindergartens and nurseries use a handbook that, according to Opper's 1990 report, "the child takes home at the end of a preschool session and returns to the preschool the next day with the parents' written response. This handbook usually contains comments from the teacher, often includes homework or suggested activities for the child to do at home, and provides an end-of-term and end-of-year report on the child's progress in the preschool" (pp. 33–34). Consequently, there is often daily *written* communication between parents and educators about children's work, despite the limited amount of other types of educator–parent contact.

As mentioned earlier, one major problem of Hong Kong's preschool situation is the existence of two separate service systems—child care centers (nurseries) and kindergartens. Although the Phase 1 study did not collect information from families specifically related to the operation of the two separate systems, some of the problems that sample families identified could be indirectly related to differences between the systems.

Considering that the *quantity* of early childhood services offered in the Hong Kong Territory is nearly sufficient to meet the needs of its population, it is likely that early childhood professionals and policymakers in Hong Kong will concentrate next on improving the *quality* of services. As Opper (1989) noted, the major issues to be focused on will probably include improvements in the training of teachers/caregivers, increased support by the government to stabilize the teaching staff and increase the proportion of experienced teachers/caregivers, new guidelines for curriculum development and for implementation of developmentally appropriate teaching methods, and unification of standards and delivery of early childhood services within the dual system. One final overarching question, of course, that looms for the Hong Kong early childhood community concerns what will happen to early childhood services in 1997, when Hong Kong reverts to China.

Italy—Two Systems, Regional and Urban–Rural Variations

Background Information

The history of preschool provisions in Italy, according to profile author Filomena Pistillo is closely tied to the country's political, social, economic, and structural changes (1989, pp. 151–202). Pistillo's profile described the care and education of young children as a "terrain on which to defend rival interests, . . . a political battleground." The rival interests have been governmental and religious.

Up until World War II, the Roman Catholic Church was responsible for most of the development of preprimary education. After the Liberation in 1943, government inattentiveness to preprimary affairs continued until the Christian Democrats, "with no small help from the church," won parliamentary control in 1948. Finally, preschool education got the government's attention in the form of a study by the National Committee for School Reform. The study publicized the ills of the preschool system, ranging from inadequate facilities, equipment, curriculum, and teacher qualifications to inadequate geographic distribution. The government, while assuring Church officials that it had no intention of taking over the system, pledged its help in expanding and subsidizing private preschool services.

Toward the mid-1950s, lay political parties began to be concerned about early childhood needs and to denounce the lack of direct government involvement and the "excessive religious control" over preschools. This concern coincided with Italy's "boom years"—its rapid industrial development and the resultant changes in social values and family lifestyles. Against this backdrop, in 1958, for the first time, government guidelines for activities in *nonstate* preschools appeared. By 1960, a government Three-Year Plan allocated money not only for expansion of the nonstate system but also for building a few state-run preschools. A law passed in 1968 at last officially recognized the government's right to be directly involved in preprimary education. This was quickly followed by the 1969 issue of government guidelines for activities in *state* nursery schools.

Today Italy has two preschool systems that between them enroll almost all children 3, 4, and 5 years of age: *state nursery schools* (run directly by a ministry or agency of the national government); and *nonstate nursery schools* (run by private organizations or by communal, provincial, or regional government), but subject to supervision by the Ministry of Education, and subsized by state funds.

Official 1985–1986 statistics showed the two systems enrolling almost equal numbers of children, but with nonstate nursery schools slightly ascendant. Rural areas depend mostly on state-run provisions, whereas urban areas have a concentration of nonstate nursery schools. Attendance at state schools (which have a combination of communal, regional, and national support) is free of charge; parents must pay fees for their children's attendance at nonstate (private) nursery schools. About two-thirds of state nursery schools remain open as much as 8–10 hours a day (two half-day sessions) for 10 months of the year. Nonstate nursery schools sometimes have longer and more flexible hours of operation.

At the outset of Italy's participation in the IEA Preprimary Project, the principal national issues under debate included updating of staff training, organization of state and nonstate nursery schools into a single national system, lowering the starting age for compulsory education, improving the quality and quantity of nursery schools in the South and the Islands, resolving the issue of teaching religion in preschools, and adjustment of the nursery school calendar to coincide with the compulsory-school calendar.

The Findings about Italy's Preprimary Care/Education

Phase 1 researchers found that 85% of families typically use at least one extraparental early childhood care/education setting each week. This figure comprises the 80% whose children attend nursery schools and the 5% whose children are cared for in home settings. In her 1989 profile, Pistillo reported that according to official records, the nursery school coverage rate for 1985–1986 was 88%, a percentage slightly higher than the one found in the IEA study.[1]

The IEA study also revealed that 60% of sample children attend only one setting, while 25% attend two or more settings. When children's second and third settings are examined, it appears that they are usually home settings—either the child's own home or someone else's home. As shown in Table A.1 (Appendix A, p. 198), all of Italy's home-based care is provided by relatives. Indeed, in a detailed analysis of the Italian IEA study findings (1990), Pusci found that grandparents provide most of the extraparental home-based care:

> Since nursery school and grandparents prove to be the two prominent settings, . . . this also turns out to be the most significant and best represented combination. Usually nursery school is the first setting, and grandparents the second one, but there are a few cases (6%) in which grandparents are the first setting (according to the number of hours of weekly attendance) and nursery school is the second (pp. 52–53).

The findings for organized facilities (nursery schools) in Italy show that children spend an average of 6 hours a day in such settings, a finding consistent with the hours of operation reported for these settings in Pistillo's 1989 profile. Regarding sponsorship, the Italian IEA study found that two-thirds of the settings are government-sponsored, over half of these being state-sponsored. Religious organizations (primarily the Roman Catholic church) sponsor 23% of the nursery schools, and private agencies sponsor 7%. When these percentages are combined, they reveal a picture of 52% *state* sponsorship and approximately 45% *nonstate* sponsorship, findings very close to those reported in the 1989 profile.

In his 1990 report of the results of Italy's Phase 1 study, Pusci presented usage rates of extraparental services for the 16 substrata used as a basis for sampling (the intersection of 4 geographical regions and 4 levels of demographic density). These rates, given in Table 7.3, indicate greater extraparental service usage in the northern and central regions of Italy than in the southern region and the Islands. In her 1989 profile, Pistillo noted a similar disparity in availability of services between the North (including the northern and central regions) and the South (including the southern region and the Islands).

Another finding of the Phase 1 study is that service usage is higher in urban areas than in rural areas in all regions except the Islands. Pistillo's

---

[1]It is worth noting that the official statistics are based on the actual *enrollment* rates, whereas the IEA study records only the data on actual *attendance*. A number of children enroll in nursery school but do not really attend, or attend only for a few months. So the gap between official statistics and the IEA study may be due to the percentage of children who fail to attend nursery school for the entire school year.

Table 7.3
Percentages of Families in Italian Communes Using
Extraparental Care/Education Services, by Commune Location and Density

Demographic density of commune	Geographical region of commune				
	North	Central	South	Islands	Total
Very high	95	94	90	69	88
High	100	96	78	62	83
Moderate	95	87	79	78	84
Low	83	89	87	88	86
All communes	89	92	83	77	85

The extraparental care/education used is primarily nursery school (94 %). *Very high* indicates communes with more than 1,500 target-age children; *high* indicates communes with 501–1,500 target-age children; *moderate* indicates communes with 101–500 target-age children; *low* indicates communes with 1–100 target-age children.

1989 profile noted that nonstate nursery schools were more likely to be located in urban areas, and the greater usage indicated in the table may correspond to the greater availability of such settings in urban areas.

As mentioned, Italy has two systems of nursery schools, a state system and a nonstate system. The systems differ in their operating guidelines, personnel requirements, and methods of financing. In discussing the organization of the state and nonstate nursery schools into a single national system, Pistillo (1989) wrote:

> Everyone accepts the idea of a national system capable of overseeing relations between the various managements and of unifying nursery education, but diversity and the principle of institutional pluralism must be respected, as provided by the Constitution. . . . [One] proposal could be summed up in the following terms: a national public system (state plus local-authority nursery schools), backed up by a set of national-level guidelines . . . that would regulate state, regional, and local authority measures to support autonomous schools and that would set certain conditions for the autonomous schools (p. 191).

Pistillo also proposed that there be state involvement in improving nursery school services in the South of Italy, including the Islands. She noted not only that there are fewer nursery schools in operation in these areas but also that many of those operating have one or more serious problems (temporary quarters, inability to provide hot meals, lack of support services).

During the next few years, both the quantity and the quality of services for young children will be the focus of early childhood professionals and policymakers in Italy.

Nigeria—Mostly Home-Based Care

Background Information

Nigeria, which became fully independent in 1960 and a republic in 1963, has a fairly recent history of child care institutions and an even more recent history of government involvement in them. The first preschools appeared in the 1950s, when Nigerians returning from studying abroad established them for their children.

It was not until 1969, which marked the first official statement of school-entry age, that the government spoke out on the role of preschools. The government's emphasis, at that time, on their *primary-school preparatory* role for 3 to 5-year-olds may explain what Onibokun (1989) described as "the rigorous academic content of Nigerian preschool programs."

The 1970s were Nigeria's oil-boom era, and this period also saw a boom in the setting up of preschools. As a result, a preprimary section was set up in the Ministry of Education to draw up guidelines for the establishment and supervision of the schools. Besides this, there has been no federal funding and no direct participation of the federal government in preschool education. Responsibility for control, supervision, and administration of preprimary programs is delegated to the states, who in turn leave pre-primary service provision in private/corporate hands.

Onibokun's own 1987–1988 survey in 7 states revealed that over 90% of preprimary institutions were run by private individuals, religious bodies, or voluntary organizations, and fewer than 10% were government-sponsored (connected to universities, teacher-training colleges, or polytechnics). The private institutions are supported by proprietors' capital and by fees collected from parents. According to Onibokun, "most Nigerian families do not earn the income to support their children in preprimary institutions."

Because each state keeps its own records, it is difficult to determine the total number of preschool institutions nationally. It is also difficult to get information from private proprietors about per-center populations and teacher–pupil ratios. However, Onibokun's 7-state survey was able to roughly gauge the adequacy of preprimary facilities by comparing numbers of preprimary institutions with numbers of primary schools in each state. The best ratio found was 1 preprimary for 8 primary schools; the worst was 1 preprimary for more than 100 primary schools. Not surprisingly, Onibokun found a preponderance of preprimary institutions in urban, rather than rural, areas.

Nursery or *kindergarten* is the name most often given to an institution serving 3 to 5-year-old children in Nigeria, though some children in this age-range are in *day-care centers* (which usually provide custodial care for children 0 to 2 years old). Typical operating hours for a nursery school are 7:30 a.m. to 2:00 or 3:00 p.m., to coincide with the "working hours of public servants." However, parents are free to drop their children off and pick them up whenever it is convenient. Day care centers often have somewhat longer hours, such as 7:00 a.m. to 6:00 p.m.

Onibokun explained that the purpose of preprimary services is to provide "social and educational services in looking after children of working mothers," which accounts for their concentration in towns, where the rate of female employment is very high. However, the profile also stated that "the vast majority of Nigerian women, whether in urban or rural areas, whether educated or illiterate, are economically active to insure their immediate families against financial inadequacy." Mothers working in the informal sector—on the farms, in the markets—often work and care for their children at the same time. It is the educated mothers employed in the formal sector of the economy, outside the home for a fixed period each day, who seek extrafamilial care for their children. Recruiting house-help (maids, or nannies, who are "young school-leavers and dropouts migrating into the cities") or recruiting unemployed relatives for child care has in recent times become less of a possibility for these mothers, because the potential "childminders" are able to find better-paying jobs in service industries.

Onibokun (1989) presented a profile of a country with increasing need for extrafamilial child care. Existing preprimary institutions fail to provide large numbers of Nigerian children with much-needed stimuli for optimum physical, social and intellectual development. Onibokun cited the need for government provision of services for economically disadvantaged children, for better state regulation and supervision of preschools in general, and for teacher training more suited to early childhood needs. Underlying all this is the need for data about the preschool population and families' needs.

The Findings about Nigeria's Preprimary Care/Education

Survey researchers questioning Nigerian mothers of 4-year-old children found that 67% of the mothers were employed for pay. It is not surprising that the percentage of "economically active" women reported in Onibokun's profile was higher than 67%, because that estimate referred to all adult women, whereas the Phase 1 study's percentage includes only mothers of 4-year-olds. Other factors explaining the difference might include some distinction between "working for pay" and "being economically active," or respondents' reluctance, for various reasons, to admit their employment to a federal interviewer.

Despite the reported large percentage of mothers of 4-year-old children employed, the family survey found that only 33% of sample families typically used extraparental care/education services each week. The most common form of service involved having a person come into the child's home; nonrelatives provided nearly 90% of this type of care. Children attending an organized facility was less common (reported by 8% of sample families). The type of extraparental service least used was care in another person's home, with nonrelatives once again providing the majority of this type of care.

What these findings show is less-than-expected extraparental care use, and among families using such services, a reliance on home-based settings rather than organized facilities. This is understandable in view of the fact that the population (and sample) in Nigeria is predominantly rural, while the few organized facilities that do exist are located in the urban areas of the country.

When interviewers asked families using extraparental care/education services their reasons for using these services, nearly half cited *parental employment* as the major reason, while another 12% gave *parental educational commitments* as a response. Only 15% of parents stated that the major reason they used extraparental services was to provide *early educational experiences* for their 4-year-old children. These findings confirm Onibokun's assertion that parental employment is an important factor in the use of early childhood care/education services.

Onibokun's 1989 profile noted that over 90% of preprimary institutions were run by private individuals, religious groups, or voluntary organizations. The findings of the IEA Preprimary Project support this statement. Of the organized facilities for which researchers obtained sponsorship information, 94% were sponsored by private organizations/individuals, religious groups, or voluntary organizations.

Since Onibokun discussed the differential between services in urban and rural areas, it may also be useful to examine the IEA study's urban

Table 7.4
Nigeria's Urban/Rural Information for Selected Family and Household Characteristics

Characteristic	Total sample N	Mean	Urban sample N	Mean	Rural sample N	Mean
Mother's yr of education	677	6.2	238	7.7	470	5.9
Father's yr of education	711	7.5	225	9.2	505	4.9
Mother's hr away	713	31.0	187	42.7	525	29.1
Father's hr away	810	53.9	233	55.7	586	53.6
	N	%	N	%	N	%
Mother works for pay	1,295	67	267	56	662	69
Father works for pay	1,295	78	248	79	599	78

and rural findings separately. Table 7.4 presents the sample characteristics for urban families, for rural families, and for the total group.

Table A.2 (Appendix A, p. 199) presents the percentages of families in urban and rural areas typically using various types of extraparental early childhood services each week. In urban areas 43% of families use such services, while in rural areas the corresponding figure is 36%—a fairly small difference. However, when the findings for the urban and rural areas are examined separately, some differences in service usage appear. In urban areas 19% of families enroll their children in organized facilities, whereas in rural areas only 7% of families use this type of setting. This finding supports Onibokun's contention that the organized facilities are located largely in urban areas. Having a person come into the family's home to care for the child is the type of care arrangement used by 17% of urban families and 26% of rural families—a difference almost equal to the rural–urban difference regarding use of organized facilities. Care by a person in another home is rarely used by families in either type of area.

In her profile Onibokun referred to mothers working in the informal sector of the economy often working and caring for their children at the same time. Assuming that this type of employment occurred largely in rural areas, we examined the daily routine information separately for the two subsamples of 4-year-old children, urban and rural. We expected the data to indicate that rural children spend a larger proportion of their waking time in the parental workplace than urban children do. However, whereas urban children spend an average of only 0.3 hour in the parental workplace, the corresponding figure for rural children is not much greater, only 0.4 hour per day. So the parent's workplace appears to be a significant location for only a very small number of children in either urban or rural areas. Perhaps, in rural areas, families only consider their children to be "in the workplace" when they travel with their parents to the market; otherwise, children are considered to be at home, even if they accompany their parents into the farm fields. The study's finding that Nigeria's rural 4-year-olds spend approximately 2 more hours per day at home (13.5 hours) than urban 4-year-olds (11.4 hours), would appear to support this explanation.

As Onibokun wrote in her 1989 profile:

> Early childhood care and education today is largely a family responsibility in Nigeria . . . . The existing child care arrangements [organized facilities] appear elitist, because they are available only to those who can pay for them (pp. 237–238).

The IEA Preprimary Project findings appear to confirm this statement.

In a country such as Nigeria it would seem that government involvement will be necessary if there is to be any significant increase in the provision of early childhood services either to children at the lower socio-

economic levels or to children in rural areas. In 1987 the Nigerian government launched the Mass Mobilization Program for Social and Economic
Recovery (MAMSER), a program that encompasses social justice, economic
recovery, and self-reliance. MAMSER is "directed at improving the conditions in rural areas and elevating the status of women" (Onibokun, 1989,
p. 238), and the expansion of the government sponsorship of preprimary
services would increase the availability of these services and assist women
in combining their roles of mother and wage earner. The findings from
the IEA Preprimary Project can now serve as an important source of
information for the government as it plans early childhood policies and
programs as part of the MAMSER program.

Portugal—Kindergartens and Grandparents

Background Information

Despite a brief period between 1910 and 1926, when the government
attempted to establish kindergartens, Portugal had very little preprimary
provision until the early 1970s, when under the Veiga Simão Reform,
preprimary education was reinstated as part of the public educational
system.

Implementation of the Veiga Simão Reform plan was interrupted
by Portugal's April 25 Revolution in 1974. Nevertheless, since that time,
there have been significant increases in the numbers of kindergartens (for
3-, 4-, and 5-year-olds) and of training schools for preschool teachers.
Bairrão *et al.*'s (1989) profile showed the number of Ministry of Education
public kindergartens, for example, increasing twentyfold between 1978 and
1988. During the same time, Ministry of Education private kindergartens
increased by about one-fifth. The result has been that the ministry's public
kindergartens outnumber private kindergartens by more than six to one.

By 1984, about a third of Portuguese children aged 3, 4, and 5 were
attending public or private kindergartens. A pre-Revolution legacy was that
services for young children were dispersed among several ministries besides
the Ministry of Education. Therefore, coordination of efforts to help young
children has been another public policy thrust during the past two decades.
The ministries sponsoring early childhood care and education are now
just two: the Ministry of Education (ME) and the Ministry of Work and
Social Security (MWSS). The ME sponsors just kindergartens; the MWSS
sponsors many institutions connected with care and education of children
aged 3 months to 6 years, and among these are various kindergartens and
joint nursery/kindergartens that service 3-, 4-, and 5-year-olds.

The ME-sponsored kindergartens include both public and private ones,
with the public kindergartens being located mostly in the poorer, rural

areas. Compared with private ME kindergartens, public ME kindergartens tend to have better child–teacher ratios (no more than 25 to 1), and in 1987–1988, about a quarter of them (mainly located in rural areas) even had fewer than 15 children. The profile authors, noting that "only 60% of Portugal's available kindergarten places are actually occupied," hinted that better adaptation of child care options to the desires and characteristics of local populations might be in order.

The various kindergartens and nursery/kindergartens under the MWSS include ones that are private nonprofit, private for-profit, cooperative, factory-sponsored, and publicly sponsored (by autarchies, or local authorities).

The result of having both the ME and MWSS systems of preprimary services is that there are multiple financing arrangements and management structures, as well as different requirements for teacher-training. Only the ME public kindergartens require no fees of parents. Kindergartens under the ME follow the "educational model," which means that available space and age are the criteria for enrollment, and programs operate 6 hours per day, Monday through to Friday, closing down 45 days for summer holidays and 2 weeks around both Christmas and Easter. Kindergartens under the MWSS follow the "social welfare model," meaning that enrollment depends on various family/child needs and considerations, and programs operate 10–12 hours per day, Monday through to Friday, with usually only 1 month off for summer holidays.

Though the preprimary programs are targeted primarily to meet children's needs, they are also intended to meet the needs of families. The female-employment rate, as well as the social and cultural deprivation of the area and the population of 3 to 6-year-olds, is taken into consideration both by the ME and the MWSS in selecting where to establish kindergartens. However, the profile authors stated that "there are children where there are no kindergartens and there are kindergartens where there are not enough children." For example, in rural areas, where geographical isolation is a problem, a large percentage of public ME kindergartens operate with small numbers of children. This fact points out the need for adapting child care options to the characteristics and needs of local populations, to optimize the benefits of public investment in preschool education. Furthermore, the reverse condition, "children where there are no kindergartens," suggests that some employed mothers resort to informal care arrangements for their 3 to 5-year-olds, such as care by home day care mothers.

The 1989 profile mentioned a government goal to increase kindergarten enrollment to approximately 80% of preprimary-aged children by early 1991–1992. The IEA Preprimary Project's Phase 1 findings not only clarify how Portugal is doing in reaching this goal, but they shed some interesting light on where children are who are not in ME or MWSS kindergartens. Portugal's IEA Phase 1 findings have been able to provide statistics about the incidence and frequency of grandparent care, a common phenomenon in that country.

The Findings about Portugal's Preprimary Care/Education

The Phase 1 family survey in Portugal revealed that 71% of Portuguese families with 4-year-old children use extraparental early childhood services. This 71% is made up of 29% who use organized facilities (kindergartens) and 41% who use either own-home or other-home care/education settings (1% are classified as using "other" types of settings). This finding of 29% kindergarten attendance agrees closely with the 32% kindergarten attendance reported in the 1989 profile by Bairrão and colleagues.

Phase 1 researchers found that Portugal's 4-year-old children are typically in extraparental settings for 44 hours per week, a figure very similar to the number of hours that mothers spend away from their 4-year-olds each week.

For the sizable group of 171 families (29%) choosing *not* to use extraparental care/education services, the most frequently given reason for this choice was the mother's nonemployment (i.e., availability to care for her 4-year-old child; 45% of mothers gave this explanation). Two other reasons for this choice were cited by nearly equal percentages of families: 24% said that no service was available or the available service was too expensive, and 22% said they received personal satisfaction either from caring for the child or from teaching the child at home.

As mentioned earlier, the Phase 1 findings allow a closer look at the caregiving role that Portuguese grandparents play, which is a subject that Portugal's 1989 profile, based on government statistics, was unable to shed light on. The findings presented here were drawn from supplemental analyses of Phase 1 data either by the ICC or by the Portuguese NRC (Barbosa *et al.*, 1990).

The method that Portuguese researchers used to locate their survey sample—a search of children's birth records—is a method that can only be used in a country with a very low rate of family mobility. Its successful use implies that families rarely move and that succeeding generations of the same family either live in the same household or live near each other. Among the 581 Portuguese households surveyed in Phase 1, interviewers found grandparents present in 21%. However, even when grandparents do not live in the household of a Portuguese 4-year-old, there is a good chance that they live nearby and consequently may be available to serve as the child's caregiver.

As noted earlier, Phase 1 findings indicate 41% of families using own-home or other-home care as their child's first setting. Table A.1 (Appendix A, p. 198) shows that nearly all this home care is provided by relatives. Further examination of the data indicates that nearly *all* care by relatives is provided by grandparents; very little is provided by siblings or other relatives. An examination of the data for children's second settings shows that 15% of families use relative (i.e., grandparent) care either in the child's home or in the relative's home, while only 2% make use of organized facility care.

Considering all settings selected by Portuguese families for the care/education of their 4-year-olds, it is clear from the Phase 1 findings that more families use grandparents as caregivers/educators than teachers. Of sample children, 207 were typically cared for by grandparents each week, while 177 attended kindergartens. Some of this care/education by grandparents took place in children's own homes, and some of it took place in the grandparent's home. The children in grandparent care spent 30 hours per week (median) in that setting; the median time spent with teachers was 40 hours per week. Thus, although more families entrust their children to grandparents than to teachers, the weekly time children spend with grandparents is less than that spent with teachers.

These Phase 1 findings, obtained in the late 1980s, show Portugal to be short of its 1991–92 goal of 80% kindergarten enrollment, which was mentioned at the beginning of this summary. Large percentages of 4-year-olds, at the time of the household survey, still remained at home with their mothers or in mostly relative-tended home-care settings, while less than a third attended kindergartens. Although a quarter of the mothers keeping their children at home said they did so because of the personal satisfaction they derived from it, another quarter expressed the opinion that programs in organized facilities were unavailable or too expensive. If the government hopes to reach its 80% enrollment goal, they will need to increase the availability of kindergartens to families with 4-year-old children and look for solutions to make kindergartens financially accessible to more families. Also, if the proportion of women active in the labor force continues to increase in Portugal, as it has in so many countries, the result may be a decreased availability of grandparents to serve as caregivers—a situation that would drastically alter life for families in Portugal.

Spain—From Schoolmasters and "Friendly Women" to Public and Private Preprimary Centers

Background Information

Evidence of early childhood services in Spain goes back as far as the fifteenth through to seventeenth centuries, when young children were taught by town-hall-hired schoolmasters or by "friendly women" paid by mothers to look after their children. Palacios, in his 1989 profile of Spain's early childhood services, described increasing government involvement over the last 20 years, as Spain's 17 regions go about assuming more and more responsibilities from the central government.

A most significant turning point in Spain's preprimary service provision was the "new period of democracy" that began in 1975, when after 40 years of dictatorial rule, Spain became a federation of "autonomous communities" (regions). Since 1977, with its 17 autonomous communities all in various stages of assuming responsibilities from the central government, the country has been aiming at providing school places for all 4- and 5-year-olds. In 1986 this goal had almost been met: over 90% of these children (85% of 4-year-olds and 95% of 5-year-olds) were in kindergartens. Approximately two-thirds of the kindergartens they attended were government-run, and one-third were privately owned or church-sponsored.

Most kindergartens—especially the public ones—are staffed by teachers specialized in preprimary education, and most operate for a full day. The public kindergartens linked to the Ministry of Education and Science are free, and those linked to other ministries are either free or charge on a sliding, income-based scale; the private and church-sponsored kindergartens charge parents fees commensurate with the prestige or quality of the institution.

Kindergarten attendance is not compulsory, but the almost universal enrollment in these schools is due not only to the large supply of public kindergartens but also to parents' growing awareness of the preparatory role of preprimary education. There has also been, in some cities and their surrounding areas, a shortage of primary school places, and enrolling their child in kindergarten has been a way that parents can assure the child's acceptance into the affiliated primary school.

Spain is a country that is in the process of forging a new identity. In addition to the rapid growth of preprimary services in the last 15 years, other changes have been occurring: extensive migration to the cities in the 1960s and, more recently, gradual improvement in the unattractive rural social conditions that caused this migration; a birthrate drop in the early 1980s to below that needed for generation replacement; an emergence of government policies in support of families—especially of families with employed mothers—in the 1980s; and a gradual assumption by the autonomous communities of responsibilities formerly held by the central government.

This last process, because it is unevenly completed as of now, may account for much of the diversity in preprimary provisions throughout Spain. For example, at the time Palacios's profile was written (1989), Spain had no official curriculum for children below school age, although the central Ministry of Education and Science did establish official guidelines in 1981. At the same time, some autonomous communities have developed their own specific preschool curricula. According to the profile, what actually happens in classrooms may ultimately depend on the degree of training of the teacher. Those with some level of specialization are likely to develop innovative programs and be interested in pedagogic techniques; those with little or no training depend more on textbooks and methods that encourage passive learning, focusing on acquiring skills more appropriate for older children.

There are also differences among the autonomous communities regarding how well the demand for preprimary services are being met, regarding the predominance of public versus private preschools (the latter have fewer specialized teachers), and regarding preprimary teacher–pupils ratios (which are higher in the private than in the public sector). When one adds to this the lack of regulation of private providers and the lack of statistics about unlicensed providers, it is no wonder that as recounted in the profile, a 1984 report on preprimary education described "a conglomeration of schools over which there is little control."

In 1987, a ministry proposal suggested a major change in attitudes towards preprimary education. The proposal would view birth to age 6 as the first (noncompulsory) link in the education chain, emphasizing the *educational* as well as the *care* aspect of all preprimary services. A new law, to be promulgated by 1989, was the anticipated outcome of the ongoing debate over the proposal. Palacios, in concluding Spain's profile, expressed hope that the new law would bring about real change.

The 1989 profile, noting that the country's ongoing process of decentralization made it difficult to present "national" statistics, presented data from both government reports and research studies about families and their early childhood services. Also, as Palacios explained, and as with many other countries, preprimary situations falling outside of government control are underrepresented in the profile's statistics. Phase 1 of the IEA Preprimary Project supplies some of these missing statistics.

The Families Surveyed in Spain

The response rate for the IEA Phase I study in Spain was 29%, and the refusal rate, 35%. When the ICC explored with the Spanish research team the reasons for the low response and the high refusal rates, they learned that when a family could not easily be contacted, the interviewer had replaced that family with another one, with little effort at repeated attempts to contact the "original" family. This extensive use of "replacement" families, as well as the unavailability of national population characteristics, makes it difficult, if not impossible, to assess the representativeness of the achieved sample in Spain. Consequently, the reader should approach the Phase 1 findings of the IEA Preprimary Project in Spain with a certain degree of caution.

The Findings about Spain's Preprimary Care/Education

Phase 1 researchers in Spain found 79% of families with 3- and 4-year-old children to be using extraparental care and education services. This included 69% who enrolled their children in preprimary centers and 10% whose children were cared for in home settings. The 1989 profile reported that in 1986, approximately 16% of 3-year-olds and 85% of 4-year-olds were enrolled in preprimary centers; so the profile's statistics and the recent findings seem to be in general agreement. Approximately one-quarter of the sample families in the present study typically used two or more settings each week, and the second and third settings were nearly always home settings.

With nearly four-fifths of sample families using extraparental services and 35% of sample mothers employed, maternal employment must be only one of several reasons families use early childhood services. Thus, it is interesting to examine the reasons that families gave for turning to extraparental services. When families in the IEA study were asked their major reason for service use, 63% cited child-related reasons, including 43% who mentioned *education of the child* as the specific reason. Only 28% of families said that *parental employment* was their major reason for using early childhood services.

The IEA Phase 1 findings and the findings included in the Palacios profile are in general agreement on the following matters regarding Spain's preprimary centers: (1) children spend 5–6 hours per day in these settings; (2) a moderate proportion of the settings (40–60%) offer health services for children, while a smaller proportion have transportation services; and (3) there is little educator–parent contact beyond informal meetings. However, the two studies reported different findings regarding how children travel between their home and the care/education setting. In the IEA study, 74% of families reported that their children traveled by foot, while in the 1983 study included in the Palacios profile, 97% of families indicated that they used either private or public transportation to convey their children to their settings. This difference in percentages may be explained by the fact that the earlier study was limited to urban areas, whereas the Phase 1 study included rural areas, small towns, and urban sites.

Since the 1989 profile also included data (from the 1983 study) about the amount of time fathers spend with their children daily, these data can be compared with the daily caregiver findings of the IEA Preprimary Project. In the IEA study, families reported that alone, fathers supervised their 4-year-olds for approximately 20 minutes daily, and together with mothers, they supervised for approximately 2 hours 20 minutes a day. In the 1983 study, families reported that 46% of fathers played with the child for 1 hour or less per day and 29% engaged in this activity for 2–3 hours per day. The findings of both studies seem to indicate that there is limited involvement of fathers in the care or education of young children in Spain.

Among the group of countries participating in Phase 1, Spain belongs to a subgroup in which organized facilities are available to and utilized by the majority of families. Spain is also one of only 4 countries in which parents citing child-related reasons for using extraparental services outnumbered those citing parent-related reasons. These findings suggest that Spanish parents are generally aware of the importance of preprimary education.

Considering the current state of early childhood education in Spain (i.e., general availability of services, parent awareness of the importance of early childhood education), the nation's early childhood policymakers and professionals may now begin to focus on how the quality of existing services affects children, families, professional staff, and society. It is time to explore such questions as these: what is the quality of experiences for children in these preprimary centers? Do these centers adequately meet the needs of families trying to integrate early childhood services with other segments of their lives (e.g., employment)? Are the equipment and facilities in the preprimary centers sufficient to allow professionals to plan and execute a variety of developmentally appropriate activities for young children? How does the preprimary education system fit into the overall educational goals for the various regions of Spain, and are sufficient resources allocated to this system?

Thailand—working Toward a Goal

Background Information

Thailand, a Southeast Asian country with over 1 million 4-year-old children, has had early childhood care and education programs since the late-nineteenth-century reign of King Rama V. As recounted in Thailand's 1989 profile (Passornsiri *et al.*, 1989), during the country's 100-year history with early childhood services, the government has initiated different types of programs in both urban and rural areas.

After Thailand's change to a constitutional monarchy in 1932, the first constitution upheld the government commitment to preprimary programs by calling for the establishment of kindergartens to prepare children for formal schooling. Gradually government 2-year kindergartens were set up, but these were confined mostly to Bangkok and other urban areas.

Since that time, preprimary care and education has spread to other parts of Thailand, and numerous kinds of preprimary services have developed. A series of government reports and national development plans in the 1970s and 1980s emphasized the need for coordinating efforts "on all fronts"—for making the care of the young child the joint responsibility of the family, the community, and the government.

At the time Thailand's profile was written (1989), the *Sixth National Education Development Plan (1987–1991)* had set a goal of expanding preprimary programs to serve at least 37% of 3-, 4-, and 5-year-old children. (About the same time, an expansion program called The Rural Kindergarten was launched, assuring that this goal would be met.) The *Sixth Plan* emphasized giving disadvantaged children more opportunity to receive "readiness training." It also addressed improving the quality of preprimary education in the following ways: developing service models appropriate to local conditions, improving methodology in accordance with the psychology of child development, upgrading health and nutrition standards, and improving supervision and evaluation. The *Sixth Plan* stated clearly that different agencies should coordinate and cooperate, so that services could effectively be given to children throughout the country.

"Coordination and cooperation" are indeed the key to Thailand's early childhood care and education future, since types and sponsors of programs have proliferated over time. Presently, preprimary services continue to be both government-run and private, as they have been from early times. Private sponsors include voluntary or nonprofit councils, associations, and foundations; government sponsors include three different kinds of local government and four different central-government ministries.

The types of preprimary programs offered by this multitude of sponsors fall into three major categories:

(1) Two-year (or 3-year) formal education in kindergarten for children aged 4–6 (age 7 is compulsory school-age).

(2) One-year preprimary classes annexed to primary schools for children aged 5–6.

(3) Nonformal education in centers of various types, such as child development centers, child nutrition centers, day care centers, and child care centers. In these centers, the children's ages can range from birth to 7 years.

In the 1980s, the number of Thai children enrolled in preprimary institutions grew rapidly in comparison with the growth of the preschool-aged population. Although the population of children 3–6 years old increased by only 3%, preprimary enrollment more than tripled betwen 1979 and 1987. The number of preprimary institutions almost quadrupled in that time. As in many other countries, Thai families' needs for out-of-home care and education programs are increasing as female labor force participation (at 65% in 1985) increases and as family structure changes from extended to nuclear.

An analysis of types and sponsors of institutions, by regions, indicates that government-sponsored services are found primarily outside of Bangkok.

Preprimary children in Bangkok are served mainly by private kindergartens and private day care centers. Children in areas outside of Bangkok are served mainly by child development centers, child nutrition centers, and preprimary classes annexed to primary schools. Participation in the IEA Preprimary Project, with the data it produces, may help Thailand with the task of "coordinating efforts on all fronts." Since the data collection for Phase 1 of the IEA Preprimary Project took place in 1989, this summary examines the Phase 1 statistics in the light of *Sixth Plan* government goals and efforts.

The Families Surveyed in Thailand

It is important to note that the Phase 1 household survey in Thailand was conducted with a large number of families (2,466) from 33 provinces located throughout the country. The response rate was 99%, and the comparison of key characteristics of the sample and the population indicated that the sample was generally similar to the population. Considering all these factors, a comparison of Phase 1 findings with *Sixth Plan* goals seems indeed appropriate.

The Findings about Thailand's Preprimary Care/Education

Researchers working on Phase 1 of the IEA Preprimary Project found that in 1989, 12% of Thailand's 4-year-old children were enrolled in preprimary programs in organized facilities: 8% in educational programs and 4% in programs that were primarily care-oriented. The researchers also found that a total of 36% of 4-year-old children were cared for by extraparental caregivers in all major types of settings (own-home, other-home, and organized facility). If one considers the 12% in organized facilities, this leaves 24% receiving extraparental care/education in home settings (either their own home or someone else's home). In these two kinds of home settings, relatives provided nearly all of the extraparental care. This finding was not surprising, since adult family members often live near one another in Thailand, especially in the rural areas.

The government's *Sixth Plan* goal (for 37% of 3-, 4-, and 5-year-olds to be in preprimary programs) referred only to organized facilities, therefore the Phase 1 finding would seem to fall short of the goal—at least if the 37% goal meant equal percentages of each age group (3-, 4-, and 5-year-olds). If coverage for 5-year-olds was intended to be almost universal, with lower percentages for the younger age groups, the goal might well have been met at the time of the Phase 1 survey.

Considering the large percentages of sample mothers and fathers employed for pay and the long hours parents spent away from their children, it was not surprising to find that 4-year-old children in Thailand typically received extraparental care/education services for an average of 56 hours each week. Of the total group of families in the Thailand study who regularly made use of extraparental care/education services, 70% gave *parental employment* as the major reason.

A study of Phase 1 findings about the organized facilities attended by Thailand's 4-year-olds shows that the government is frequently a sponsor of these settings, either as the sole sponsor or as one of multiple sponsors along with educational institutions, religious institutions, and so forth. Approximately 20% of organized facilities offer health services to children, but fewer than 10% offer special education services or social services. While only 25% of families to whom special education services are available actually use these services, a large percentage of families use the available health services (85%) or social services (71%).

Nearly two-thirds of Phase 1 sample families reported that they had at least one informal meeting with the teacher/caregiver in the organized facility during the previous 3 months, and 38% reported that they had this type of contact at least weekly. Meetings requested by the teacher/caregiver and parent group meetings were other types of parent-setting contact reported by the parents, but these meetings occurred infrequently (less than once per month).

Since approximately two-thirds of Thailand's sample children were cared for solely by their parents/guardians, it is interesting to look at the daily routine data for these children. The findings indicate that for the average child, the mother was the caregiver for half of the child's 16 waking hours each day. Only two other categories of persons (both parents, grandparents) served as caregivers for more than 1 hour of the child's waking time. Thus, the largest proportion of the 4-year-old child's time was spent with a parent or grandparent, a finding that is consistent with Thailand's Phase 1 data about family use or nonuse of extraparental care/education settings.

Because of the nature of Thailand, it is interesting to examine some major findings separately for urban areas (16% of the sample) and for rural areas (84% of the sample). Table 7.5 presents data separately for urban and rural areas for several selected family and household variables.

The table highlights the contrast in the percentages of urban and rural families who have running water and who own a television set. (These variables were of interest because availability of running water is one of several factors that determines how much time family members spend in routine daily household activities, while the presence of television is an indicator of the young child's access to the world beyond his or her immediate surroundings.)

Table A.2 (Appendix A, p. 199) presents separate urban and rural percentages for 4-year-old children in extraparental care/education settings. The percentages of children cared for solely by their parents/guardians are similar for urban and rural areas. However, in urban areas, more than three

Table 7.5
**Thailand's Urban/Rural Information for Selected Family and
Household Characteristics**

Characteristic	Total sample		Urban sample		Rural sample	
	N	Mean	*N*	Mean	*N*	Mean
Mother's yr of education	2,249	4.8	349	6.6	1,899	4.5
Father's yr of education	2,194	5.4	340	7.9	1,853	5.0
Mother's hr away	1,116	43.7	170	47.9	945	42.9
Father's hr away	1,873	76.4	302	70.8	1,570	77.4
Number of children	–	–	386	2.2	2,079	2.4
	N	%	*N*	%	*N*	%
Mother works for pay	2,466	57	353	58	1,921	57
Father works for pay	2,466	95	345	97	1,868	94
Indoor water	2,466	18	385	81	2,071	7
Television	2,466	44	386	81	2,079	37

A dash indicates that no data were available.

times as many children attend organized facility preprimary programs as in rural areas.

The Phase 1 findings present a picture of Thailand as a country in which the majority of parents use exclusively parent/guardian at-home care for their 4-year-olds. The reasons that families gave for choosing this type of care were largely parent/guardian-related and included such responses as the parent enjoying having the child around and thinking it is important for parents to be the major persons in the child's life during this period. Also, many families had not considered using extraparental early childhood services. The families who did use extraparental care/education services tended to choose home settings (own-home or other-home) rather than organized facilities, and in these home settings, relatives provided the care/education.

With the Phase 1 results as a basis, Thailand must now consider the next steps in the government's involvement with early childhood care and education services. Questions that emerge from the results of this study include the following: are the government's goals and purposes for early childhood programs consistent with the lifestyles and preferences of families? If the government views early childhood education in an organized facility as important, how can it communicate this information effectively to parents to increase their use of these programs?

The U.S.A.—A Multifaceted System of Preprimary Services

Background Information

As in many other countries, preprimary provisions in the U.S.A. have developed in response to children's care and school-preparation needs. But the U.S. profile (Olmsted, 1989) also cited two strong American beliefs that have influenced the course of provision development: The first is a belief that childrearing is the private province of family members (especially the mother), to be carried out, in a pluralistic society, as each family sees fit. The second is a belief that personal fulfillment comes through work (increasingly, in modern society, work for pay, outside the home). The tension created by these two beliefs has heightened over the years as more and more American mothers, for personal or economic reasons, have entered the labor force. The tension manifests itself in the variety of arrangements families make for child care (often informal, family-based arrangements) and in the ongoing controversy over who (family, community, national government) should be responsible for child care.

The U.S. profile traced the history of "two strands" of early childhood services. The first strand concerns the provision of care for young children, while the second strand concerns the provision of early education.

Throughout the 1970s, families' needs for early care and education increased as more mothers of young children continued to enter the labor force and as more families saw early education programs as beneficial for their children. However, in this decade a congressional bill that would have established a national child care program for the first time in the U.S.A. was vetoed by President Richard Nixon, who opposed "[committing] the moral authority of the national government to the side of communal approaches of childrearing over against the family-centered approach."

The 1980s witnessed three trends in the federal government's role regarding early childhood provisions: *decentralization* (federal funding cutbacks and elimination and matching-fund requirements for states); *privatization* (open support for a diverse child care market through employer incentives, easing of requirements for private providers, and tax benefits to families); *deregulation* (failure to enact federal guidelines for child care services, thereby leaving regulation up to individual states). The result of these policy trends has been a highly decentralized system of childhood care and education services, with federal, state, local, and private (for-profit and nonprofit) providers. There is considerable variation among the 50 states as to relative state and federal funding levels, regulations and licensing standards, and populations served. Also, a large variety of forms of child care and education exist, with some states continuing a two-strand system and others blending the care and education strands into one.

Federal funding of services, in keeping with a national policy of noninterference in family affairs, has primarily targeted families with special needs or families at risk because of economic or social circumstances.

The profile revealed that in 1987, slightly more than half of U.S. 3- and 4-year-olds had mothers active in the labor force. Also, about a third of U.S. 3- and 4-year-olds were in institutional education or care programs, but almost half of these children had mothers who were *not* employed. Of employed mothers, almost half chose to entrust their 3- and 4-year-olds to in-home care, relative care, or a family day care home.

Leaving responsibilities up to states has produced not only a great variety of program types but also much state-to-state variation in licensing, staff-training requirements, and program requirements (for staff–child ratios, space, curriculum). For family day care, in particular, there are states that lack home licensing requirements and states that require no experience or education of providers.

This summary of the United States' IEA/PPP Phase 1 study methods and findings looks at the family survey results to see how they compare with information in the 1989 profile and to present findings for subgroups of families.

The Findings about the U.S.A.'s Preprimary Care/Education

The Phase 1 family survey revealed that 61% of American families with 4-year-old children use extraparental early childhood services. This 61% is made up of 35% who use organized facilities, 17% who use other home arrangements, and 9% whose children are cared for in their own homes by others. Service usage as reported in the 1989 profile and as found in the present study, reveals a close correspondence between the two sets of findings.

Phase 1 researchers found that American 4-year-olds are typically in extraparental settings for 28 hours per week. This closely agrees with the weekly hours mothers spend away from their 4-year-olds. Also, 43% of American 4-year-olds typically attend one extraparental care/education setting each week, and 18% attend two or more such settings. American parents are generally satisfied with the care/education services their children receive, and report few problems.

When American parents were asked to state the major reason for their use of extraparental services, 51% cited parent-related reasons (such as *employment, family obligations*), while 42% cited child-related reasons (such as *education, social-emotional development*). Of the 9 countries reporting data for this question, the U.S.A. is the only one in which nearly equal percentages of parents cited parent-related and child-related reasons. These findings suggest that both the "care strand" and the "education strand" of services described in Olmsted's 1989 U.S. profile continue to exist.

Regarding average annual service costs in the U.S.A., Phase 1 findings were these: US$1,200 per year for in own-home care, US$1,440 per year for other-home care, and US$1,728 per year for organized facility care (in a child care center, preschool). In general, American families pay 5–7% of monthly household income for care/education services for their 4-year-olds. These figures are lower than those reported in the 1989 profile, perhaps because the earlier figures came from studies in predominantly large urban areas.

The Phase 1 study found that of the organized care/education facilities identified by sample families (*n* = 170), 25% were sponsored by private organizations, 19% were sponsored by religious organizations, 15% were sponsored by the government, and 12% were sponsored by educational institutions. These data support the 1989 profile's information about the multiplicity of sponsors of American early childhood care/education settings.

Phase 1 findings indicated that 37% of organized facilities in the U.S.A. offer health services, while approximately a quarter offer each of the other categories of service—special education services, social services, and transportation services. Whereas three-quarters of children to whom health services are available use these services, about half use available transportation services, and only a third use available special education and social services.

When organized facility users in each country were asked about types and frequencies of home-setting contact in the previous 3 months, American parents were among those reporting the most contact. Over 60% of U.S. sample parents reported having three different types of home-setting contact (informal meetings, group meetings, telephone/written communication). The most striking finding was that nearly half of parents reported having assisted in the setting. Also, 44% noted that they had attended a meeting requested by the teacher/caregiver.

The daily routine information for 4-year-olds in the U.S.A. shows that the mother serves as caregiver for 10–11 hours of the child's daily waking hours; the organized facility teacher/caregiver serves for the second-longest period (1.8 hours daily). The American father typically provides little primary supervision of the young child, either alone or in the presence of the mother. Other relatives tend to serve as caregivers for only a small portion of the child's day. Findings about the various settings attended by the 4-year-old child during his or her waking hours are consistent with findings about the persons serving as caregivers. American 4-year-olds typically spend about 12 hours a day in their own homes and 1–2 hours a day in either an organized facility or another home (e.g., a family day care home).

Since both *family structure* (two-parent or one-parent) and *employment status of parents* could be related to use/nonuse of extraparental services and to type of services used, it is useful to examine the data separately for the four categories of families formed by these two characteristics (see Table 7.6). Among families with both parents or the sole parent in the labor force (i.e., *no unemployed parent*), it is not surprising that only a small percentage of 4-year-olds in one-parent households are in *parental care only*; however, in a two-parent household where both parents are employed outside the home, a sizable percentage of 4-year-olds are in *parental care only*. This may be because it is sometimes possible for two parents to work alternating schedules in order to provide the child's total care between them.

From Table 7.6 data this further observation about families with *no unemployed parent* can be made: when the one-employed-parent family uses extraparental services, they are more likely than the two-employed-parent family to use a single care/education setting.

Another interesting conclusion from Table 7.6 is that when one examines the use of extraparental services for two-parent, one-unemployed-parent families and one-parent, unemployed-parent families, very similar

Table 7.6
U.S. Early Childhood Care and Education Service Usage
for Families with Various Characteristics

Service usage	No unemployed parent		At least 1 unemployed parent	
	% of 2-parent households ($n = 163$)	% of 1-parent households ($n = 49$)	% of 2-parent households ($n = 131$)	% of 1-parent households ($n = 81$)
Parental care only	**24**	**14**	**56**	**58**
1 extraparental setting per week				
Own-home care	9	14	2	5
Other-home care	15	27	4	3
Organized facility	26	19	28	25
Subtotal	**50**	**60**	**34**	**33**
2 or more extraparental settings per week				
Own-home and other(s)	3	4	2	0
Other-home and other(s)	13	8	2	2
Organized facility and other(s)	10	14	6	7
Subtotal	**26**	**26**	**10**	**9**
Total	**100**	**100**	**100**	**100**

patterns emerge regarding both numbers and types of settings used. Comparable pattern-similarity cannot be found in comparing the two kinds of two-parent households or the two kinds of one-parent households. The data in Table 7.6 would thus suggest that in the U.S.A., *parental employment status is more related to service usage than family structure is*.

In the Phase 1 family survey, U.S. researchers added questions about medical and dental insurance coverage. The findings indicate that 85% of children are covered by medical insurance, with employer-provided insurance accounting for 55%, family-purchased insurance accounting for 13%, and Medicaid accounting for 12% (5% responded with "other"). The findings also indicate that 56% of children are covered by dental insurance, and this agrees with the percentage of children receiving dental examinations in the year previous to the survey.

In summary, the U.S. Phase 1 findings confirm recently reported government statistics about the use of extraparental care/education services by families with preschool-aged children. The additional information that was obtained through the family survey, however, enriches the total data set and facilitates more in-depth analyses.

8

Questions Answered, Questions Raised—A Summary

DAVID P. WEIKART

With the worldwide increase in out-of-home care and education of young children, the issues involved in developing and providing such services have become the subject of much debate. Information to guide this debate and to serve as a basis for public policy formation, though scarce at first, is increasingly available.

To begin with, the United Nations (UNESCO, 1989) provides statistical information related to early child development from 150 countries. In addition, Myers (1992) in *The Twelve Who Survive* provides a comprehensive summary of policy and research in developing countries. Cochran (1993) and authors from 29 countries, in the *International Handbook of Child Care Policies and Programs*, also supply information from a wide range of countries, including modern, industrialized states such as Sweden and Italy as well as struggling Third World countries such as Vietnam and Zimbabwe. What is notable is that *none of these sources examines the use of child care and education services from the family's perspective*. That investigation is the goal of the IEA Preprimary Project reported here.

Initially, Phase 1 of the multiphase IEA project documented 14 nations' official government policies, both historically and most recently, toward early childhood services for families. This documentation took the form of the book *How Nations Serve Young Children: Profiles of Child Care and Education in 14 Countries* (Olmsted & Weikart, 1989). Phase 1 researchers then went on to their major task of surveying families in each country about their use, or nonuse, of the services that are available. The aim has been to let families speak—to learn firsthand how parents accommodate family needs and beliefs in light of the child care/education services they are offered by the public and private sectors. Such information, because it has been obtained in as accurate a manner as possible, should serve as a sound basis for national decision making. By gathering identical data from a wide range of countries—those with comprehensive, well-formed child care/education systems and those with

179

patchwork or nonexistent systems, those with large-scale private-sector services and those with predominantly government provision—the IEA study provides a picture of the full range of policy options.

Until now, the field of child service has been clouded with extensive statements about what families need or want expressed by advocates of various points of view. Often these statements are not research-based, and even government statistics—narrow as they are—are of little use in validating them. The purpose of the Phase 1 study, then, has been to provide reliable information, comparable across countries, that can be used for careful discussion of the issues. It should set a standard for other studies as well as contribute to the understanding of the problems families face in this age of new opportunities.

The Context of the IEA Preprimary Project

The IEA Preprimary Project comes at a good time. In addition to parents' growing needs for out-of-home care for their preschool-aged children, there is growing recognition that the early childhood period establishes the foundation for later adult performance. That high-quality early childhood education can significantly improve the life chances of children from poor homes and environments is confirmed by such longitudinal studies as the (American) High/Scope Perry Preschool Project (Schweinhart *et al.*, 1993) and the Turkish Early Enrichment Project (Kağitçibaşi *et al.*, 1988). While there is little or no comparable research showing that preprimary programs can benefit children who are not poor to the same extent, policymakers as well as parents recognize the importance of adequate support for all children during this crucial period of development. In short, need for child care and realization of the value of early childhood education converge to generate today's extensive support for the provision of preprimary programs. The information that the three phases of the IEA Preprimary Project will provide should guide development of programs to meet the needs of both families and children in the twenty-first century.

The most important aspect of this study was the commitment to searching out a representative sample of parents of 4-year-olds in each country and asking them what early childhood services they used, if any, and their opinions about them. So often, studies in the early childhood field start with the care/education setting and select parents whose children already participate in that setting. This practice makes a project easier to carry out but does not survey an unbiased sample of users and does not give information about those who elect *not* to entrust their children to the out-of-home setting.

Also, until now, most of the studies conducted in this area of research have focused on the "structural" characteristics of settings and/or have limited themselves to studying just one type of setting. Those studies that have included some on-site observation or assessment of children have typically limited the scope of their investigation to children's development as it relates to the care/education program's structural features. In the U.S.A., for example, one can cite several such studies.

The National Day Care Study (Ruopp *et al.*, 1979) was a study of U.S. center-based day care only. Using child observation and assessment, it explored the relationships among three structural features (staff–child ratio, group size, and caregiver qualifications), program quality and cost, and effects on children. Similarly, the considerable amount of research documenting the impact of the United States National Head Start programs on children's development (e.g., cognitive, socioemotional), has been limited to only one type of center-based program and has evaluated the relationship between structural features of Head Start programs and children's development during and after Head Start participation (Hubbell, 1983; McKey *et al.*, 1985).

Another U.S. study concerned with just one type of setting, the Public School Early Childhood Study (Mitchell, 1988a, b; Marx & Seligson, 1988), gathered descriptive data at the state, district, and program levels on issues in early childhood education and characteristics of public school preschool programs for children under the age of 5. However, once again, this study produced information focusing on structural features, such as the classroom setup and types of activities provided for children.

A second study concerned with day care in the U.S.A., the National Day Care Home Study (Singer *et al.*, 1980), explored a wide range of characteristics of family day care homes by conducting limited observations of individual children and adults to collect data about such behaviors as children's involvement in activities, interactions with other children and adults, and expressions of emotion. These observations provided researchers with behavioral data to assist in determining the influence of structural characteristics (e.g., caregiver training, enrollment) on adult and child behaviors.

While each of the studies just mentioned may have determined that within a single type of early childhood care/education setting, certain structural characteristics are *necessary* to produce specific developmental outcomes, that is not to say what characteristics are *sufficient* to do so. For this latter type of conclusion, a study across a wide range of settings, encompassing more than structural characteristics of settings, is called for. This is the multiphase IEA Preprimary Project.

What Makes this IEA Project Unique?

From the first meeting of the Preprimary Project's National Research Coordinators (NRCs), it was clear that the participating countries would need to survey a wide range of formal and informal systems that had been developed for child care/education both in and out of the home. Thus the preprimary study is taking great care to incorporate both formal and informal, both in-home and out-of-home care systems: not the official care/education policies in participating countries, but the care/education arrangements that parents piece together to meet child and family needs.

Whereas some studies spend a great amount of time trying to select care settings from education settings or vice versa, the IEA Preprimary Study has included all types of early childhood settings, so comparisons across all settings can be made. As various countries reported their data, it became clear that this decision was a good one. While it might have been relatively simple within a given country to distinguish between what are considered "care" and what are considered "education" settings, across countries it made no sense. For instance, Hong Kong's day care settings literally look more like Hong Kong's education settings than like day care settings in Finland or the U.S.A.[1]

Another aspect of the IEA study that lends it special value is that it includes information on the total care and education of the child throughout the week. While most children in most countries attend only one major setting outside the home, significant numbers in many countries attend a second setting, and in some countries (such as Belgium and Germany) they attend more than two. From the point of view of public policy, creating and financing a system to provide one major setting for children is task enough, but where two or more settings a week are involved, how are these settings supported and monitored? What is their quality? How are they staffed? Finally, what is the overall public policy regarding adequacy of service if families must seek out so many different forms of support in caring for their children?

While there are several international early childhood studies, the IEA preprimary study is the largest survey with internationally devised and agreed-upon data collection procedures and instruments. One of the principal decisions in creating the study was that it would represent a cross-national consensus regarding the types of information to be collected. Because childrearing, a subject close to each country's cultural life and

---

[1] In connection with Phase 2 of the IEA Preprimary Project, High/Scope Educational Research Foundation has prepared a set of videotapes showing typical early childhood settings in the countries participating in Phase 2, including Hong Kong, Finland, and the U.S.A. For information about the videotapes, contact High/Scope Press.

national temperament, cannot be forced into any externally devised mold, it was important that the instruments not be unilaterally developed (by the ICC) and then "imposed upon" participating countries. Instead, instruments were developed by cooperating national planning teams. Then, once the instruments were approved by all countries on an item-by-item basis, local field trials were employed in each country to assess item response and time required for administration. While this consensus method often made steady progress in a timely fashion difficult, all participants agreed that it was the only method that would respect each country's needs and sensitivities.

A special goal of the project was to obtain a representative sample of parents in each country. Aside from the difficulties encountered in doing so in Spain, this goal was reached. In cooperation with the project's sampling referee, different but equivalent sampling procedures were devised for each country (as described in Chapter 2). Thus the data give a representative picture of families' views and use of care and education services in each participating country.

In an effort to reach a sample of all parents, an entire country was included in the study in nearly every case. Although it would have been tempting and certainly easier to include only the city where a particular National Research Center was located or just a neighboring province or state, IEA researchers strove to achieve a good balance between, for example, urban and rural populations. This was true in vast countries, such as China and the U.S.A., as well as in countries/territories of more manageable size, such as Hong Kong and Belgium.

A final point of uniqueness is this: the IEA Phase 1 study has been able to obtain high response rates from the nationally selected samples. Whereas high refusal rates have negatively affected the quality of the findings of many studies both nationally and internationally, this project was able to minimize such a problem (the response rate in Spain was the exception). Through the household survey method used, the national data collection teams were evidently able to convey to parents a sense of purpose and responsibility that encouraged them to cooperate with the study. This accomplishment, which attests to the careful supervision that NRCs provided during the survey, has greatly influenced the quality of the data obtained.

A small number of well-conducted international comparisons of early education services have been carried out in recent years. One of these was an intensive study of specific preschool settings and used video and other methods to gain insight as to how teachers viewed their own preschool and a preschool in each of two other countries (Tobin *et al.*, 1989). However, one must be wary of the fact that studies using this approach frequently mention "Chinese preschools" or "U.S.A. preschools" as though a single case represents the whole system.

Other approaches to international studies have brought together a number of reports by experts on individual countries to describe the state of early childhood care and education internationally (Kamerman & Kahn, 1978; Cochran, 1993). The IEA Preprimary Project's initial Phase 1 report, *How Nations Serve Young Children*, used this latter approach to document past and present official policy and data from governmental sources in 14 nations.

Both the case-study and expert-report methods stand in contrast to the method used in the IEA Preprimary Project to gather its major Phase 1 data. As described in Chapters 2 and 3, this project surveyed a representative sample of households to discover what kinds of settings preschool-aged children in each country experience on a daily or weekly basis. Therefore the findings are an indication of what typically happens in each country rather than an in-depth study of a single selected preschool setting or practice.

The Phase 1 Findings

Earlier chapters of this book presented country-specific data from the Phase 1 survey. The following sections of this chapter lift out from that data some overarching issues concerning all the participating nations.

Workforce Participation and Utilization of Care/Education Services

One of the principal policy findings from this study is that the trend from parent care to out-of-home (or at least extraparental) care/education for preschool-aged children is linked to the movement of women into the formal, paid workforce. In all countries, this trend is stronger in urban than in rural areas, as might be expected. Indeed, the only countries recording a majority of children exclusively in home care by parents are China (55%), Nigeria (65%), and Thailand (63%)—all countries where rural populations predominate. No other country reported more than 40% of 4-year-olds exclusively under parental care.

Perseverance of the Trend

The second principal policy finding is that for two major reasons, this trend toward extraparental care/education is unlikely to be reversed. First, the majority of parents using extraparental services (most parents in 5 of the 9 countries reporting data) cite their employment as the reason. Where service usage is approximately 80% or higher, as in Germany, Hong Kong, Italy, and Spain, the child's need for education or for social–emotional development is cited.

Second, the one thing that might cause a halt or shift in the trend— parental concern about the quality of extraparental care/education the child receives—did not surface in any country. Indeed, at least 92% of parents in every country reported that they were "somewhat satisfied" or "very satisfied" with the services their children were receiving. Furthermore, when asked for specific problems encountered with services, most parents in most countries reported few or none.

There were some exceptions. Hong Kong parents reported a range of concerns, including problems with program philosophy, with facilities and equipment, with other children who attend, and with cost. Parents in China reported problems with facilities and equipment, and with qualifications of staff. Otherwise, the 10,913 parents using extraparental services were largely uncomplaining. For example, no problem area (including "sick child not accommodated") merited even 1% mention across all those interviewed.

This lack of parental dissatisfaction does not mean that from a professional point of view there is no room for improvement in program quality or delivery. It also does not mean that from the regulatory perspective, no health or safety shortcomings can be found. It means that while a few families, especially those with special needs, may experience problems, the average parent, found through a household survey, either truly has adequate, problem-free services or does not perceive any inadequacies. This finding may be one reason why advocates for meeting the needs of special subpopulations of young children and their families find it difficult to gain widespread support for their causes.

The Number of Settings Attended

A third finding from this study is that most children (a majority in 8 countries) who experience extraparental care/education each week are served in no more than one extraparental setting. However a considerable number of children—ranging from 5% in Nigeria to 41% in Belgium— attend a second setting, as well. In 2 countries, small to moderate numbers of children typically attend third and fourth settings each week (Belgium reported 23% in a third and 5% in a fourth setting; Germany reported 8% in a third and 8% in a fourth setting). Thus, since the principal "cause" of extraparental care/education is the need for child care while parents work, the need to resort to more than one setting was reported by significant numbers of families in countries where children's services do not cover the full parental work day. Belgium, Germany, Italy, and the U.S.A. are instances of this phenomenon.

Extent of Time in Extraparental Settings

A fourth finding is that when children are in extraparental care/ education, they spend significant time in such settings. While Hong Kong (17 hours per week), Germany (25 hours), and the U.S.A. (28 hours) represent the low end of the scale, more typical are the 35 hours found in Spain, Nigeria, and Italy and the 55 hours found in Thailand and China. This time in extraparental care/education settings represents a large proportion of a child's life—in the case of a child in Thailand or China, more than half the child's waking hours during the five or six parental workdays each week. Thus, in many countries, one might expect that the extraparental setting the child experiences plays a large part in forming the child's physical, intellectual, and social–emotional growth. Leaving the conduct of these settings to chance, whim, or even unquestioned tradition, would seem an unwise course for a nation. Phase 2 of the IEA Preprimary Project will examine, through direct observation, the quality of the settings where children spend much of their time—including the quality of home settings.

Education: A Goal for the Home Setting

A fifth finding is that in all countries, parents electing to keep their children at home overwhelmingly cited parent-related reasons for doing so. Primarily, these reasons involved parent goals, for example, the goal of being the child's "first" teacher or educator. (Education of the child is, of course, also a reason cited by parents who use extraparental settings.) Noteworthy, however, is the fact that a number of parents who keep their children at home do so because they lack an alternative—services are either unavailable or are unsatisfactory in some way. *Lack of an alternative* was cited especially in China and to a lesser extent in Finland, Germany, Italy, Nigeria, and the U.S.A.

Sponsors of Out-of-Home Child Care and Education

A sixth finding is this: across the 11 countries participating in the Phase 1 survey, the out-of-home child care and education services that families use are sponsored primarily by governmental or religious organizations. In Finland, Italy, and Portugal at least half of all programs are under government auspices, whereas religious organizations sponsor the majority (60%) of programs in Germany and Hong Kong. In Belgium all settings have multiple sponsors, with the government always being one of those sponsors, and religious organizations being another for 41% of settings. Private organizations also play some role, providing 25–28% of programs in Hong Kong, Nigeria, and the U.S.A. In spite of the extensive interest in and discussions about employer-provided care, only China reported a significant percentage of programs with such sponsorship (28%), while Finland, Spain, and the U.S.A. reported only 2% or less; no other countries reported any employer sponsorship. Clearly, corporate- or workplace-sponsored care, while an interesting alternative, is relatively rare.

These findings about service sponsorship suggest that governments and religious organizations will continue to be the primary funders and administrators of early childhood care and education programs. They are also the likeliest source of funds for the vast early childhood service expansion envisaged in most countries. While private institutions will continue to play their part, it appears unlikely that families will have their service needs met through corporate or workplace sponsorship.

Auxiliary Services to Children

A seventh finding of the Phase 1 study is that few organized facility programs in the participating countries offer families and children comprehensive services such as health care, special education services, social services, and transportation. The most offered and best used service is health care. However, the services offered are not necessarily used. Only 6 countries reported health care usage by more than 50% of those to whom health services were available, and only Belgium reported health care usage by more than half of all children in its survey sample.

Special education and social services, when provided, are lightly used. As a percentage of total sample, fewer than 8% of children in any country receive special education or social services through their early education and care programs. These findings are in spite of the fact that the usual service providers—governmental or religious agencies—are those likely to promote and encourage auxiliary service usage (as does the national Head Start program in the U.S.A.). Fewer than half of the 4-year-olds in any country are offered transportation to their early childhood programs. Among those to whom transportation is offered, usage ranges from 22% in Belgium to 65% in China. However, since the survey found that most children live within a few minutes of the facility they attend, availability of transportation does not appear to be an issue.

Mothers as Principal Caregivers

An eighth finding concerns children's principal caregivers. In every participating country, regardless of its stage of economic development, mothers have the most responsibility for young children's care and supervision. Of the 4-year-old's 16-hour waking day, the time spent with mother (alone or with father) ranges from 8.4 hours (or 53% of the day) in Belgium to 11.9 hours (or 74% of the day) in Germany. This contrasts sharply with the hours that fathers are present (with or without mothers), which ranges from 0.9 hour (or 6% of the day) in China and Hong Kong to 3.7 hours (23% of the day) in Belgium and 3.5 hours (22% of the day) in Thailand. Indeed, no country reports "father only care" amounting to even an hour a day; father's daily time alone with the child ranges from 0.1 hour (6 minutes) in Hong Kong to 0.9 hour (54 minutes) in China. Child care, in spite of the rhetoric about equality and role sharing in the western countries, is still very much care by mothers in all participating countries, regardless of the various cultures and levels of development involved in this study.

Nonfamilial Caregivers or Teachers

A ninth finding has to do with caregivers other than parents. Further investigation of children's daily routines indicates that the time children spend with caregivers/teachers other than their parents or relatives varies greatly from country to country. While Belgium reported children spending 6 hours per day in nonfamilial care, Germany—also a developed European country—reported only 2.1 hours (although more than Thailand's 1.0 hour, this is below the U.S.A.'s 2.8 hours). One of the most interesting facts to come out of the daily routine information is that preschool-aged children in a few countries are left alone for extended periods of time without direct adult supervision. This occurs in China, where "alone time" constitutes 2.9 hours of the child's day, and in Thailand, where it is 0.8 hour of the child's day. (See Chapter 6 for more information on children spending time alone.) Another fact worth noting is that while Belgium comes closest to having nonfamilial services (in multiple settings) that cover a full workday for parents (6 hours), across all participating countries, the average early childhood service coverage is only a portion of the full workday.

Location of Children's Services

A tenth and final finding: as the findings about *care by mother* would indicate, most children spend a large part of their waking hours at their own homes. The second-most frequented location is the school or organized care center. An exception is found in Finland, where children average more time in a family day care home (2.4 hours) than in an organized facility (2.1 hours). Time spent in all other settings is minimal. The wide variety of locations that this study hypothesized *does* exist—parks and playgrounds, family day care homes, workplace arrangements, neighbors' homes—but to a far lesser extent than a worldwide survey might be expected to uncover. Worthy of special note is the finding that transition times (traveling to and from education/care settings) are not a problem, since the average travel time is no more than 15 minutes in most countries. However, there are some children who travel more than 15 minutes, which is the case in China for 27% of children. Most countries reported an average of 5 minutes travel time, and since for many children this is walking time, one can conclude that settings are generally close at hand. Private auto use is high in the U.S.A. and also typical in Belgium and Finland.

Final Comments

The IEA Preprimary Project has undertaken a difficult Phase 1 task. The international research team was committed to developing survey instruments that represented the best ideas that were acceptable to all. By working as a team, the NRCs achieved this goal without compromising the quality of information attained. Through teamwork, the problems in data collection were resolved, and the complex work was carried out.

Perhaps the most noteworthy finding of this study to date is this: although preschool-aged children in all countries are in extraparental or out-of-home care in significant numbers (in most countries, over half typically experience more than 2 hours of care each week from someone other than a parent), mothers still provide the greatest share of children's care. While the national patterns of early childhood services differ considerably, mothers and paid nonfamily adults provide the most supervision, and fathers the least, everywhere. There appear to be two reasons for the increasing use of child services: mothers are entering the paid workforce in increasing numbers throughout the world, and families are seeking advantages for their children in a world they see as highly competitive.

While some social policy analysts may see the spread of the feminist movement or the economic pressures of industrialized society as the issues behind the worldwide demand for early childhood services, it is probably not useful to dwell on these issues. Such a view only draws the focus away from children. The very real situation the world's children face demands our careful attention, because in a substantial number of societies children are right now being raised by young people or adults paid to undertake the task rather than by parents or family members. How qualified are these caregivers and educators? What is the content of the settings these children find themselves in, and what is the quality of children's social interactions in these settings? Are children having the kinds of early childhood experiences that lead to sound child development? Do children's early childhood settings provide the appropriate framework for the development of good workers and good citizens? Are families better off for having such settings to turn to?

The second phase of the IEA preprimary project asks these questions by addressing the quality of life of the child in care and education settings both inside and outside of home. Finding the answers to such questions is vital to the life of every nation involved.

References

Abreu, J. G., Abreu-Lima, I., Bairrão, J., Barbosa, M., & Cruz, O. (1989). *IEA Preprimary Project Phase 1 sampling report: Portugal*. Porto: University of Porto.

Bairrão, J., Abreu-Lima, I., Barbosa, M., & Cruz, O. (1989). *IEA Preprimary Project Phase 1 data collection report: Portugal*. Porto: University of Porto.

Bairrão, J., Barbosa, M., Borges, I., Cruz, O., & Macedo-Pinto, I. (1989). Care and education for children under age 6 in Portugal. In P. P. Olmsted & D. P. Weikart (Eds.), *How nations serve young children: Profiles of child care and education in 14 countries* (pp. 273–302). Ypsilanti, MI: High/Scope Press.

Barbosa, M., Cruz, O., Abreu-Lima, I., Rangel-Henriques, M., Bairrão, J., & Borges, M. I. (1990). *IEA Preprimary Project Phase 1 findings report for Portugal*. Porto: University of Porto.

Berrueta-Clement, J. R., Schweinhart, L. J., Barnett, W. S., Epstein, A. S., & Weikart, D. P. (1984). *Changed lives: The effects of the Perry Preschool Program on youths through age 19* (Monographs of the High/Scope Educational Research Foundation, 8). Ypsilanti, MI: High/Scope Press.

Bronfenbrenner, U. (1979). *Ecology of human development.* Cambridge, MA: Harvard University Press.

Cochran, M. (Ed.). (1993). *International handbook of child care policies and programs.* Westport, CT: Greenwood Press.

Delhaxhe, A., & Hindryckx, G. (1989). *IEA Preprimary Project Phase 1 sampling report: Belgium*. Liège: University of Liège.

Delhaxhe, A. (1989). Early childhood care and education in Belgium. In P. P. Olmsted & D. P. Weikart (Eds.), *How nations serve young children: Profiles of child care and education in 14 countries* (pp. 13–37). Ypsilanti, MI: High/Scope Press.

Delhaxhe, A., & Hindryckx, G. (1991). *IEA Preprimary Project Phase 1 findings report for Belgium*. Liège: University of Liège.

Epstein, A. S. (1993). *Training for quality: Improving early childhood programs through systematic inservice training* (Monographs of the High/Scope Educational Research Foundation, 9). Ypsilanti, MI: High/Scope Press.

Hindryckx, G., & Delhaxhe, A. (1989). *IEA Preprimary Project Phase 1 data collection report: Belgium*. Liège: University of Liège.

Hoas, H. (1990). *IEA Preprimary Project Phase 1 data collection report: United States*. Ypsilanti, MI: High/Scope Educational Research Foundation.

Hoas, H., & Olmsted, P. P. (1989). *IEA Preprimary Project Phase 1 sampling report: United States*. Ypsilanti, MI: High/Scope Educational Research Foundation.

Hubbell, R. (1983). *A review of Head Start research since 1970 (Head Start Evaluation, Synthesis, and Utilization Project)*. Washington, DC: CSR.

International Labour Office (1990). *1989–90 yearbook of labour statistics*. Geneva: Author.

Kağitçibaşi, Ç., Sunar, D., & Bekman, S. (1988). *Comprehensive Preschool Education Project: Final report*. Ottawa: International Development Research Center.

Kamerman, S. and Kahn, A. (Eds.). (1978). *Family policy: Government and families in 14 countries*. New York: Columbia University Press.

Katz, L. (1975). Early childhood programs and ideological disputes. *Educational Forum*, **34**(3), 267–271.

Kish, L. (1965). *Survey sampling*. New York: Wiley.

Kish, L. (1987). *Statistical design for research*. New York: Wiley.

Lazar, I., & Darlington, R. (1979). *Lasting effects after preschool* (Summary report). Washington, DC: U.S. Department of Health, Education and Welfare.

LeVine, R. (1970). Cross-cultural study in child development. In P. H. Mussen (Ed.), *Carmichael's Manual of Child Psychology* (Vol. 2, pp. 559–612). New York: Wiley.

Marx, F. & Seligson, M. (1988). *The Public School Early Childhood Study: The state survey*. New York: Bank Street College of Education.

McKey, R. H., Condelli, L., Ganson, H., Barrett, B. J., McConkey, C., & Plantz, M. C. (1985). *The impact of Head Start on children, families, and communities (Final report of the Head Start Evaluation, Synthesis, and Utilization Project)*. Washington, DC: CSR.

Mitchell, A. (1988a). *The Public School Early Childhood Study: The case studies*. New York: Bank Street College of Education.

Mitchell, A. (1988b). *The Public School Early Childhood Study: The district survey*. New York: Bank Street College of Education.

Myers, R. (1992). *The twelve who survive*. London: Routledge.

Ojala, M. (1989). Early childhood training, care, and education in Finland. In P. P. Olmsted & D. P. Weikart (Eds.), *How nations serve young children: Profiles of child care and education in 14 countries* (pp. 87–118). Ypsilanti, MI: High/Scope Press.

Ojala, M. (1990). *IEA Preprimary Project Phase 1 findings report for Finland*. Joensuu: University of Joensuu.

Ojala, M., & Siekkinen, M. (1989a). *IEA Preprimary Project Phase 1 data collection report: Finland*. Joensuu: University of Joensuu.

Ojala, M., & Siekkinen, M. (1989b). *IEA Preprimary Project Phase 1 sampling report: Finland*. Joensuu: University of Joensuu.

Olmsted, P. P. (1989). Early childhood care and education in the United States. In P. P. Olmsted & D. P. Weikart (Eds.), *How nations serve young children: Profiles of child care and education in 14 countries* (pp. 365–400). Ypsilanti, MI: High/Scope Press.

Olmsted, P. P. & Weikart, D. P. (Eds.), (1989). *How nations serve young children: Profiles of child care and education in 14 countries*. Ypsilanti, MI: High/Scope Press.

Olmsted, P. P., Kish, L., & Weikart, D. P. (1987). *IEA Preprimary Project Phase 1 sampling questionnaire*. Ypsilanti, MI: High/Scope Educational Research Foundation.

Onibokun, O. (1989). *IEA Preprimary Project Phase 1 sampling report: Nigeria*. Ibadan: University of Ibadan.

Onibokun, O. (1991). *IEA Preprimary Project Phase 1 data collection report: Nigeria*. Ibadan: University of Ibadan.

Onibokun, O. (1989). Early childhood care and education in Nigeria. In P. P.Olmsted & D. P. Weikart (Eds.), *How nations serve young children: Profiles of child care and education in 14 countries* (pp. 219–240). Ypsilanti, MI: High/Scope Press.

Opper, S. (1989). Child care and early education in Hong Kong. In P. P. Olmsted & D. P. Weikart (Eds.), *How nations serve young children: Profiles of child care and education in 14 countries* (pp. 119–142). Ypsilanti, MI: High/Scope Press.

Opper, S. (1990). *IEA Preprimary Project Phase 1 findings report for Hong Kong*. Hong Kong: University of Hong Kong.

Opper, S. (1989a). *IEA Preprimary Project Phase 1 data collection report: Hong Kong.* Hong Kong: University of Hong Kong.

Opper, S. (1989b). *IEA Preprimary Project Phase 1 sampling report: Hong Kong.* Hong Kong: University of Hong Kong.

Palacios, J. (1989). *IEA Preprimary Project Phase 1 sampling report: Spain.* Seville: University of Seville.

Palacios, J. (1989). Child care and early education in Spain. In P. P. Olmsted & D. P. Weikart (Eds.), *How nations serve young children: Profiles of child care and education in 14 countries* (pp. 303–341). Ypsilanti, MI: High/Scope Press.

Palacios, J., González, M. M., Hidalgo, V., Moreno, C., Capote, M., & Ruiz, A. (1989). *IEA Preprimary Project Phase 1 data collection report: Spain.* Seville: University of Seville.

Passornsiri, N. (1989a). *IEA Preprimary Project Phase 1 data collection report: Thailand.* Nonthaburi: Sukhothai Thammathirat Open University.

Passornsiri, N. (1989b). *IEA Preprimary Project Phase 1 sampling report: Thailand.* Nonthaburi: Sukhothai Thammathirat Open University.

Passornsiri, N., Kutintara, P., & Suwannapal, A. (1989). Child care and early education in Thailand. In P. P. Olmsted & D. P. Weikart (Eds.), *How nations serve young children: Profiles of child care and education in 14 countries* (pp. 343–363). Ypsilanti, MI: High/Scope Press.

Pistillo, F. (1989). Preprimary education and care in Italy. In P. P. Olmsted & D. P. Weikart (Eds.), *How nations serve young children: Profiles of child care and education in 14 countries* (pp. 151–202). Ypsilanti, MI: High/Scope Press.

Pusci, L. (1990). *IEA Preprimary Project Phase 1 findings report for Italy.* Frascati: European Center for Education.

Pusci, L. (1989a). *IEA Preprimary Project Phase 1 data collection report: Italy.* Frascati: Centro Europeo dell'Educazione.

Pusci, L. (1989b). *IEA Preprimary Project Phase 1 sampling report: Italy.* Frascati: Centro Europeo dell'Educazione.

Rossbach, H.-G. (1988, April). *Daily routines of young children.* Paper presented at the annual meeting of the American Educational Research Association, New Orleans, LA.

Rossbach, H.-G. (1989a). *IEA Preprimary Project Phase 1 data collection report: Germany.* Münster: University of Münster.

Rossbach, H.-G. (1989b). *IEA Preprimary Project Phase 1 sampling report: Germany.* Münster: University of Münster.

Ruopp, R., Travers, J. Glantz, F., & Coelen, C. (1979). *Children at the center: Summary findings and their implications* (Final Report of the National Day Care Study, Vol. 1). Cambridge, MA: Abt Associates.

Shi, H. Z. (1989a). *IEA Preprimary Project Phase 1 data collection report: China.* Beijing: Central Institute of Educational Research.

Shi, H. Z. (1989b). *IEA Preprimary Project Phase 1 sampling report: China.* Beijing: Central Institute of Educational Research.

Schweinhart, L. J., Barnes, H. V., & Weikart, D. P. (1993). *Significant benefits: The High/Scope Perry preschool study through age 27* (Monographs of the High/Scope Educational Research Foundation, 10). Ypsilanti, MI: High/Scope Press.

Shi, H. Z. (1989). Young children's care and education in the People's Republic of China. In P. P. Olmsted & D. P. Weikart (Eds.), *How nations serve young children: Profiles of child care and education in 14 countries* (pp. 241–254). Ypsilanti, MI: High/Scope Press.

Shi, H. Z. (1990, September). *Some implications for China's early childhood education from Phase 1 of IEA Preprimary Project.* Paper presented at the IEA General Assembly Meeting, Beijing, China.

Shi, H. Z. & Xiang, Z. P. (1990). *IEA Preprimary Project Phase 1 findings report for China (PRC)*. Beijing: China Central Institute of Educational Research.

Singer, J., Fosburg, S., Goodson, B., & Smith, J. (1980). *Final Report of the National Day Care Home Study*. Cambridge, MA: Abt Associates.

Tietze, W., Rossbach, H.-G., & Uferman, N. K. (1989). Child care and early education in the Federal Republic of Germany. In P. P. Olmsted & D. P. Weikart (Eds.), *How nations serve young children: Profiles of child care and education in 14 countries* (pp. 39–85). Ypsilanti, MI: High/Scope Press.

Tobin, J. J., Wu, D. Y. H., & Davidson, D. H. (1989). *Preschool in three cultures: Japan, China, and the United States*. New Haven, CT: Yale University Press.

United Nations Educational, Scientific, and Cultural Organization (UNESCO) (1991). *Early childhood care and education: A world survey*. Paris: Author.

United Nations Educational, Scientific, and Cultural Organization (UNESCO). (1989, September). *1988 world survey on early childhood care and education (ECCE): Summary of findings*. Paris: Author.

Weikart, D. P., Kish, L., & Olmsted, P. P. (1988). *IEA Preprimary Project Phase 1 interim sampling report*. Ypsilanti, MI: High/Scope Educational Research Foundation.

Note Regarding Appendices

Only Appendices A and B are included in this volume. A separate volume containing Appendix C, the Parent/Guardian Interview data, is available at no extra charge from the publisher.

To obtain a copy of Appendix C please contact the Editorial Department, Social Sciences, Elsevier Science Ltd, The Boulevard, Langford Lane, Kidlington, Oxford OX5 1GB, U.K.

Appendix A
Supplementary Tables

Table A.1
Percentage Distribution of 4-Year-Old Service-Users According to Type of First Setting

Country/Territory	N	n Who attend 1 or more settings (% of N)	(% of n) Own home		(% of n) Own home		(% of n) Organized facility				% of n in other settings
			Relative	Non-relative	Relative	Non-relative	Care	Education	Unclassified	Miscellaneous	
Belgium (Fr.)	424	416 (98)	1	0	3	1	0	95	0	0	0
China (PRC)+	12,835	5,469 (43)	12	0	10	0	11	65	0	2	0
Finland	576	431 (75)	4	3	4	43	0	31	0	15	0
Germany (FRG)	509	417 (82)	14	4	18	4	0	60	0	0	0
Hong Kong+	947	947 (100)	—	—	—	—	4	96	0	0	0
Italy	1,000	852 (85)	3	0	3	0	0	94	0	0	0
Nigeria+	1,295	435 (33)	6	60	1	8	2	13	10	0	0
Portugal	581	410 (71)	21	2	26	9	0	0	41	0	1
Spain	480	379 (79)	4	2	5	1	0	0	87	0	1
Thailand	2,466	894 (36)	41	1	24	1	12	21	0	0	0
U.S.A.	432	264 (61)	9	5	10	18	18	40	0	0	0

The symbol + indicates that weighted data were used for analysis.

Table A.2

Percentage Distribution of Urban/Rural 4-Year-Olds According to Use or Nonuse of First Settings

Country/Territory	N		n	% of N	Own home parent care only	Own home (nonparent)	Other home	Organized facility	Other
Belgium (Fr.)+	—		—	—	—	—	—	—	—
China (PRC)+	12,591	U	3,540	28	22	4	6	67	1
		R	9,051	72	70	6	4	19	1
Finland	576	U	345	60	18	6	32	44	—
		R	231	40	37	4	39	20	—
Germany (FRG)	509	U	396	78	19	13	17	51	—
		R	113	22	17	19	21	43	—
Hong Kong+	—							—	—
Italy	1,000	U	551	55	11	3	3	83	—
		R	449	45	20	2	2	76	—
Nigeria+	1,172	U	191	16	57	17	7	19	—
		R	981	84	64	26	3	7	—
Portugal	—		—	—	—	—	—	—	—
Spain	480	U	273	57	18	3	4	75	0
		R	207	43	26	7	4	62	1
Thailand	2,448	U	381	16	57	10	5	28	0
		R	2,067	84	65	16	10	9	0
U.S.A.	432	U	401	93	38	9	16	37	—
		R	31	7	52	6	29	13	—

The symbol + indicates that weighted data were used for analysis. U indicates urban, and R indicates rural. Dashes indicate that no urban/rural comparison data were available.

Table A.3
Median Hourly Cost and Median Weekly Cost to Parents in U.S. $ for Services in Extraparental Care/Education Settings

Country/Territory	N	Own home (nonparent)				Other home				Organized facility			
		No. using	Median cost per hr	Mean hr used per wk (SD)	Median cost per wk	No. using	Median cost per hr	Mean hr used per wk (SD)	Median cost per wk	No. using	Median cost per hr	Mean hr used per wk (SD)	Median cost per wk
Belgium (Fr.)	424	—	—	—	—	2	1.85	19.0 (4.2)	33.00	65	0.04	25.3 (2.8)	1.14
China (PRC)[+]	12,835	—	—	—	—	—	—	—	—	—	—	—	—
Finland	576	19	2.24	31.2 (8.7)	57.50	170	1.11	37.4 (9.0)	34.21	148	1.07	30.2 (15.1)	33.92
Germany (FRG)	509	10	2.97	23.5 (11.4)	68.00	12	1.44	30.0 (11.9)	41.50	242	0.44	20.5 (8.9)	8.75
Hong Kong[+]	947	—	—	—	—	—	—	—	—	947	0.40	17.2 (7.0)	6.63
Italy	1,000	2	0.06	15.0 (8.9)	0.97	—	—	—	—	15	0.02	32.7 (9.1)	0.80
Nigeria[+]	1,295	214	0.05	41.4 (8.9)	1.79	32	0.04	37.4 (11.5)	2.04	80	0.03	23.8 (5.5)	0.51
Portugal	—	—	—	—	—	—	—	—	—	—	—	—	—
Spain	480	—	—	—	—	2	0.55	28.8 (5.3)	15.89	212	0.30	29.6 (8.9)	7.77
Thailand	2,466	33	0.08	73.6 (42.0)	4.47	29	0.05	61.4 (47.9)	1.95	277	0.01	38.1 (6.7)	0.58
U.S.A.	432	20	1.50	21.3 (17.2)	25.00	53	1.11	28.5 (14.7)	30.00	114	1.61	24.4 (16.3)	36.00

The symbol [+] indicates that weighted data were used for analysis. Dashes indicate that no information was available.

Table A.4
Mean and Standard Deviation of Variables Used for Regression Analysis on Hours of Use of Early Childhood Services

					Variables			
Country/ Territory	*n*[a]	Hr per week (*SD*)	Urban/ Rural[b] (*SD*)	No of children (*SD*)	Education, father (*SD*)	Education, mother (*SD*)	Hr away, mother (*SD*)	Hr away, father (*SD*)
Belgium (Fr.)	226	36.8 (11.8)	2.2 (.8)	2.2 (.8)	13.1 (3.0)	13.2 (3.6)	32.5 (15.3)	48.4 (14.4)
China (PRC)[+]	8,814	33.0 (32.6)	.3 (.5)	1.5 (.9)	7.4 (3.9)	8.4 (3.3)	51.8 (24.6)	63.5 (32.8)
Finland	385	29.1 (17.2)	.6 (.5)	2.3 (1.1)	12.9 (3.3)	12.3 (3.3)	33.4 (16.6)	47.5 (16.5)
Germany (FRG)	178	22.0 (16.4)	.7 (.4)	1.8 (.7)	10.3 (2.3)	10.9 (3.1)	17.2 (16.7)	50.7 (12.4)
Hong Kong[+]	866	17.2 (7.0	– –	– –	9.1 (2.7)	10.0 (3.1)	– –	– –
Italy	158	36.8 (10.8)	.7 (.5)	1.9 (1.0)	10.7 (4.5)	11.3 (4.8)	30.7 (12.2)	47.5 (12.5)
Nigeria[+]	242	34.6 (12.9)	.2 (.4)	– –	9.0 (4.9)	11.0 (4.3)	42.2 (16.6)	54.8 (15.6)
Portugal	341	45.2 (20.6)	– –	1.9 (1.1)	6.3 (3.4)	6.2 (3.4)	43.9 (20.3)	62.9 (26.0)
Spain	191	36.6 (18.4)	.7 (.5)	1.9 (1.0)	13.0 (4.8)	13.4 (5.0)	31.3 (16.5)	50.4 (16.7)
Thailand	986	36.6 (34.5)	.2 (.4)	2.4 (1.4)	5.2 (3.2)	5.8 (3.6)	42.6 (30.0)	73.0 (39.1)
U.S.A.	209	21.5 (18.5)	.9 (.2)	2.6 (1.3)	13.6 (3.3)	14.1 (3.7)	26.5 (16.4)	52.7 (22.0)

The symbol [+] indicates that weighted data were used for analysis.
[a]The regression analysis deleted cases with missing values (listwise).
[b]Rural is coded as 0 and urban is coded as 1, except for Belgium, for which rural area is coded as 1, middle (combined urban and rural) area as 2, and urban area as 3.

Table A.5
Correlation between the Variables Used for Regression Analysis on Hours of Use of Early Childhood Services

Country/Territory	n[a]	Hr/Wk & Urban/rural[b]	Hr/Wk & no. of children	Hr/Wk & education, mother	Hr/Wk & education, father	Hr/Wk & hr away, mother	Hr/Wk & hr away, father	Urban/Rural & no. of children	Urban/Rural & education, mother	Urban/Rural & eduaction, father	Urban/Rural & hr away, mother	Urban/Rural & hr away, father
Belgium (Fr.)	226	-.072	-.267*	-.094	-.098	.378*	.076	-.133*	.024	.032	.010	.084
China (PRC)[+]	8,814	.351*	-.359*	.332*	.254*	.434*	.229*	-.309*	.403*	.318*	.155*	-.020*
Finland	385	.172*	-.339*	.077	.085*	.786*	.058	-.173*	.120*	.260*	.110*	.012*
Germany (FRG)	178	.026	-.264*	.116	.008	.483*	-.012	-.162*	-.005	.012	.038	-.148*
Hong Kong[+]	866	–	–	.069*	.081*	–	–	–	–	–	–	–
Italy	158	-.034	-.106	.018	-.057	.387*	.062	-.045	.104	.149*	.011	.119
Nigeria[+]	242	-.164*	–	-.016	.374*	.273*	.245*	–	.140*	.037	.195*	.065*
Portugal	341	–	-.206*	.059	.083	.649*	.082	–	–	–	–	–
Spain	191	.131*	-.036	.095	-.001	.639*	.178*	.037	.295*	.175*	.204*	.006
Thailand	986	.003	-.151*	.101*	.099*	.829*	.248*	-.101*	.326*	.391*	.028	-.088
U.S.A.	209	-.025	-.219*	.098	-.023	.653*	.068	.026	.089	.053	-.041	-.026

Table A.5 (*continued*)

Country/Territory	n[a]	No. of children & education, mother[b]	No. of children & education father	No. of children & hr away, mother	No. of children & hr away, father	Education, mother & education, father	Education, mother & hr away, mother	Education, mother & hr away, father	Education, father & hr away, mother	Education, father & hr away, father	Hr away, mother & hr away, father
Belgium (Fr.)	226	.108	.165*	-.179*	.052	.615*	-.073	-.120*	-.063	-.055	.151*
China (PRC)+	8,814	-.447*	-.322*	-.112*	-.035*	.521*	.143*	.052*	.085*	.044*	.340*
Finland	385	-.090*	-.075	-.347*	-.024	.573*	.047	-.006	.021	.051	.095*
Germany (FRG)	178	-.006	.045	-.284*	.071	.465*	.059	-.098	-.060	-.038	-.202*
Hong Kong+	866	—	—	—	—	.720*	—	—	—	—	—
Italy+	158	-.151*	-.127	.039	-.050	.737*	.093	-.009	-.029	-.013	.065
Nigeria+	242	—	—	—	—	.433*	.071*	-.044	.015	.024	.379*
Portugal	341	-.259*	-.198*	-.195*	.048	.718*	-.066	-.129*	-.077	-.163	.164*
Spain	191	-.080	-.038	-.054	.025	.605*	.083	.036	-.007	-.093	.076
Thailand	986	-.205*	-.192*	-.107*	-.059*	.705*	.084*	-.071*	.091*	-.059*	.279*
U.S.A.	209	-.149*	-.188*	-.058	.063	.670*	-.050	.037	-.185*	.137*	-.057

The symbol + means that weighted data were used for analysis.
[a] Regression analysis deleted cases with missing data (listwise).
[b] Rural is coded as 0 and urban is coded as 1, except for Belgium, for which rural area is coded as 1, middle area as 2, and urban area as 3.
* $p \leq .05$

Appendix B

IEA Preprimary Project Phase 1 National Research Centers and Coordinators

Belgium

        Service de Pédagogie Expérimentale
        Faculte de Psychologie et Sciences de l'Education
        B 32 Université de Liège au Sart-Tilman
        B 4000 Liège

      Coordinators: Arlette Delhaxhe
                 Genevieve Hindryckx

China (PRC)

        China Central Institute of Educational Research
        Beisanhuan zhong lu 46
        100088 Beijing

      Coordinators: Shi Hui Zhong
                 Xiang Zong Ping

Finland

        Early Childhood Education Department
        University of Joensuu
        P.O. Box 111
        80101 Joensuu

      Coordinator: Mikko Ojala

Germany (FRG)
    Universität Münster
    FB Erziehungswissenschaft Institut III
    GeorgsKommende 33
    4400 Münster

    Coordinator: Hans-Günther Rossbach

Hong Kong
    Department of Education
    University of Hong Kong
    Pokfulam Road

    Coordinator: Sylvia Opper

Italy
    Centro Europeo dell'Educazione
    Villa Falconieri
    I-00044 Frascati
    Rome

    Coordinator: Lucio Pusci

Nigeria
    Institute of Education
    University of Ibadan
    Ibadan

    Coordinator: Olayemi Onibokun

Portugal
    Faculdade de Psicológia e de Ciências da Educaçáo
    Universidade do Porto
    Rua das Taipas, 76
    4000 Porto

    Coordinator: Joaquim Bairrão

Spain

Departamento Psicologia Evolutiva
Universidad de Sevilla
Apartado 3128
41071 Sevilla

Coordinator: Jesús Palacios

Thailand

School of Educational Studies
Sukhothai Thammathirat Open University
Jaengwattana Road, Bangpood, Pakkred
Nonthaburi 11120

Coordinator: Nittaya Passornsiri

U.S.A.

High/Scope Educational Research Foundation
600 North River Street
Ypsilanti, MI 48198

Coordinators: Patricia P. Olmsted
Helena Hoas

International Coordinating Center
High/Scope Educational Research Foundation
600 North River Street
Ypsilanti, MI 48198

International Coordinator: David P. Weikart
Deputy International Coordinator: Patricia P. Olmsted

Index